Integrating CMMI® and Agile Development

Praise for *Integrating CMMI® and Agile Development*

"When Alistair Cockburn gave the keynote for our Software Engineering Process Conference in San Jose, I knew that the issues that had separated CMMI and Agile were far more about perceptions than about principled development. This book fills a critical need in bridging two communities that share a common purpose—producing high-quality software systems that excite the customer and win repeat business opportunities."

*—Mike Phillips, CMMI Project Manager, Software Engineering Institute;
coauthor,* CMMI®-ACQ: Guidelines for Improving the Acquisition
of Products and Services

"The client cases Paul describes are easily relatable and can be extrapolated to many organizations. He spends most of his efforts in these cases on the basics that are common to CMMI and Agile. In particular, he dutifully applies Lean principles and practices to empower Agile practices and facilitate CMMI practices. . . . Chapter 9 is the book's best stuff—not because it's about golf, but because this is the point at which you get answers to your key question: What's in it for me?"

*—Hillel Glazer, Principal and CEO, Entinex, Inc.; Certified High Maturity
SCAMPI Lead Appraiser; CMMI Instructor*

"This book will challenge many of your (mis)understandings about both Agile delivery and CMMI. Paul thoughtfully applies his years of practical experience to help bridge two disparate communities who are working toward the same goal—improving an organization's IT productivity. It's about time someone wrote a book like this."

*—Scott W. Ambler, Chief Methodologist for Agile and Lean, IBM Rational;
author,* Agile Modeling, *and coauthor,* Enterprise Unified Process

"This book can provide great help to a variety of organizations figuring out how best to implement CMMI, including large and small enterprises, even if their starting point is not 'Agile.' All in all, this book contains a lot of 'pearls of wisdom' that can make a much-appreciated contribution to the software engineering community."

*—Mike Konrad, Chief Architect, CMMI, Software Engineering Institute;
coauthor,* CMMI®: Guidelines for Process Integration and
Product Improvement, Second Edition

"No two software development programs are identical. Each has requirements, resources, schedules, and users that necessitate an equally unique development strategy. The strength of this book lies in its ability to identify strengths from CMMI and Agile methods, which helps both managers and technical professionals tailor a balanced hybrid approach."

*—Doug Parsons,[1] Chief Software Engineer, Future Force (Simulation);
Army PEO Simulation, Training and Instrumentation*

---

1. The views expressed here belong to the author and do not necessarily represent the views of PEO STRI, the U.S. Army, or the federal government.

"This book will measurably improve how systems and software systems are developed."

"Having experience with both CMMI and Agile, I find this book very insightful. I keep taking notes. I think it is a great aid to anyone who has been through the process."

"I consider the discussion of model-based improvement in the early chapters of this book to be one of the best I have seen. Paul has great insight into effective software process improvement and is articulate in describing both the issues and ways in which they should be considered."

"This is a good topic presented with lots of practical points, helpful summaries, and interesting case studies. The idea of 'Doorway Risk Management' in Chapter 4 is great!"

"I found several really nice nuggets throughout the book (lessons, cautions, insights, etc.). I also liked the summary sections at the end of each chapter and the extensive use of case studies. Finally, I discovered some real gems in the Epilogue, which provides a very nice conclusion for the book."

Integrating CMMI® and Agile Development

Case Studies and Proven Techniques for Faster Performance Improvement

Paul E. McMahon

✦ Addison-Wesley

Upper Saddle River, NJ • Boston• Indianapolis • San Francisco
New York • Toronto • Montreal • London • Munich • Paris • Madrid
Capetown • Sydney • Tokyo • Singapore • Mexico City

CarnegieMellon
Software Engineering Institute

The SEI Series in Software Engineering

Library of Congress Cataloging-in-Publication Data

McMahon, Paul E.
  Integrating CMMI and agile development: case studies and proven
techniques for faster performance improvement / Paul E. McMahon.
    p. cm.
  Includes index.
  ISBN 978-0-321-71410-7 (pbk. : alk. paper)
  1. Capability maturity model (Computer software) 2. Capability
maturity model (Computer software)—Case studies. 3. Agile software
development. I. Title.
  QA76.758.M35 2010
  005.1—dc22
                                                        2010018025

ISBN-13: 978-0-321-71410-7
ISBN-10:   0-321-71410-5

Text printed in the United States on recycled paper at RR Donnelley in Crawfordsville, Indiana.
First printing, August 2010

This book is dedicated to my wife Jan, my children Lindsey and Patrick, and my son-in-law Dan for their continual support and help in keeping me focused on the things that matter most.

Contents

Foreword by Mike Phillips

As I write this, the CMMI Product Team is crafting our next release of CMMI models—CMMI V1.3. A critical element of the V1.3 release is to improve the models' coverage of the unique elements that Agile methods have provided to accelerate software development in innovative ways. We on the product team believe that the synergies that Agile methods and CMMI models have when used together demands this expansion of model coverage. In our update of CMMI models for V1.3, we were directed by criteria that required that we minimize the models' growth. (As of this writing, we have over 110,000 people trained in CMMI models, and over 4,000 organizations that have demonstrated their adoption of the practices using CMMI benchmark appraisals. Therefore, a large amount of change would require them to be retrained and reduce the overall benefit to users.) The product team has chosen to add supporting material to process areas that have the strongest correlation with Agile methods, and where Agile methods might be perceived as significantly different in approach from CMMI practices.

Release of this book precedes the release of Version 1.3 models. The book provides some of the key insights from Paul's work with a number of organizations to show ways that CMMI and Agile methods can effectively be teamed for success. The collection of examples that Paul uses to illustrate effective process improvement confirms our conclusion that these two approaches are complementary and are not, in fact, competitors. Each can complement the other and add value to any organization's development efforts.

Paul's book allows you to gain many more hints, tips, and insights than we can ever include in a CMMI model. I particularly like the mixture of "myths," "lessons," "insights," and straightforward "questions and answers" that he has sprinkled throughout the book. The lessons from real organizations that he has renamed to be RAVE, BOND, LACM, NANO, and GEAR, are part of Paul's delightful way of sharing his consulting experiences with you. Each of these lessons provides a potential "takeaway" for your process improvement journey—ideas that will make your application of Agile methods and CMMI better for having read them.

With this book, Paul is providing invaluable leadership that will fuel the move forward with various mixes of Agile methods and CMMI models. Your use of the tools and techniques captured within this work will enable you to join us in the effort to grow these ideas and improve your organization's performance.

—*Mike Phillips*
CMMI Program Manager

Foreword by Hillel Glazer

Looking back at writing and discussions that brought CMMI and Agile concepts together, arguably, the conversation, at best, entered the mainstream between the years 2004 and 2006. As of the publication of this work, many people are still skeptical about whether CMMI and Agile can truly co-exist. (I suppose, when there are more than 20 years of history associated with a brand (e.g., SEI's CMM), it might take a few more years for the broader market to catch on. Thanks to social media and the Internet, it will hopefully take less than two decades to drill the message into people's minds.)

There are several things I like about Paul's book, which make it worthwhile reading for people interested in this topic. His case studies are typical across many types of companies and many situations. As I reviewed an early version of the work, I found myself believing he was working with many of my own clients and former employers. Prior to reviewing the manuscript, I had never met Paul or collaborated with him. For us to have such similar experiences merely provides further evidence that Pareto was right: 80% of the problems *can* be explained by 20% of the issues. The cases Paul describes can be easily related and extrapolated to many organizations. Even if/when his case studies don't match a reader's experience precisely, that doesn't mean they are not relevant or there aren't lessons to be learned and applied.

Another attribute I like is that Paul seems to spend most of his efforts in these client cases on the basics that are common to CMMI and to Agile. In particular, he dutifully applies Lean principles and practices to empower Agile practices and facilitate CMMI practices. If I had to point to one "take away" from this book, it would be this.

I should point out that, like many of us, Paul's been doing this for a while. His experience pre-dates the named "Agile" movement just as "Lean" is a progenitor of the Agile movement. An important meta-observation about Paul's work, in general, is that it often takes an expert like Paul to effectively (and objectively) bring "Lean" principles into a software development organization. There's something about the manner in which software and "processes" have been brought together over the years that have established many challenges in this space. Paul demonstrates several techniques to create conditions that allow for both flexibility and disciplined improvement that are worth emulating—both as a consultant, in general, but with respect to Lean principles, in particular. Readers without a firm grounding in "Lean" principles and practices would be well advised to have a guide or coach to try them out the first few times.

The same things I like also carry precautions to the broader reader audience. One thing is clear about both the companies Paul included in his cases, and about Paul's approach: improvement as a business driver is a key to success. Implementing CMMI for the ratings or "Agile" for bragging rights won't work. It must be human nature that causes people to continue to seek "silver bullet" solutions to their business challenges. Were there such solutions, there would be no challenges. Paul's techniques and approach were adapted from his experience addressing his clients' needs. They were not prefabricated in Paul's office and then installed in his clients' conference rooms. Paul generated appropriate solutions in the context of his clients' needs. The caution is this: experiment, inspect, and adapt. For either CMMI or Agile to benefit an organization or from each other, and, for either to truly take advantage of experimenting, inspecting, and adapting, there are several attributes an organization must embody: self-awareness, learning, brutal honesty, trust, and refusal to settle for mediocrity as a goal. Organizations who merely try to copy Paul's work clearly don't "get it."

Enjoy the work and I hope you all achieve your state of "excellence."

—*Hillel Glazer, Principal and CEO, Entinex, Inc.*
CMMI High Maturity Lead Appraiser

Preface

Why You Should Read This Book

This book explains why combining an Agile approach with the CMMI[1] process improvement framework [1] is the best route to quickly achieve your business objectives[2] and it gives you practical and proven techniques to do it. But the book's greatest value might lie in its insights into how real performance improvement is achieved by focusing on "repeating specific weaknesses" that tend to be unique and closely related to culture in each organization. The book also provides

- Proven alternatives to traditional approaches to implement CMMI practices that can increase your agility
- Proven criteria to help make timely and effective decisions
- Proven techniques to extend Agile methods to Systems Engineering and Project Management
- Big picture insights, lessons, and cautions
- Specific "how-to" examples to quick-start a successful Agile and CMMI integration
- Common mistakes to avoid when implementing an Agile approach

First, to understand why more companies are not jumping at this great opportunity, you need to understand the problem.

---

1. The Capability Maturity Model Integration (CMMI) is a process improvement maturity model for the development of products and services developed by the Software Engineering Institute (SEI).

2. An organization's "business objectives" might not include "process improvement." Why it is important to start with business objectives is discussed in Chapter 2. Examples of business objectives are provided in Chapter 3.

The Problem

The mistaken belief persists that the Capability Maturity Model Integration (CMMI) and Agile approaches are at odds. In a Technical Note[3] appearing on the Software Engineering Institute (SEI) Web site in November 2008 [2], a call to action is issued to both Agile and CMMI camps. CMMI experts are encouraged to engage the Agile community by including examples from multiple types of organizations. Agile experts are encouraged to learn about the CMMI and how its practices can complement Agile practices. The authors of the Technical Note universally agree that Agile methods and the CMMI "can not only coexist, but successfully integrate to bring substantial benefits to both Agile and traditional software development organizations."

Why Conflicts Continue to Arise

One reason for many of the conflicts that arise when using the CMMI together with an Agile approach traces back to the origins of the CMMI found in the development of its precursor CMM model. As stated in the referenced technical note:

> *If we look at the genesis of the CMM, it predates the internet and nearly everything associated with internet technology. For that matter, CMM predates many software development, deployment, and infrastructure technologies, languages, and methods...*

> *...In today's frequent discussions of increasing globalization and the important role played by trust in making effective collaboration happen across stakeholders, one might describe such a development context as exhibiting low trust. Users were typically not direct contributors to the evolution of the end product prior to field-testing. They instead had to depend on the contracting relationship, requirements, and standards to deliver the product they needed. These comments may be an over-generalization, but they are intended to summarize the DoD software acquisition environment that existed at the time. Further, these comments explain why the practices in the CMMI sometimes exhibit some of these same high ceremony and low trust characteristics found in the high-risk, government-contractor environment in which software failure could equal lives lost.*

---

3. Technical Note CMU/SEI-2008-TN-003, November 2008, "CMMI or Agile: Why Not Embrace Both!"

Another reason for many of the conflicts is the differing views on just what "Agile" is. Some view "Agile" simply as quick when making a decision or light when it comes to writing things down, but these popular misunderstandings of agility have led many organizations down unsuccessful paths.

Why I Wrote This Book

I wrote this book to help bridge the chasm described previously. Through this book, I explain where the heart of the conflict exists, and what you can do about it. A fundamental claim made through the case studies is that:

> *Most of the conflicts that arise between the CMMI and Agile are based in either a historical view of what a "good practice" should look like when implemented—which may no longer be accurate given the world we live in today—or a misunderstanding of what "Agile practices" really are and how they should be executed.*

It is my hope that CMMI experts, including lead appraisers, will consider this material and potentially re-think messages that might be being inadvertently shared related to what a "good CMMI-compliant" practice should look like when implemented. It is also my hope that organizations currently *misapplying Agile concepts* will begin to understand where their practices are deficient and see how the CMMI could help them locate their right level of agility given their business situation.

Throughout this book, I share numerous examples of how the CMMI can help Agile, and how Agile can help the CMMI.

How CMMI Can Help Agile

One goal of the book is to expose characteristics of Agile misapplications common in growing "Agile-like"[4] organizations and share how the CMMI can help these organizations by providing "reminders" of critical practices that frequently lose visibility as organizations grow and project pressures rise. I also share how the CMMI can help even successful growing organizations that are applying fundamental Agile practices as intended.

---

4. When I use the phrase "Agile-like" or "wannabe Agile" in this book, I am referring to organizations that are trying to use an Agile approach but are missing key ingredients of true agility.

How Agile Can Help CMMI

In this book, I also provide numerous options to traditional "how-to" approaches to implement CMMI practices. Some of these options are not well known, and in one personal case study, I present some "out of the box" thinking with respect to the use of the CMMI to help an organization move beyond consistency to the kind of performance required to effectively and continually rise above the competition.

What This Book Is Not

This is not a book about the fundamentals of the CMMI, nor is it a book about Agile methods such as Scrum, Extreme Programming, and the Crystal Methodologies—although you will read about lessons learned from applying these software methods as well as many proven systems engineering and project management techniques that evolved consistent with these methods.

What This Book Assumes about the Reader

Some of the chapters in this book assume the reader is familiar with either traditional CMMI-based development and management approaches or Agile development approaches, and is interested in learning how the other could be used effectively to help an organization achieve its business objectives fast.

The book is intended for managers at all levels, systems engineers, software engineers, and process professionals in large and small organizations that currently employ traditional CMMI-based processes, Agile methods, or a mix of both. The book is also intended equally for both CMMI and Agile experts, as well as less experienced personnel, and those just starting out with new process improvement initiatives looking for the most effective implementation approach for their organization.

How This Book Is Structured

In this book, I share six major case studies, each with related lessons, insights, myths, and cautions. *Lessons* contain key fundamental information. *Insights* contain key information that might require deeper reflection by the reader. *Myths* contain a belief about the CMMI model or an Agile approach that most people know is not true, but that organizations often treat as though it were. *Cautions* raise awareness of commonly observed pitfalls.

In Chapters 2 through 10, you will find 16 insights, 15 myths, 16 cautions, and 62 lessons. Lessons are numbered sequentially within each chapter. The book is structured into five major parts. Part I provides an introduction and a CMMI and Agile primer. Part II focuses on techniques to help CMMI process mature organizations increase their agility. Part III demonstrates how a successful Agile organization can increase its CMMI process maturity without compromising the agility that has brought it success. Part IV provides multiple examples demonstrating how the CMMI can help organizations that are trying to be agile but are missing key ingredients of true agility.

Part V focuses on the role of *repeating specific weaknesses* in achieving real performance improvements. Chapter 9 is intended to help you think a little "outside the box" by demonstrating the use of an Agile approach together with key CMMI practices to help solve a non-work-related challenge. Through this personal challenge, I draw some nontraditional conclusions— but conclusions backed up by case study data. This case study takes us beyond the fundamentals, examining how real "consistent high performance" is best achieved. This story brings us closer to the personal side of process improvement, and looks at how great organizations continually outperform the competition. In the concluding chapter, we step back, summarize what we have learned from these case studies, and provide an insight into real and consistent performance.

How Different Audiences Can Use This Book

This book can be used by different audiences in multiple ways. First, executives and senior managers looking for the big picture are encouraged to read the introductory material at the start of each of the five major parts of the book. Then scan the book, focusing on the *Scenarios* at the start of each chapter, the "What You Will Learn in This Chapter" paragraphs following the Scenarios, the highlighted *Insights, Lessons, Cautions,* and *Pause, Reflect, and Glance Forward* features throughout the chapters, and the summarizing tables at the end of each chapter entitled "How Agile Helps CMMI" and "How CMMI Helps Agile." You can then go back and read more specific case study information related to topics of greatest interest. You can also use the Roadmap in the Part I Introduction to help locate specific key information.

Second, technical leaders and developers looking for a deeper understanding can read the full case studies, which provide the rationale for approaches taken and the thought process we went through in applying the CMMI model to varying situations. This level of detailed information is necessary to understand why the options were chosen within each of the specific organizations. This information can in turn help you make better decisions given your own situation.

Third, process professionals and those looking for more detailed "how-to" information should first take the time to digest the case study information, understanding both what was done and why. This will lead to "how-to" questions. To help with the "how-to," specific examples are provided in the appendices. These "how-to" annotated examples are referenced from footnotes within the case study chapters and can help your process improvement effort get started on the right track toward a successful Agile and CMMI integration.

Fourth, the novice (i.e., software engineer fresh out of college or college student) or those looking for the fundamentals are encouraged to first read Chapter 1, the introduction, and CMMI/Agile primers. Then, after reading the Summary tables at the end of each chapter, read Chapters 4, 5, and 8 and Part V. Chapters 4 and 5 provide a good foundation in fundamentals, while Chapter 8 demonstrates some of the most common challenges observed in traditional organizations when initially attempting an Agile approach, along with practical and proven solutions.

Acknowledgments

I thank the following people for reviewing and commenting on the multiple draft versions of this book: Scott Ambler, Dr. Alistair Cockburn, Jim Convery, Erin Convery, Neil Crowder, Bob Epps, Kyle Gabhart, Hillel Glazer, Gary Hafen, Elaine Harmon, Mike Konrad, Rich McCabe, Jan McMahon, Dr. Mark Paulk, Doug Parsons, Mary Lynn Penn, Mike Phillips, Dr. Jeff Sutherland, John Troy, Dr. Richard Turner, David Webb, and Jason Yip.

I thank all those who helped in the production of this book especially Peter Gordon, Kim Boedigheimer, and Dmitri Korzh.

I thank clients, colleagues, and friends who have helped through ongoing support and insightful conversations. I especially thank Craig Button, Dr. Dave Cavitt, Christina Chick, Paul Curtis, Sue Franciscus, Dave Gdovin, Ed Harvey, Toni Goad, Jeanie Kitson, David Kitson, Jack McGinn, Steve Noel, Dr. Mike Oakes, Don Reifer, Beth Starrett, Leslie TerHaar, Howard Stein, Graham Upton, and Mike White.

Special thanks to my wife Jan for her detailed review and edit of this manuscript; John Troy for his multiple detailed and late night reviews and discussions; Bob Epps for his life-time of insightful comments and discussions; Dr. Richard Turner for his overall structural comments on an early version of the book; Rich McCabe for his key comments on an early version of the book that helped me focus on what was most important to say; Hillel Glazer for recommending the sidebars to help pull the reader through early sections by glancing forward at important material to come later; Alistair Cockburn for suggesting the addition of more "how-to" examples; Mike Konrad for his detailed review and suggested additions with respect to the CMMI Version 1.3; Hillel Glazer and Mike Phillips for writing Forewords to the book; and Bob Demer for inviting me to his week-long golf marathon sixtieth birthday celebration.

PART I

Introduction

Part I of this book includes an introduction, along with CMMI and Agile primers to lay the groundwork for the discussions that follow. Table Intro-1 provides a roadmap to key information in this book.

Table Intro-1 *Roadmap to Key Information in the Book*

Proven alternatives to traditional approaches to implement CMMI practices that can increase your agility	Ch 2 Prune Overweight Processes
	Ch 2 Lean Peer Reviews
	Ch 3 Selecting Subprocesses for Statistical Control
	Ch 4 BOND Case Study (Gap Analysis, Running Process Improvement Project, Peer Reviews, Organizational Repository Structure, Packaging Processes, Formalizing Informality)
	Ch 6 Priority-based Incremental Process Deployment
	Ch 6 Pre-tailoring Alternative

Continues

1

Table Intro-1 *Roadmap to Key Information in the Book (Continued)*

	Ch 6 Alternative Approach to Tailor Roles and Responsibilities Ch 7 Process Improvement Project Optimizations Ch 7 Quality Assurance Alternatives
Proven criteria to help people make timely and effective decisions	Ch 3 Special Circumstances and Alternative Decisions Ch 4 Tailoring/Guides, Where "How-to" Decisions Are Made Ch 5 Criteria to Aid Decision for PMP Ch 6 Supporting an Agile Culture Through Better Decisions Ch 7 Criteria for Tailoring Templates Ch 7 Criteria for Tailoring Ch 7 Criteria for Testing Ch 7 Criteria for Peer Reviews Ch 8 Criteria to Decide Priority Work Ch 8 Criteria to Help Decide if I Can Meet a Commitment
Proven techniques to extend Agile methods to Systems Engineering and Project Management	Ch 3 Diddling in DOORS Story Ch 5 Agile Five Steps to Planning Ch 8 Technique 1: Sutherland 10 Percent Rule Ch 8 Technique 2: Scope Document to Manage Collaboration Ch 8 Technique 3: Push-Pull Technique Ch 8 Example 1: Estimating Tasks and Assessing Commitments Ch 8 Example 2: Prioritizing Work Ch 8 Example 3: Managing Work Scope Ch 8 Example 4: Progress Assessment Ch 8 Example 5: Training
Proven innovative approaches to help your organization continually outperform the competition	Chs 2 and 3 Case Study of LACM Ch 9 Your Repeating Specific Weaknesses: Finding Them, Why They Are Bad, Eliminating Them and Keeping Them from Coming Back

Table Intro-1 *Roadmap to Key Information in the Book (Continued)*

	Ch 10 Conclusion Epilogue: What Does Passion Have to Do with Performance?
Big picture insights, lessons, and cautions	**INSIGHT** Insights are boxed and shaded **LESSON** Lessons are boxed **CAUTION** Cautions appear in bold print
Specific "how-to" examples to quick-start a successful Agile and CMMI integration	Ch 5 Example CMMI Evidence Generated Using a PMP Template Ch 5 Example Agile Schedule Guidelines Ch 6 Example Stakeholder Matrix Appendices B through F Annotated Examples Referenced from Applicable Chapter Case Studies in Footnotes
Common mistakes when implementing an Agile approach	Ch 6 NANO Case Study Ch 7 GEAR Case Study Ch 8 DART Case Study

Chapter 1

Introduction and CMMI/Agile Primers

1.1 Introduction and CMMI Primer

The Capability Maturity Model Integration (CMMI) for development is a process improvement maturity model for the development of products and services developed by the Software Engineering Institute (SEI).

There is no single prescribed best way to use the CMMI model. If one examined the breadth of possibilities, at one extreme is what could be called the "imposition" method. This is the method that "imposes" a documented process for each of the process areas and related practices within the model. The imposition method is the easiest answer to the common question, "Can't you just tell me what the CMMI says I have to do?"

At the other extreme is what could be called the "nonimposition" method. This method is best reflected by the common response to a new CMMI initiative in an Agile organization: "I already know how to do my job" or "I'm sure we can find something to prove that we do that."

The intent of the CMMI model is not to "impose" a set of practices on an organization, nor is it to be applied as a standard to which one must "prove compliance." Used appropriately, the CMMI can help you locate the specific areas where change in your organization can provide the greatest value given your business objectives.

To apply the model this way requires an understanding of the choices you face, the options you have, and related consequences of your decisions. To understand your choices and options requires first a high-level understanding of the structure of the CMMI model.

CMMI Primer

The CMMI model is composed of a collection of *Process Areas* (PAs) each containing a set of *Specific Practices* (SPs) and *Generic Practices* (GPs). Refer to Table 1-1 for key CMMI PAs discussed in this book, and a brief description of each.

Table 1-1 *Key CMMI Process Areas Discussed in the Book*

Process Area	Brief Purpose Description
Project Planning (PP)	To establish and maintain the project's plan
Project Monitor and Control (PMC)	To provide an understanding of the project's progress so corrective actions can be taken
Risk Management (RSKM)	To identify potential problems before they occur
Quantitative Project Management (QPM)	To quantitatively manage the project's defined process
Requirements Management (REQM)	To manage the requirements
Requirements Development (RD)	To produce and analyze requirements
Technical Solution (TS)	To design, develop and implement solutions
Verification (VER)	To ensure selected work products meet requirements

Table 1-1 *Key CMMI Process Areas Discussed in the Book (Continued)*

Process Area	Brief Purpose Description
Validation (VAL)	To demonstrate that a product fulfills its intended use
Product & Process Quality Assurance (PPQA)	To provide objective insight into products and processes
Measurement & Analysis (MA)	To develop and maintain a measurement capability to support management information needs
Decision Analysis & Resolution (DAR)	To analyze possible decisions evaluating alternatives against established criteria
Causal Analysis Resolution (CAR)	To identify causes of defects and other problems and take action
Organizational Process Focus (OPF)	To plan, implement, and deploy organizational process improvements based on strengths and weaknesses
Organizational Process Definition (OPD)	To establish and maintain a usable set of organizational process assets
Organizational Training (OT)	To develop skills and knowledge of people so they can perform their roles effectively and efficiently
Integrated Project Management (IPM)	To establish and manage the project and involvement of relevant stakeholders according to the defined process

Practices are grouped under *Specific* and *Generic Goals*. The SPs are expected practices that are specific to each process area, whereas the GPs are common across all PAs. The GPs discussed in this book (all level 2, and 3 GPs) along with a brief description of each, are provided in Table 1-2.

Table 1-2 *Key CMMI Generic Practices Discussed in the Book*

Generic Practice	Brief Description
GP 2.1	Establish an Organizational Policy
GP 2.2	Plan the Process
GP 2.3	Provide Resources
GP 2.4	Assign Responsibility
GP 2.5	Train People
GP 2.6	Manage Configurations
GP 2.7	Identify and Involve Relevant Stakeholders
GP 2.8	Monitor and Control the Process
GP 2.9	Objectively Evaluate Adherence
GP 2.10	Review Status with Higher Level Management
GP 3.1	Establish a Defined Process
GP 3.2	Collect Improvement Information

Key SPs discussed in this book, along with a brief description of each, are provided in Table 1-3.

Table 1-3 *Key CMMI Specific Practices Discussed in the Book*

Specific Practice	Brief Description
CAR SP 1.1	Select Defects and Other Problems for Analysis
CAR SP 2.1	Implement Action Proposals
MA SP 1.1	Establish Measurement Objectives
MA SP 1.2	Specify Measures
MA SP 2.4	Communicate Results
OPD SP 1.1	Establish Standard Processes

Table 1-3 *Key CMMI Specific Practices Discussed in the Book (Continued)*

Specific Practice	Brief Description
OPD SP 1.3	Establish Tailoring Criteria and Guidelines
OPF SP 1.1	Establish Organizational Process Needs
PMC SP 1.1	Monitor Project Planning Parameters
PMC SP 2.3	Manage Corrective Action
PP SP 1.2	Establish Estimates of Products and Task Attributes
PP SP 1.3	Define Project Life Cycle
PP SP 2.7	Establish the Project Plan
PP SP 3.2	Reconcile Work and Resource Levels
QPM SP 1.3	Select Subprocesses to Statistically Manage
REQM SP 1.3	Manage Requirements Changes
RSKM SP 3.1	Develop Risk Mitigation Plans
VER SP 1.2	Select Work Products for Verification
VER SP 1.3	Establish Verification Procedures and Criteria

Practices are expected, but can be achieved by what is referred to as "alternative" practices that achieve the intent of the practice. All goals related to a process area must be achieved when seeking a rating associated with a process area.

The purpose of the GPs is to aid what is referred to as *institutionalization* of a PA, which effectively means ensuring the organization has an infrastructure in place to support the PA when new people come in or other changes happen within the organization. While there is only one set of PAs, the model can be employed using two different representations referred to as the *Staged* Representation and the *Continuous* Representation. With the Staged Representation, process areas are viewed as collections at five distinct maturity levels.

With the Continuous Representation, decisions on the use of the model can be made in a more flexible way supporting an organization's unique business objectives. The Continuous Representation is the preferred representation when using the CMMI model and an Agile approach together.

A question that sometimes arises relates to what appears to some as redundancy between the generic practices and certain process areas. For example, GP 2.5 Train People and the Organizational Training Process Area, or GP 2.6 Manage Configurations and the Configuration Management Process Area, or GP 2.9 Objectively Evaluation Adherence and the Product and Process Quality Assurance Process Area.

One reason for this is the options you have when applying the model using the Continuous Representation. The generic practices ensure you are addressing these practices for whatever process area you decide to focus on even if you haven't selected its related full process area.

Use of the Phrase "CMMI Compliancy" in This Book

The phrase "CMMI compliancy" in this book means achieving the intent of the CMMI practices.

1.2 Agile Primer

Agile methods have evolved from grassroots movements based on proven practices of successful small software teams. Popular Agile methods include Scrum [3], Crystal [4, 5], Extreme Programming [6], and Agile Modeling[1] [7]. The term "method" as used here means a collection of techniques intended to work together. The term "technique" refers to a specific "how to" approach to implement some aspect of an Agile principle.

Agile Principles and Practices

Agile "principles" refers to the 12 principles behind the Agile Manifesto that was drafted by 17 methodologists in February 2001 to help address challenges faced by software developers. Refer to Appendix A for the 12 principles.

---

1. According to a Gartner study in autumn 2009, Agile Modeling driven approaches (www.agilemodeling .com) was the second most popular strategy after Scrum.

The Agile Manifesto also identifies four values:

- We value individuals and interactions over processes and tools.
- We value working software over documentation.
- We value customer collaboration over contract negotiation.
- We value responding to change over following a plan.

It also states as a point of clarification with reference to the four values, "That is, while there is value in the items on the right, we value the items on the left more."

Key Agile practices discussed in this book, along with a brief description of each, are provided in Table 1-4.

Table 1-4 *Key Agile Practices Discussed in This Book*

Agile Practice	Brief Description
Incremental and multigrain planning	"Coarse" and "fine" grain plans developed and used to guide work.
Continual refinement of plan	Plans are continually refined as new information is acquired.
Short iterative development cycles working closely with customer	To help ensure requirements are understood, work is done in short cycles using frequent customer feedback to aid course correction.
Daily team standup meetings with current work kept visible to the full team	Ensures team is communicating and staying on the agreed-to course.
Teams self-manage the work	Team members measure their own velocity/productivity and commit to work based on the team's measured performance.
Frequent delivery of working product to customer based on customer priorities	Helps team stay focused on customer high value items.
Time-boxing work	Schedules are maintained by reducing delivered functionality, if necessary.

Continues

Table 1-4 *Key Agile Practices Discussed in This Book (Continued)*

Agile Practice	Brief Description
Team retrospectives	Team periodically reflects on its processes, frequently making improvements the team agrees can help their performance.
Rapid response to changing customer needs	By keeping the iterations short and continually communicating with the customer, the team is able to change priorities on shorter cycles, if required.

Agile Terminology Used in This Book

The phrase "Agile approach" refers to the extension of Agile concepts to include the critical domains of Systems Engineering and Project Management, and software. By "Agile organization," I mean an organization that uses an Agile approach on the majority of its projects.

The term "hybrid Agile" refers to the use of a blend of traditional and Agile techniques. The phrase "Agile-like" or "wannabe Agile" refers to organizations that are trying to use an Agile approach, but are missing key ingredients of true agility.

For more information on Agile methods, refer to [7, 8, 9].

1.3 General Information about the Case Studies

What I share in the case studies in the book is what happened, and the thought process we went through using the CMMI model to make process-related project management and systems engineering decisions. It is my hope that by sharing this level of detail, those on both sides of the Agile–CMMI divide can begin to see how using the CMMI model in the manner discussed supports the common goal we all strive for.

Each case study focuses on specific subjects related to CMMI and Agile, explained further at the start of each chapter. Earlier case studies in the book sometimes begin to touch on a subject that is more germane to a later case study. In these situations, footnotes are employed to let the reader know where in the book more information is available.

In this book when I refer to "high maturity," I include maturity levels 3, 4, and 5. As a point of clarification, today when the SEI refers to "high maturity," it is now reserved for levels 4 and 5. "Level 3" in this book means CMMI Maturity level 3.

1.4 General Information about Terminology Used in the Book

Many terms are clarified throughout the book on first use in the text or footnotes to aid communication. For ease of later reference, these terms are summarized in Appendix G.

PART II

Helping Mature Organizations Increase Agility

In this part of the book, I share stories about the LACM organization, a large CMMI process mature organization that is successfully increasing its agility.

Here you will learn techniques to improve existing traditional CMMI-based processes in support of increased agility while maintaining CMMI compliancy. In Chapter 3 you will learn about nontraditional approaches LACM employed using the higher CMMI level practices effectively together with an Agile approach.

CMMI experts, especially those working inside large traditional CMMI-based process organizations, should be interested in the LACM case study to learn effective options in using the higher-level CMMI practices to help an organization align improvement efforts with the true needs of the organization.

Chapter 2

Techniques to Increase Agility in CMMI Mature Organizations

Scenario: *You are a large CMM[1]/ CMMI process mature organization. The good news is that you already have documented processes, have been through a formal CMMI appraisal, and have been appraised at a high CMM/CMMI level (3, 4, or 5). But internally you are hearing complaints from your workforce, including: "The company processes don't help me do my job," or "The company processes require me to do extra work that isn't adding value,"[2] or "We need to increase our process agility to respond more rapidly to changing customer needs." You'd like to make your processes more Agile to help position your company to be more competitive in the future, but you are afraid of making changes that could put your CMMI compliance[3] at risk. So what can you do? What options do you have?*

---

1. CMM refers to a precursor maturity model to the CMMI that focused only on software.

2. In this book when I use the term "value," I mean usefulness with respect to achieving business objectives.

3. In this book, the phrase "CMMI compliant" means "achieving the intent of the practice."

2.1 What You Will Learn in This Chapter

- Where to start a process improvement effort to get the most value for your investment
- Why the way many organizations use the CMMI model costs more than necessary and fails to provide the promised payback
- Techniques to align process initiatives with real business objectives
- How one process mature organization increased its agility using the CMMI model
- Two specific examples to increase agility
- CMMI appraisal options not well understood
- An alternative approach to increase agility along with related advantages and disadvantages

2.2 LACM Case Study Background

LACM is a successful high-tech organization focusing on the U.S. defense market. In 2007, the organization experienced its greatest success in the history of the company. With over fifty active projects, only two were experiencing any difficulty with respect to cost, schedule, and customer satisfaction goals. The organization achieved a CMM level 3 many years ago and a CMMI level 3 in 2008. The 2008 CMMI process improvement effort was initiated high up in the organization.

2.3 Where to Start When Using the CMMI Model to Increase Agility

When you begin a CMMI-based process improvement effort, there is not a single required starting point or specific method for using the model, but the approach taken at LACM might be the best I have ever witnessed at a large U.S. defense company.

While this initiative was partially motivated by the drive to achieve a CMMI level 3 formal rating because new business opportunities were demanding it, a few of the executives at this company also understood how the CMMI could help them achieve their business goals by addressing known weaknesses within the company.

When this process improvement effort was initiated, the Vice President (VP) of Engineering was adamant that any process changes resulting from the effort must be clearly aligned with business goals. He knew the company needed to make a number of very specific changes because the future needs of his customers were changing. He also knew the right time to make these changes was now when the company was successful, because if he waited any longer the results would come too late.

To get the right process efforts started, he told some of his directors that when he looked at the company processes he couldn't tell anything about what the company did. That comment led to a great deal of discussion as to whether one should be able to tell what a company does just by looking at its processes—and if so where in the process descriptions this should be evident.

The VP also challenged the engineering organization with a series of questions. He asked:

- Why are our customers coming back to us now over the competition?
- What is the unique value this organization brings to its customers?

These questions led to an improved business value statement, which led to more questions being asked by those reporting to the VP related to process needs directly supporting customer value. The results of these discussions were captured and communicated throughout the organization via a series of presentations and open forum discussions deeper in the organization. These presentations and discussions drove specific process improvement actions that were reviewed prior to approval against the agreed-to current business needs and future customer needs.

Understanding the changing business needs and resultant process needs was not arrived at easily. Nevertheless, the investment in the time to allow the people in the organization to attend presentations and discuss their real process needs in light of the business direction and changing customer needs helped the organization see clearly where they should spend their process improvement dollars to best help achieve their goals. In this chapter, I share specific process improvement efforts that resulted from this activity.

> **INSIGHT**   You have a choice where to start a process improvement effort when using the CMMI Model.

2.4 Where Many Organizations Wrongly Start When Using the CMMI Model

Often, organizations start their process improvement effort when using the CMMI model at a level 2 process area such as Project Planning (PP). Unfortunately, this creates more work in the long run for a number of reasons. First, when organizations start at level 2 without first giving some thought to level 3, they often end up reworking what was done at level 2.

Second, most organizations don't have an unlimited process improvement budget so they have to make decisions how to spend their limited resources. By starting your effort at the level 3 Organizational Process Focus (OPF) SP 1.1, you can create powerful criteria to aid process improvement related decisions right from the start.

OPF SP 1.1—"Establish and maintain the description of the process needs and objectives for the organization."

2.5 How the CMMI Model Is Often Used, and Options Not Well Understood

Today, many organizations in search of a certain CMMI level rating just go out and implement every practice expected at that level and don't think about how much money they should be investing in each area first. Unfortunately, many of these organizations don't know they have options within the model that allow them to make intelligent decisions related to how they spend their process improvement dollars based on their business objectives. An example of a choice you have is the data you decide to collect when doing peer reviews. To help make a good decision here, ask yourself the following two questions:

- Who is going to use this data if we collect it?
- How does this data relate to our business objectives?

If no one is going to use the data, then don't waste valuable resources collecting it. Why data is often collected today that is not used in large high-tech companies often is found on investigation to tie to historical experiences that are no longer valid in today's world.[4]

2.6 Aligning Your Process Initiatives with Your Real Business Objectives

At LACM, the VP of Engineering realized that there were many process improvement initiatives going on throughout the organization, but they were not being coordinated or assessed against clear criteria. The result was redundant efforts without measurable goals. To ensure all process efforts were aligned with business objectives and coordinated across the organization, he identified a single point in the organization for approval and monitoring of process efforts. Resources to execute the process improvements were distributed across the organization, with cost, schedule, and performance reporting consolidated under a single source who reported status weekly directly to him.

That VP at LACM was not a CMMI expert, and I don't believe he even knew about SP 1.1 of OPF. He just knew from experience what he had to do to get his organizational process improvement effort aligned with the business needs and get the related cost and schedule under control.

Starting at OPF SP 1.1 makes sense if you are a high maturity[5] organization initiating a new improvement effort, or if you are just starting out with your first process improvement effort as the following lesson indicates.

> **LESSON 1**
>
> By first establishing the process needs within your specific business context, you can provide criteria to help make more cost-effective decisions on how to focus and drive your process improvement priorities.

---

4. This subject is discussed in the next chapter where we examine more closely the implementation of CMMI level 4 and 5 practices and their relationship to agility.

5. In this book, "high maturity" includes maturity levels 3, 4, and 5. As a point of clarification, today when the SEI refers to "high maturity" it is now reserved for levels 4 and 5.

One of the reviewers of this book commented that he read the Lesson 1 six times, wondering how this was possible. I told him the story of what one CMMI lead appraiser, who had actually worked with Watts Humphrey developing the material that led to the original CMM model, told me. He had impressed upon me the power of SP 1.1 of OPF by stating that the developers of the model knew that different businesses had different process needs because of the nature of their product and customers. By spending time to capture your true business needs, you can provide a context to make decisions about where to focus your priorities. Today, many organizations in search of a CMMI Maturity level 3 just go out and implement every specific practice in every level 2 and level 3 process area, and don't think about how much effort they should be investing in each area first. If you have created a good, documented process needs description, you can use that to explain why you might decide to focus more on one area rather than another. *Unfortunately, many organizations don't know they have these options at their disposal to make intelligent decisions related to how they focus their effort based on their business needs.*

2.7 Aligning Process Descriptions and Training with the Real Process

Through the presentations and the discussions initiated by the VP, people in the organization became increasingly aware that the company achieved great value through product reuse. But as this discussion evolved, people began to realize that many of the company processes had been written solely for new development. This included the systems engineering requirements and design processes. Further discussions occurred on the relationship between design and product reuse, and the reuse of requirements. Because of these discussions, specific process improvement initiatives were identified and approved to better align systems engineering processes and training in the company with its reuse-centric approach.

The discussions initiated by the VP also led to an increasing awareness of the need for more rapid response to changing customer needs. Further questions and discussions on where current processes were failing led interestingly to human resources and personnel turnover in the company.

The driving force behind these discussions related to experiences at the company the year before initiating the CMMI effort. In 2007, LACM had experienced a large number of technical resignations, which in turn had stressed engineering's response time due to the time it took to hire and train new people and the need to stretch experienced personnel beyond normal expected limits.

This discussion in turn led to questions as to why people were leaving the company. Analysis of the data from exit interviews found that the most common reason given was they didn't know what management's expectations of them were in doing their job. The common phrase used was "thrown into the fire, don't know what to do." They had been hired to do a job, but then felt they had received very little relevant training.

What is interesting is that this company did have a comprehensive formal training program, but the people in the organization were indicating that there was a disconnect between the training that was formally being given and what they were being asked to do on real projects.

As a result, the company took a very innovative approach to increase their process agility and align the processes and training with the real work people were doing. One specific part of this effort became known as *pruning* the processes.

2.8 Two Specific Examples to Increase Agility: Pruning and Leaning

Pruning Overweight Processes to Improve Response Time

Because they had received the feedback from those leaving the company indicating people had difficulty understanding management's expectations of them on the job, the company initiated an effort to build flow diagrams of what people really did to complete the real work they were being asked to do. Then they annotated these diagrams with the process assets[6] the people said they really used to do their job. These were not theoretical diagrams; they were built based on what people said they did every day to get their job done. Anything that didn't end up on a flow diagram was a candidate for elimination. These diagrams were followed up with further questions:

- If no one used something, why was it there?
- Were we wasting time training people on the use of certain process assets?

---

6. By "process asset" I mean any artifact that supports people in carrying out their jobs, such as a template or guide.

- Did we believe people should be using certain process assets that weren't being employed?
- Did we believe if they did use them, it would help the people get their job done more effectively?

This approach helped to "prune" the processes, making them easier to use, and served to further ensure those processes were aligned[7] with the real process needs of the business in supporting customers' rapidly changing needs.

In the case where we thought certain process assets or steps would help people get their job done more effectively but weren't understood, initiatives were undertaken to communicate the purpose of the process asset that wasn't being used along with improved training in how it could help. In many cases it turned out that most of the items not completed, but documented in a current process, were put there because someone believed the CMM or CMMI required them when in fact this was not the case.

Leaning the Peer Review Process

As an example, this company had a very onerous Peer Review process. This process required a great deal of data to be collected about each defect written at a Peer Review. It also had processes requiring periodic analysis of this data. When we did the real flows, we found that people were entering all the data because the Peer Review tool required by the company mandated it. It was also determined that no one was following the process to analyze this data and use the results. So the question was asked:

Why are we making people enter all this data, if no one is using it?

We had to explain that this data was not required by the CMM or the CMMI. The *Peer Review Practice under the Verification Process Area* of the CMMI does expect you to analyze data about preparation, conduct, and results of peer reviews, but it doesn't dictate what this data needs to be. This is an example where many organizations have gone overboard in interpreting the model to create non-value-added work for its people.

The flow analysis led to a streamlining or a "leaning" of the Peer Review process, making the process more effective and consistent with the intent of the Peer Review practice within the CMMI model. Through these process improvement efforts at LACM, the following insight was uncovered.

---

7. The term "align" in this book means in agreement with, or consistent with.

> **INSIGHT**   Historically there has been a tendency for people to read
> things into the CMMI model that are not there and thus create unneces-
> sary non-value-added work for themselves. By understanding and using
> the CMMI model practices as they were intended, you can help align your
> real processes with your real process needs and objectives.

2.9 Why More Organizations Don't Prune and Lean Their Processes Today

One comment I have repeatedly heard is that "pruning" is a great idea, so why don't more organizations do this? I have never heard any organization indicate they didn't like this idea, but the reason many organizations don't do it is that it requires a commitment of the time of key people in the organization who really use the processes. Usually these people are just too busy with direct contract work and the priority doesn't allow this to happen.

Nevertheless, if your organization is experiencing a high percentage of resignations as LACM was, consider allocating a percentage of the time of key people to such an effort. A small investment in pruning and leaning just might pay high dividends in the long run.

2.10 Understanding the CMMI Model Intent to Help Your Organization Succeed

When an organization uses the CMMI model as LACM did, you can expect to find yourself asking questions leading to different decisions related to process needs and priorities. When used this way, the model becomes more of a tool or an aid assisting the decision-making process—which leads to Lesson 2.

> **LESSON 2**
>
> The CMMI model is not a set of dictated practices. It is a model that is
> intended to be used to "reason" about our processes to help us ask the
> right questions leading to an understanding of our weaknesses and areas
> of needed improvement.

Unfortunately, not all organizations understand this lesson or use the model as it was intended. Too often, we find that organizations are just "going through the motions" when it comes to SP 1.1 of OPF, and creating an abstract process needs statement that doesn't really get to the real issues affecting the business. As a result, such statements are rarely used to drive real process related decisions within the organization.

I don't mean to make this sound easy. When I challenged one organization by telling them their process needs description was too general to be useful, the response I got was that if they made it more specific it would soon be out of date. I replied that is why the practice starts with the words "establish and maintain." Those words mean not just to document it, but "document and use" it, which implies it needs to have enough value to be usable.

It also implies that when it is no longer accurate because business conditions change, you should want to update it, so you can continue to use it as active criteria to make on-going continuous value-added process improvement decisions.[8]

2.11 Options You Have in Using the CMMI Model for Appraisals

Multiple options are available using the CMMI model when appraising an organization. Some organizations only think about using the model for a formal appraisal (referred to as a SCAMPI[9] A) with the goal of obtaining a rating. Experience has shown that great value can be achieved by using the model less formally to appraise an organization with the goal of determining the as-is process situation and identifying potential opportunities for improvement. This type of appraisal effort can also be used to aid discussions leading to a better understanding of the organization's real process needs. We did this at LACM prior to the formal appraisal in 2008 and its benefits were enormous in terms of helping the organization focus its follow-on process improvement efforts.

My experience indicates when an appraisal team faces the pressures of Senior Management's expectations on achieving a certain CMMI level

---

8. In the GEAR case study discussed later, you will see an example of the cost of misalignment between real process needs and on-going process improvement initiatives.

9. SCAMPI stands for Standard CMMI Appraisal Method for Process Improvement.

because potential new business is riding on the assessment's results, this situation often creates a strong inhibitor to the identification of the most valuable potential opportunities for real improvement. Potential real value-added opportunities for improvement under these conditions tend to get lost in the pressures to ensure all the necessary supporting evidence is attained to achieve the desired rating.

By conducting a less formal appraisal early (referred to as a SCAMPI B, C, or gap analysis), often clarifying focus and priorities can be brought to a challenging improvement effort.[10]

2.12 An Alternative Approach to Agility

RAVE Case Study

The approach taken by LACM is not the only route for large process mature organizations looking to increase their agility. RAVE is a large CMMI level 5 organization that also focuses primarily on the U.S. defense market similar to LACM. In 2005, RAVE recognized a number of their projects were attempting to move in the Agile direction through an informal grassroots movement (referred to in some organizations as "stealth" Agile),[11] despite the fact that the company formal processes did not recognize the validity of an Agile approach. To address this need, RAVE initiated a Six Sigma team to tackle the problem. I was asked to participate on the team to provide an independent Agile and CMMI perspective.

The outcome resulted in the development of an Agile Developer's Guide, which was viewed as one of many options within the company's available toolkits. The strategy taken at RAVE was different from LACM in that RAVE decided not to modify its existing CMMI level 5 processes to accommodate potential Agile approaches, but rather handle Agile through its normal tailoring and standard project planning processes. The fundamental idea of implementing agility through the normal tailoring and project planning processes makes sense, but I have a number of cautions to share based on my experiences observing this kind of approach to increasing an organization's agility.

---

10. Conducting a gap analysis using the CMMI model in an Agile organization is discussed in Chapter 4, in the BOND case study.

11. When I use the phrase "stealth Agile" in this book I mean an informal Agile initiative that isn't part of a documented and approved plan.

> **CAUTION**
>
> If you implement agility through a Developer's Guide approach, make sure your process identifies clearly the limits allowed through your tailoring guidelines. Otherwise, you are likely to fall into the common trap of losing fundamental practices (e.g., Systems Engineering critical practices) that are necessary[12] [10].

An example of a potential lost fundamental systems engineering practice is the appropriate degree of requirements analysis.[13]

When I was asked to help RAVE develop their Agile Developer's Guide, one of the first questions I asked related to how their tailoring process works. While they were explaining the process to me, I asked:

What is the minimum everyone must do?

They were unable to provide an answer because they had no clearly defined limits.

When Agile approaches are implemented appropriately together with CMMI processes, effective implementation of required practices results, not their deletion.

> **CAUTION**
>
> If you implement agility through a Developer's Guide approach, be aware of the potential consequence of redundant efforts.

While the Agile Developer's Guide approach can be sound, it also presents the risk of process redundancy and extra work when we are seeking the reverse. A common tailoring mistake I have observed is to add the Agile approach not as an implementation alternative, but rather on top of existing required traditional practices. Specific areas in which to be on the lookout for this costly mistake relate to product reviews and progress reporting.

---

12. See reference for a related article with more examples. In Chapter 4, I discuss a CMMI process asset structure that supports agility and can help avoid the common trap described previously.

13. The subject of appropriate degree of requirements analysis when using an Agile approach is discussed in the DART case study.

2.13 Summary: How CMMI Helps Agile

The following table provides a summary of how CMMI areas discussed in this chapter help Agile.

CMMI Area	How It Helps Agile
OPF SP 1.1	Used as intended helps make most effective decisions with limited process improvement dollars

2.14 Summary: How Agile Helps CMMI

The following table provides a summary of how Agile approaches discussed in this chapter help the CMMI.

Agile Approach	How It Helps CMMI
Pruning processes	Processes reflect what people really do
Leaning processes	Ensures data collected is used

Chapter 3

Agility and the Higher CMMI Level Practices

Scenario: You are a CMMI level 3 organization, and you've been considering taking your organization to level 4 and 5, but you are unsure if this is the right path to help your organization achieve its efficiency and productivity goals. You've heard level 4 means statistical process control[1] and you are worried that the control charts you'll need to develop won't provide the real payback in project performance. So what can you do? What options do you have?

3.1 What You Will Learn in This Chapter[2]

- The real intent of CMMI level 4 and 5 practices and how one organization achieved this intent by using Agile and Lean techniques with the CMMI
- How one organization modified its measurement program to align with its real information needs

---

1. This is a myth. Statistical process control is just one possible approach, and you will learn in this chapter about other possible approaches.

2. This chapter is not intended to tell you everything you need to know before you initiate process improvement in CMMI high maturity process areas; rather, it addresses issues relative to Agile. Reference the "Understanding CMMI High Maturity Practices" course and the CMMI and Six Sigma courses at the SEI for more information.

- Why the approach taken in many higher CMMI mature organizations with respect to Quantitative Project Management (QPM) has failed to provide the promised payback, and how you can avoid this pitfall
- A different way to view subprocesses that can help you achieve your business objectives fast

3.2 Background on the Higher CMMI Level Practices

There continues to be significant controversy over the value of moving an organization to CMMI level 4 and 5 even though over the past few years increasing evidence has accrued as to its value[3] [11]. First, the motivation isn't there for many organizations to the same degree as it is for CMMI level 3 because in the past, the Department of Defense (DoD) has only required a level 3 for many of its contracts. Second, many organizations tend to shy away from level 4 due to the fear that statistical management of subprocesses, which is an expected practice in the level 4 QPM process area, will become an academic exercise without real payback in project performance.

At the 2008 Systems and Software Technology Conference (SSTC), I spoke on the subject of using Lean[4] and Agile techniques together with CMMI level 4 and 5 practices to help organizations achieve business objectives fast[5] [12]. That work was based on a specific case study of a situation that occurred at LACM a few years before they had reached the high level of success discussed in the previous chapter. The case study in this chapter, which is based on that previous work plus what happened at LACM afterward, caused me to start taking a different view of the higher CMMI level practices.

This chapter is divided into two sections. In Section I, I share key points from the previously published case study at LACM. In Section II, I move beyond that work to share updated information on how LACM is gaining the value of the higher CMMI level practices by using them *less formally* along with an *Agile* approach.

---

3. Jeff Sutherland, co-founder of Scrum, has also discussed the value of using Scrum and CMMI level 5 practices together. See the reference.

4. Lean refers to a collection of techniques related to Agile that improve cycle time by focusing on process flow and speed.

5. Material referenced here can also be found in the referenced *CrossTalk* article.

Section I
Key Case Study Points

3.3 Case Study Background

Many years ago, I assisted LACM in a discussion of their business objectives, and during that process, we used the Goal-Question-Metric (GQM) technique [13] to help align their measures with their objectives. The company had standardized processes and training in place with a strong emphasis on product baseline management with disciplined change approvals. Their business objectives included increasing off-the-shelf product sales, reducing unique customer customizations, and meeting cost and schedule commitments. The natural question that arose was:

Are they achieving their business objectives?

While isolated success stories existed, most managers in the organization felt they had fallen far short of their goal. As an example, it was not uncommon in Senior Management reviews to hear words such as:

Why are we making all these unplanned and unbid changes?

This case is not unique. I have observed variations of this pattern in multiple organizations. To help understand why these cases commonly occur, let us start with measurement fundamentals.

3.4 Measurement Fundamentals

A fundamental purpose of measurement is *"To guide management decision-making"* [14].

But how do we manage our measurements to facilitate their use in helping to make more effective decisions?

A second question is:

What do we measure?

Watts Humphrey identifies a number of types of measures, including process measures (e.g., defects by phase responsible), product measures (e.g., defects by product component), and resource measures (e.g., hours to fix a defect) [13]. But Watts also tells us that these are *foundation measures* that should be used as a starting point, and that organizations are expected to derive more *specific measures* based on business needs.[6]

3.5 Measurement in the Case Study

In our case study, data in all three of Watt's categories were collected for years and retained in an organizational measurement repository. Due to concern over the nonachievement of business objectives, I was asked to conduct an independent analysis. I started by analyzing the data in the repository and I first noticed from this data a high percentage of defects injected late in the development cycle. I observed this from the "defects by phase responsible" measure. But when I talked to developers, I heard that the majority of their problems were due to vague requirements that did not receive appropriate attention early in the development phase.

My first key observation was this *disconnect*[7] between the *objective data* in the *organizational repository* and what I was hearing from the people in the trenches who did the work.

Trying to better understand what was going on, I kept digging and asking more questions, and as I did, I discovered more *disconnects*. I asked one developer to describe the product baseline management process I had read about in their documented processes, and he replied:

> *It's not how we really work. We propose things that are similar to what we are going to do, but not exactly. We propose based on where we think the product will be in the future when the work comes in. Often those assumptions are wrong.*

My second key observation was this *disconnect* between the documented processes and what I was hearing was happening in the trenches.

3.6 Stepping Back

I have witnessed these two key observations—to varying degrees—as common patterns in many organizations. Let us explore further how this affects business objectives.

---

6. What I mean by this is measures that have sufficient granularity and contextual data associated with them to enable their effective use.

7. The term "disconnect" in this book means an inconsistency.

When process improvement efforts are initiated in an organization, there are usually two relevant process views, referred to as the "as-is" and the "to-be." The usual approach is to first capture the "as-is," and then discuss weaknesses leading to the desired "to-be." But often the "as-is" doesn't receive appropriate attention. The argument goes like this:

> *We are looking at getting better so shouldn't we focus on the "to-be?"*

The answer is yes and no. Yes, you want to create a clear vision of where you want to go, but you also need to take the time to conduct the critical dialogue leading to an understanding of why we do what we do today, and the potential need to *stretch* the organization with changes. Without this critical dialogue first, we don't know how big of a *stretch* we face.[8]

LESSON 1

The first step is to capture the real "as-is" process.

3.7 Digging Deeper for Candidate Root Causes

I didn't yet know the root cause so I kept asking more questions. I had heard that a number of projects were currently overrunning cost and schedule, so I asked:

> *Does the company underestimate when it bids?*

I received a mix of answers. One person responded:

> *No. Our bids are okay, but we often don't get the hardware ordered and installed in time to meet the software integration schedules.*

Another said:

> *The bids are okay given the assumptions at proposal time, but when we find the assumed product functionality isn't there after award, we don't always adjust the schedule or resource needs.*

I now had candidate root causes to investigate further, including the hardware procurement and installation processes, and the plans and schedules update processes. But I didn't have *quantitative data* to back up what I was hearing, so I

---

8. We talk more about effective techniques to capture the real "as-is" process in Agile organizations in Chapter 4 in the BOND case study.

went back to the *Organizational Repository*. Unfortunately, I couldn't tie existing historical data to potential root causes because the data that had been collected for years was the typical textbook type measures, which were not *specific* enough to help.

In the book *Measuring the Software Process* [14], it is stated that:

> When planning for measurement it is important to identify the critical factors that often arise from concerns and problems and risks that threaten ability to meet goals.

In the book *Understanding Variation* [15], we find that:

> Much of the managerial data in use today consists of aggregated counts. Such data tends to be virtually useless in identifying the nature of problems... The work of process improvement requires specific measures and contextual knowledge. [15]

In our case study, traditional *foundation measures* only had been collected. *Specific context relevant measures* were not derived based on business needs.

LESSON 2

Company standard metrics are often insufficient for real process improvement.

3.8 Specific Context Relevant Measures

Examples of specific context relevant measures that could have helped include:

- Cycle time to get critical path hardware on order
- Cycle time to install and test critical hardware

How did we come up with these measures? By asking key questions.

LESSON 3

Derive specific measures for needed insight, by asking key questions.

How Did We Get Here and How Does It Affect Business Objectives?

Many of us were taught that we need to gather large volumes of data before analyzing and using it, but the flipside is that today we are using shorter development cycles and the value of data erodes quickly over time.

Think about what is going on here. We said earlier the purpose of measurements is to *guide decisions*. These decisions in turn affect how well we do at achieving our business objectives. But if the measurements we are taking do not adequately consider the *critical factors* that threaten our goals, what chance do we have of making the best decision?

I also discovered that while people had been trained in the importance of the company standard measures, due to schedule pressures the data had often been entered quickly without adequate consideration for its accuracy.

3.9 Deriving the Right Data and Caring about the Data

This leads to the question:

How do you get people to derive the right data and care about the data?

In Watts Humphrey's book [13] where he explains the Personal Software Process (PSP), the point is made that:

Because of a short feedback cycle, the engineers realize the effect of the PSP, and use their own performance data to gauge their improvements.

This same principle holds for small teams.[9] Experience indicates that when small teams are empowered to collect data and remove real obstacles in their path, the right data is derived and accurately collected because they know it is critical to achieving the goal. This is consistent with Lean and Agile principles to empower the team and remove obstacles.

LESSON 4

Use small empowered teams to derive meaningful measures, and then review and refine in short cycles.

---

9. It is worth noting that Version 1.3 of the CMMI for Development scheduled for release in November 2010 features teams more prominently. To be specific, the draft released in February 2010 has the definition for team (not in Version 1.2), as well as one new practice in OPD on teaming standards, and one in IPM on establishing teams. This could change in the final release.

3.10 What Does This Have to Do with CMMI High-Level Practices?

The CMMI guidelines with respect to QPM, a level 4 Process Area, states that:

> *The specific practices of QPM are best implemented by those who actually execute the project's defined process—not by management or consulting statisticians only.*

Another tip in the guidelines states that:

> *...when effectively implemented, QPM empowers individuals and teams by enabling them to accurately estimate and make commitments to these estimates with confidence. [1]*

The CMMI tip tells us to empower project team members. Our experience tells us this works best when the teams are small.

3.11 The Right Time to Implement CMMI Level 4/5 Practices

This leads to a question:

> *When should an organization consider implementing higher CMMI level 4 and 5 practices?*

To help answer this question, let us first look closer at the relationships among Agile, Lean, and CMMI level 4 and 5.

3.12 Relationships among CMMI, Agile, and Lean

The CMMI is a reference model that helps us understand "what" to do. The Continuous Representation of the CMMI model supports using process areas based on business needs. Lean and Agile advocates often argue against the CMMI by asking:

> *Why do I need to wait until CMMI level 5 to analyze and fix problems?*

The answer to this question is:

> *You don't need to wait, and you shouldn't!*

The reason some erroneously believe you have to wait is because the Causal Analysis and Resolution (CAR) Process Area is at level 5 in the staged representation of the model. However, when you use the Continuous Representation of the CMMI model, you can use whatever practices can help your organization based on your business needs. This is one reason why the Continuous Representation of the model is preferred for Agile organizations. Agile and Lean techniques provide effective "how-to" techniques that can work together with the CMMI practices.

Agile, Lean, and the CMMI are not in conflict, but rather can help each other and help you achieve business objectives fast.

For more information on Lean techniques, refer to [16, 17, 18, 19].

3.13 Back to the Case Study: How CMMI, Agile, and Lean Can Help Together

In our case study, we were addressing two real problems: cost/schedule overruns and late hardware. We needed specific objective data to verify we were tackling the correct root cause. As soon as the data was gathered, we needed to analyze it and act on it. The CMMI model helps us with the "what to do"; in this case, *Gather, Analyze, Act.*[10] Lean and Agile techniques help us with the "how to do it"; in this case, *Timely short cycles*, and *small empowered teams*.

It has been my experience that when organizations over-focus their attention on the level 2/3 practices, there is a tendency to miss the valuable business-focused help that can be provided through the higher CMMI level practices.

Although LACM was not formally using the CMMI level 4/5 practices at the time, we were effectively achieving the intent of these practices through this effort.

LESSON 5

Consider using selective CMMI level 4 and 5 practices with Agile/Lean techniques to address key business objectives.

---

10. Refer to QPM Process Area, Specific Practice 2.1, "Select Measures and Analytic Techniques," and CAR Process Area Specific Practice 2.1, "Implement the Action Proposals."

3.14 What Happened in the Case Study and Process Improvement Insights

Alistair Cockburn has observed a commonality between engineering and manufacturing. You can observe it as Alistair states:

> ...once you notice decisions as the product that moves through a network of people. [20]

This observation can be taken a step further to help us gain insight related to business objectives. Whenever I have investigated problems similar to our case study, I find the root cause often comes down to two possibilities: weakness in process or weakness in people skills. The CMMI model contains two similar causes of variation referred to as common causes (e.g., process) and assignable causes (e.g., weakness in people skills).

3.15 Back to the Case Study Again: What Really Happened

As it turned out, I found that most of the time the hardware was being ordered and installed on time, and most of the time the schedules and plans were maintained appropriately. But I also found that sometimes *special circumstances* occurred, perturbing the normal flow of work and requiring a person to make a *decision*. Sometimes, in these cases, decisions were *deferred inappropriately*, resulting in an impact on project schedules. I also found that sometimes *decisions* were made that should have led to *other decisions* that were not made.

More specifically in our case study, sometimes hardware was not ordered due to missing data on a procurement requisition and an inexperienced procurement specialist who didn't know how to best handle the situation. I also found that sometimes projects were under-bid because impacts weren't known at proposal time, and when identified afterward sometimes schedules were not updated. I also found that sometimes assumptions proved incorrect, and when identified sometimes plans were not updated appropriately.

The CMMI model describes two types of causes of variation that roughly correspond to process versus skills.

All of these situations lead us to a question:

Are these process problems (often due to common causes), or people problems (often assignable)?

3.16 Insight

In my experience, most often the root cause for broader problems turns out to be a mix of both. The process is never perfect, nor are the people.

> **INSIGHT** We need to take appropriate action to minimize the likelihood of the problem recurring. Often this means combining process improvement with additional mentoring and/or training for people.

Historically, many organizations who have implemented CMMI level 4 and 5 practices have spent significant effort distinguishing these categories of problems. The reason these insights are important is because they tell us that *Agile* techniques can help us attain the intent of many of the CMMI level 4 and 5 practices by executing them in an *integrated* way, rather than by trying to artificially separate them.

Examples of What We Did to Help Resolve the Problems

Specifically, in our case study, we provided the procurement specialist with some immediate *on-the-job guidance* explaining *alternative* solutions that could have been made. For example, instead of just placing the procurement requisition to the side on his desk when he didn't know

Pause, Reflect, and Glance Forward

It might be worth pausing at this point to reflect on whether what we have seen in the Procurement case study reflects a pattern at LACM. We heard that "sometimes the hardware doesn't get ordered on time." If true, is it always due to an inexperienced procurement specialist, or could there be other causes as well? If we could characterize the conditions that lead to common undesirable situations, is it also possible there are actions we could take to avoid such patterns from coming back? We will continue to explore the concept of repeating patterns as we move deeper into the book. And we will explore what you can do to detect such situations and keep them from coming back.

how to handle the missing data, he could have picked up the phone and called the individual who had submitted the requisition letting him know that the data was required. As another alternative, he could have called his manager and asked for guidance. We also recognized that a note should be added next to the field on the requisition form indicating that field was required, and if left blank the requisition could not be processed. Refer to Table 3-1.

Table 3-1 *Special Circumstances and Alternative Solutions*

Special Circumstances	Current Solution	Alternative Solution	Value of Alternative Solution
Missing data on procurement requisition and inexperienced procurement specialist	Place requisition to side on desk due to lack of data	Call person who submitted requisition	Train people performing the process
		Call manager and ask for guidance	Train people performing the process
		Add note on form indicating field required for hardware to be ordered	Improve the process

3.17 More about the Real Intent of CMMI Level 4 and 5 Practices

Although LACM was not formally using the CMMI level 4/5 practices at the time of this case study, we were effectively achieving the *intent* of these practices through this effort. Two of the level 4 and 5 Process Areas are QPM and CAR. The CMMI guidelines tell us through a sidebar tip with respect to CAR that:

> *Although this PA is commonly used for defects, you also can use it for problems such as schedule overruns and inadequate response times that should not be considered defects.*

This was exactly the type of situation we were dealing with in investigating the late hardware ordering and installation. What we did led to practical help on a project in a specific situation. My experience has been that once organizations reach a certain level of process maturity, this type of problem analysis and resolution often becomes the most valuable and therefore the type that the organization should be focusing on to help them achieve their business objectives.

By monitoring where you most often see problems on your projects (e.g., in the case study it was cycle time to get hardware ordered and installed), you are identifying the areas that become the best candidates for the sub-processes to place under statistical management. Once the right processes are identified, you then manage them quantitatively until they are back under control. Then you move on and look for the next bottleneck in your organization. But keep in mind that in all organizations, changes occur (e.g., people turnover) and therefore it is not uncommon for processes that appear to be under control today to fall out of control tomorrow. Refer to Figure 3-1.

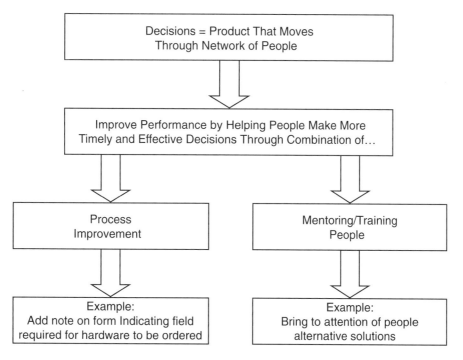

Figure 3-1 *Improved Performance Through Improved Solutions*

How Should an Organization Select Subprocesses for Statistical Control?

I have found in many large organizations that the subprocesses selected for statistical control are often *isolated to single departments* such as software engineering. Subprocess selection should meet at a minimum the following criteria:

- Being "critical" to the business
- Having "experienced problems in the past"

My experience indicates that most often subprocesses that best meet these criteria are not isolated to individual departments, but rather *cross multiple department boundaries* as we saw in the case study involving the hardware procurement difficulty.

This is because often in the past, problems occur where communication breakdown is most likely, and this tends to happen more often when the process crosses multiple organizational entities (including teams) or functional/technical competencies.

It is for this reason I recommend that organizations consider selecting subprocesses for statistical management that are not isolated to single departments.

When using *Agile* techniques we partition work into *shorter increments—* often called *iterations, time-boxes, or sprints—*where the work completed in each increment involves complete *slices* through multiple traditional development phases. This implies the involvement of multiple organizational entities (including teams) or functional/technical competencies. Incremental development supports more effectively than traditional Waterfall development the monitoring of the most valuable subprocesses for statistical control over short periods of time leading to real payback.

LESSON 6

To gain the most value when selecting subprocesses for statistical control, consider subprocesses that cross multiple organizational boundaries (including teams), or functional/technical competencies, and are used on projects with incremental development.

Section II
LACM's Current Approach to Process Improvement

Now let us look closer at LACM's current approach to continuous process improvement.

3.18 Continuous Process Improvement at LACM

In the LACM case study the organization was experiencing unprecedented success, but no one was sure why. I had a discussion with a director at LACM on this subject while the two of us were working together doing an analysis of his company's organizational assets. We were working with another process improvement professional who works for him and is very knowledgeable of the CMMI, having taken many of the advanced courses on the CMMI model from the SEI. The conversation went like this:

Director:

> At times I wonder how much all this work we are doing with the CMMI matters. Right now, our company is incredibly successful. With over fifty ongoing projects, only two are experiencing any difficulty. Almost all projects are on schedule, meeting their customer deliverables, and hitting cost targets. I'm not sure why it's happening, but I do know there are certain things in this organization that really have become institutionalized. First is weekly status reporting. Everyone knows if you don't get anything else done, you get your status report done and flowed up in time for the full report to flow to the vice president. And every week this status is used to make real decisions so people are very attentive to making sure it accurately reflects what is going on with their projects. The Senior Management Reviews also happen on a regular basis and people know what the organization is looking for at these reviews. There is an established format for these reviews. There aren't a lot of things being looked at, but it's the same few things that just keep getting hammered week after week such as staffing, schedule, requirements, and risk. And now people know what to expect, and they are preparing themselves ahead of time because they know the questions management will be asking. Something seems to be working.

McMahon response:

> *I find what you say very interesting. I have always believed that while the CMMI model is very comprehensive, when it really comes down to being successful it is a matter of organizations identifying those handful of keys to consistently focus on. When the people all get on the same page it creates a force that is almost unstoppable.*

Director reply:

> *So if what we are saying is right, why are we spending all this energy on all this other stuff?*

This wasn't the end of this discussion. Later I continued the discussion with the process improvement professional who had just sat listening to our conversation. He had done a lot of thinking about CMMI level 4, wondering if he should be pushing level 4 and 5 more formally in the organization.

Process Improvement Professional:

> *I'm glad we aren't proceeding with level 4. For example, all those statistical control charts[11] just wouldn't be of benefit to the company helping us get to where we need to go.*

McMahon response:

> *While I agree that I wouldn't recommend that the organization formally go after a level 4 or 5 right now, I actually believe that where this organization is headed is aligned with the real intent of level 4 and 5. First, the fundamental problem I see so often is that people read things into the CMMI model at level 4 and 5 just as they do at level 2 and 3. They believe the model says things that aren't really there. For example, the practices at level 4 do expect you to statistically manage subprocesses, but don't tell you which subprocesses to pick, nor what related data you need to measure.*

> *Sometimes organizations prematurely decide what these subprocesses should be based on what they hear others do rather than doing what the model says, which is to pick them based on your business need. Now, let me give you a real example.*

> *The director told me that those Senior Management Reviews are truly institutionalized. People know what to expect now. But I've sat in on a few of*

---

11. Level 4 is really about improving discipline and predictability. Using statistical control charts is one approach, but not the only possible approach.

them, and even though most of the projects are doing well, there are still issues and frequently the project engineers don't have very good answers.

For example, while the projects seem to be hitting their cost and schedule targets at an overall level, certain subsystems seem to always be in trouble still overrunning, while other subsystems actually are beating their targets regularly. Looking more closely at some of the underlying factors involved with these subsystems could be very revealing. For example, comparing the planning parameters that went into the bid, such as planned lines of code to be reused versus new development, planned discrepancies expected versus number actually written, and cost to fix a discrepancy in these subsystems versus the planned estimate.

My point is simple: We know there are still trouble spots in the organization even though overall the organization is doing well. Investigating these trouble spots could potentially help the organization do even better, and help identify where to best spend our future process improvement dollars to get real payback. This would be an example of using level 4 and 5 as intended. Note here that these provide more examples just like the procurement case where by asking deeper questions one would be likely to drive down to some very specific root causes where actions could be taken to help resolve real issues that could help on-going projects. Based on what I have seen in the past there is a good chance the issues will cross organizational boundaries.

Too often, what I have observed are subprocesses placed under control that have not been chosen for the right reasons. In other words, the digging and analysis just described does not happen first. As a result, the subprocesses placed under control and data collected is too far removed from the real issues affecting the project today. Consequently, project managers don't use the data to help them make real decisions that could help their project and the company. Thus, we don't get the payback we should from the causal analysis and resolution step.

My experience has shown that one of the best ways to select these subprocesses is by monitoring what is actually happening on active projects and taking timely action. When done right, it results in taking advantage of real opportunities and helping projects in need when they need it. It is also important to note that the subprocesses that are chosen to be monitored more closely often don't need to be watched for extended periods of time, just long enough to understand what is happening and put appropriate corrective actions in place.

3.19 Why the Unprecedented Success at LACM?

I observed two key activities at LACM that most likely accounted for the organization's unprecedented success. First, Senior Management is heavily engaged, driving process improvement alignment with business objectives from the top down.

> **LESSON 7**
>
> Identify and focus on the handful of key priorities the organization consistently uses to drive the business.

Second, there exists a continuous grassroots improvement effort engaged across the organization, and these efforts are increasingly multidisciplinary. While this organization has so far decided not to formally pursue CMMI level 4 and 5, they are reaping benefits of level 4 and 5 practices by using them informally together with Lean and Agile techniques.[12]

> **LESSON 8**
>
> Monitor what is actually happening on active projects using related information to choose subprocesses to assess more closely. This will allow you to address key trouble spots unique to your business in a more timely fashion. Then move on to the next trouble spot.

3.20 Diddling in DOORS: A Story about Real Work Management and Measurement

Following are words from a conversation I had with a Program Manager that provides another potential candidate to apply Agile techniques together with high CMMI level practices (CMMI level 4, 5). This Program Manager's responsibilities include the management of a set of core products that are commonly used across multiple projects in a CMMI high maturity organization.

---

12. The reason LACM is not formally pursuing CMMI level 4 and 5 is that they have heard from a CMMI level 5 sister division that they had experienced exorbitant costs "proving" to the appraisal team their process improvements were real. One of the main objectives of the CMMI Version 1.3 is to ensure the high maturity practices are understood the same way by lead appraisers, the organization, and the SEI, and these planned changes should lessen the frequency with which such disconnects happen.

Program Manager:

I believe there is an opportunity for some significant improvements in the way we manage our core product development. Whenever we finish an update, my developers come to me with great ideas to improve the product. These ideas are fresh in their minds because they just finished an update and know where the trouble spots are. They often have good ideas about where we need to work the product to make it more reusable to achieve real savings during the next product update. Unfortunately, no one is listening to them at this time. Then when it comes time to do the next round of updates to our product, someone from Systems Engineering gets involved and spends significant resources diddling in DOORS[13] trying to come up with the requirements for the next update. But unfortunately, the Systems Engineers who are assigned don't understand the products we use to achieve many of the customer's requirements. The way I see it, most of the work they end up doing is just a rehash of old requirements and usually provides little real value. We should be reusing more of the requirements and just making updates that make sense from the customer perspective and where we know we can improve the product. But unfortunately we spend huge sums of money continually reinventing and diddling in DOORS and we don't get the value from this effort that we should because the Systems Engineers aren't talking to the developers who understand our products.

These comments hit at a common problem I see in many large organizations. Senior Management wants more effective cost and schedule management. I hear Senior Management in Engineering in many product-oriented organizations driving for increased visibility and accountability of work effort from a product perspective. There is often a business-driven objective to gain more reuse and increase visibility of the relationship between cost expenditures and product functionality achieved.

When I see this common pattern, I have often suggested that the measures in that organization should be better *aligned* with the *goals* I am hearing. Frequently in these cases, the measures being reported are *functional* department measures rather than *product* measures.

What you measure drives what you focus on in your organization.

If an organization has this product perspective as a goal, they need to align measures correspondingly. As an example, one of the best measures of product functionality is tests passed versus tests planned (this is a common Agile

---

13. DOORS is a popular commercially available requirements management tool.

measure). Requirements should tie to tests (or verification method), and all work that is going on should be traceable to a test, or a planned verification activity. This means we have a measurement for all work, and visibility of the value of that work from an end-product perspective.

Unfortunately, what I find is that there is often in-fighting in traditional functional organizations against the product measurement perspective. The product approach would require that we measure "slices" of work allocated to increments of development that are tied to *product functionality*. Often, traditional functional organizations fight this perspective. But the words of the Program Manager explain why it is important that we keep pushing for this change in perspective.

This is not meant to imply that all organizations that have large systems engineering budgets and expend high amounts of resources on defining requirements using tools like DOORS are being unproductive. However, it is saying that we need to be able to trace those expenditures, just like any others, to value for the company based on business drivers. When we have difficulty seeing the tie between work going on in an organization and the end resultant product, there is a problem simply from the standpoint that it is not manageable.

When I investigated the situation this Program Manager was raising by asking questions inside the organization I found that the *root cause* traced to the fact that Systems Engineers who worked in DOORS rarely spoke to Product Developers, and the requirements database was not closely managed in relation to the approved work going on at the product level.

The organization had a *disconnect* between what Systems Engineering was viewing as the important requirements work and what the Software Engineering group was doing to the products. My recommendation was that a small empowered team be established to pilot a new way to do product development that engaged Systems Engineering and Software Engineering personnel more closely. My intent was to develop a way to feed the knowledge from the real developers back to Systems Engineering, affecting more productively the DOORS requirements effort.

One way to encourage this closer working relationship between Systems Engineering and Software Engineering is to have people work together in a small team environment rather than in a sequential "throw it over the fence" mode, which had been their culture. This would be a good first step to align the work in Systems with the work in Software and eventually align all reporting with end product functionality.

Thus, here is an opportunity to monitor what's going on more carefully with an eye to eliminating this divide. Again, statistical management can be a useful approach. Refer to Table 3-2 for examples of candidate subprocesses for statistical management.

Table 3-2 *Candidate Subprocesses for Statistical Management*

Subprocesses of the Following Processes Are Candidates for Statistical Management	Critical Business Need	Multiple Departments Involved
Hardware procurement process	Historical schedule problems	Hardware Engineering and Procurement
Requirements development process	Address real customer needs	Systems Engineering and Software Engineering

3.21 Finance Perspective on Work Management and Measurement

I have heard finance organizations in particular argue against the product measurement perspective discussed in the previous paragraph. Their arguments sounded shortsighted to me. When pushed to answer why they want to measure costs functionally, the best answer I have received is:

> *Because we have a validated bid system and we bid future costs based on past experience.*

The argument is that it would just *cost too much to change*. But this line of reasoning sounds *deadly* to me. Continuing with it leads one to conclude we can never change because we have to work as we bid, and we always must bid based on how we worked in the past.

Can you see how this logic will lead an organization to destruction? Certainly, change must be carefully managed. But without change, the eventual demise of an organization is just a matter of time.[14]

---

14. The subject of managing change is also covered in the NANO case study in Chapter 6.

3.22 Is the CMMI Measurement and Analysis Process Area Inconsistent with the Agile Principle of Simplicity?

Referring back to the lesson of focusing on the "handful" of key priorities that drive the business at LACM, this should not be interpreted as just affecting a "handful" of people. Those handfuls of key priorities Senior Management cared about translated into a "handful" of measures that were reported at the periodic Senior Management briefs, but supporting that data were measures that were being collected *deep into the organization*.

What is different is that through the improvement efforts at LACM, people now understood how each measure at the lower levels supported a higher-level business driver.

A question arises here:

> *Is there inconsistency between the idea of focusing on just a handful of key priorities at any one time, and the CMMI Measurement and Analysis (MA) Process Area?*

If you read much of the popular literature on the CMMI, you might be led to believe that when you use the CMMI, you will be forced to collect and manage as one text puts it:

> *A boatload of metrics.*

The "boatload" of metrics perspective often results from process development approaches that drive process definition to align physically with the CMMI model. This in turn can lead to distinct measures associated with each process area. This is not a requirement of the CMMI model, but rather an implementation choice.

The CMMI MA Process Area does expect organizations to collect, analyze, and store measurements, but doesn't dictate what those measurements need to be or how they need to be stored or used. What it does say in SP 1.1 is that organizations are expected to:

> *Establish… measurement objectives derived from… needs and objectives.*

This decision is up to you. It is a choice every organization has, and the decision should be made based on your business needs. Nothing in the CMMI Measurement and Analysis Process Area (or in any other area of the CMMI model) is inconsistent with the Agile principle of simplicity.

3.23 How LACM Handled Measurement and Analysis from the CMMI Perspective

At LACM, a measurement process was written based on the business needs of the organization. That process was mandated by Senior Management for all projects. To tailor this process required an exception by the vice president.[15]

In most cases, I recommend that only "what you must do" and not "how you do it" should be placed in nontailorable process assets. But there are certain processes in an organization where it might make sense to mandate "how to" information. This is because of culture and criticality to the business. Measurement and analysis is a good example in many organizations where mandating "how to" might make sense.

At LACM, this measurement process identified those handful of key priorities based on the business needs, and identified related measures for each. LACM had a very good reason for making this decision. By placing the measurement process at the mandated level in the process assets, they were making it very clear what measurement data needed to be collected, and ensured that no data was being required organizationally to be collected that didn't have a purpose and wasn't being used effectively. This mandate actually helped to maintain the "lean" data collection strategy throughout the organization.

3.24 Summary

In the LACM case study, I have shared practical techniques proven to work that are consistent with both the CMMI model and Agile principles to help an organization achieve business objectives. These techniques are specifically oriented toward an organization that already has formal processes in place and might have achieved a formal high CMMI rating.

But what if your organization doesn't yet have formal processes in place and you are a growing successful Agile organization? You know you need some increased formality because you also know your current processes won't scale—but you also fear losing the culture that brought you the success you have achieved to date. So what do you do?

---

15. We will discuss at greater length the structure of Organizational Process Assets in the next chapter on the BOND case study, and Tailoring later in the book in the GEAR case study in Chapter 7.

In the following chapters, we address this challenge through multiple case studies, each with its own specific challenges. In the case study in the next two chapters on BOND you will learn about specific techniques that worked to help maintain a successful Agile culture while adding the CMMI compliant processes necessary to achieve a full formal staged CMMI level 3.

3.25 Summary: How CMMI Helps Agile

The following table provides a summary of how CMMI areas discussed in this chapter help Agile.

CMMI Area	How It Helps Agile
QPM, SP 1.3 Select Subprocesses to Statistically Manage CAR, SP 1.1 Select Data for Analysis, SP 2.1 Implement Action	Helps us understand "what" practices we must follow to achieve continuous improvement

3.26 Summary: How Agile Helps CMMI

The following table provides a summary of how Agile approaches discussed in this chapter help the CMMI.

Agile Approach	How It Helps CMMI
Simplicity (e.g., identify handful of keys to business)	Helps us implement ("how-to") MA PA and QPM PA effectively by collecting the right data needed to support better decisions
Small empowered teams, rapid action, select subprocess threads that cross organizational boundaries	Helps us implement QPM and CAR PAs effectively and efficiently to provide real rapid payback to the organization

PART III

Helping Agile Organizations Increase Maturity

In this part of the book, I share stories about the BOND organization, a growing successful Agile organization that has achieved advanced CMMI process maturity.

Here you will learn techniques to develop and deploy CMMI-compliant processes within an existing successful Agile culture. In Chapter 5, you will learn the added value CMMI level 3 practices can bring to a previously successful Agile organization.

The BOND case study should be of particular interest to CMMI-knowledgeable people who want to learn how successful Agile organizations operate and how their practices can actually help a CMMI implementation. This case study should also be of interest to Agile-knowledgeable people who want to know how to effectively use the CMMI model while maintaining their successful Agile approach, and what value a CMMI effort can bring to an Agile organization. This part of the book is also recommended for novices interested in learning the fundamentals of both the CMMI and an Agile approach.

Chapter 4

Bringing Process Maturity to Agile Organizations—Part I

Scenario: You are a small Agile organization that is successful and growing, but to date you have few documented processes and no formal training program for your people. To maintain your success as you grow you are going to need more process discipline. You would like to start a CMMI process improvement effort. However, you fear losing the Agile culture that has led to your current success. So what should you do? What options do you have?

4.1 What You Will Learn in This Chapter

- Five popular myths about processes in Agile organizations
- Common challenges faced initiating a CMMI process improvement effort within an Agile organization
- Successful techniques to guide a small growing Agile organization to CMMI level 3 while maintaining an Agile culture

- Answers to common questions related to developing Agile processes
- Practical techniques to structure an organizational repository supporting agility and CMMI compliancy

Section I
Key Case Study Points[1]

4.2 BOND Case Study Background

In July 2007, I participated in a formal CMMI appraisal with the goal of achieving a full-staged (18 process areas) CMMI level 3 for a client I will refer to as BOND. I began helping this client years earlier when they had virtually no written processes, or training, and only 25 people. The company, which was started by two retired military men, had been rapidly growing at a rate of over 30 percent a year reaching over 150 people by the time of the 2007 appraisal.

The key challenge I was presented with at the onset was to help the organization add the needed process discipline the CMMI could bring to help them continue to manage their projects effectively as the organization grew. The owners also stressed the importance they placed on maintaining the successful Agile culture that they felt was an important component of their business success.

After I initially executed a gap analysis (I will explain what a gap analysis is shortly) against the CMM model for this organization in 2001, they attempted for a few years to move forward with their process initiative on their own, but were unsuccessful.

In 2003, I executed a second gap analysis (this time using the CMMI model). Subsequent to the presentation of my gap analysis findings to Senior Management, I was asked to become more involved in assisting the organization's process improvement effort.

They asked—as many clients do—if I had CMMI-compliant processes that could expedite their CMMI goals. I replied that I could help them develop

---

1. While the approaches described in this case study work for an Agile organization, they are actually intelligent ways to work in any organization.

their own processes addressing the areas the CMMI expected, and that I could share what I referred to as "starting point CMMI-based process templates." I also emphasized that we wouldn't achieve the goal they were searching for if we tried to use these process templates without taking the next important step. Now, let me explain what the next important step is and how we executed it to help BOND achieve their CMMI level 3 goal.

4.3 What Is a Gap Analysis and Why Is It Crucial for Agile Organizations?

Whenever I am asked to help a small Agile organization improve its process maturity, I always recommend we start with a gap analysis against the CMMI model.[2] The purpose of a gap analysis is to assess where an organization currently is from a process perspective and identify gaps based on the CMMI model. The result is a strengths and weaknesses report and an initial set of recommendations to help the organization achieve its current process goals.

When I present weaknesses I have observed based on the CMMI model practices, I always stress that these might or might not be actual weaknesses in the organization that require actions. Part of the follow-on plan always includes more analysis of these "potential weaknesses" to determine the proper course of action given the organization's business situation and process needs.

Executing a gap analysis is important for any organization initiating a process improvement effort because it facilitates the most effective plan based on the correct priorities for that particular organization. I now want to share the key points on how I conduct a gap analysis for an Agile organization, and why the approach you use when doing a gap analysis is crucial when it comes to agility. This will lead to a discussion of additional techniques I use to help Agile organizations move forward with a successful CMMI process maturity effort.

---

2. The discussion to follow on a gap analysis and running a process improvement effort like a project relates to the expected practices in the Organizational Process Focus (OPF) process area in the CMMI model. Examples of OPF and Organizational Process Definition (OPD) processes are provided in the appendices to this book.

4.4 Keys to Conducting a Gap Analysis for an Agile Organization

There are multiple approaches to conducting a gap analysis. You can focus on documentation including the products an organization produces, and documented processes employed in developing those products. You can also spend time interviewing people in the organization who use those processes. I have seen a gap analysis conducted using exclusively the documentation route, and at times, this can make sense. Most often, a traditional gap analysis focuses on the documentation, supplemented with a few interviews.

When I do a gap analysis for an Agile organization, I switch this traditional emphasis from the documentation to the discussions with the people. The way I conduct these interviews is crucial to the success of the approach.

I conduct my interviews individually, not in groups as is often done with more formal CMMI appraisals. I am particularly careful how I phrase my questions during these interviews. I keep the interviews informal with an emphasis on letting the people being interviewed just talk about how they do their job. I have found that by phrasing questions as simply as possible, most people tend to talk openly and with ease about their job. An interview question I often start with is:

Can you tell me how you do your job?

I spend most of my time taking notes, letting the employee speak. My follow-on questions flow naturally from responses that lead me to dig deeper. I don't use any of the words from the CMMI model in asking the questions, but I do keep the model practices in mind. I am using those practices to trigger more detailed questions based on what I hear.

Late in the interview after I have learned how they view their responsibilities and carry out their activities to achieve those responsibilities, I ask:

Do you follow a process when you do your job?

Almost everyone in Agile organizations that have just begun a process improvement effort answers that question with:

No.

By the time I ask that question, I already know the answer, and most of the people have answered it incorrectly.

By this time, I have in my notes a great deal of the information that describes the process they actually do follow when doing their job. They, of course, when asked that question assume I mean a documented process.

I assess what they tell me they do against the CMMI model, and against whatever written processes exist. I look at examples of the products they produce to corroborate what they are telling me and what their documented processes say.

When I out-brief a client with strengths and weaknesses against each process area of the CMMI model, each point I make is backed up with objective evidence from what I heard in an interview and/or saw in documentation. What I hear in interviews and see through documentation—along with my own experience based on patterns I have seen in similar organizations—is shared in my report and serves as the objective data that leads to my recommendations. I always stress in my report that any weaknesses identified against the CMMI model are "potential weaknesses" to the business.

My reports go much deeper with detailed examples than most traditional gap analysis reports. This approach is counter to what is usually done partly because of nonattribution concerns. It is important that I don't attribute specific findings to individuals in order to maintain an atmosphere in which people are willing to talk openly about their jobs.

However, too often valuable findings are raised up to an abstract set of statements leading to ultimate findings that become almost useless in helping the organization focus on the specific priority improvements needed.

Furthermore, it has been my experience that when a gap analysis does not provide specific examples with details backing up conclusions, Senior Managers do not place much value in the report resulting in minimum value to follow-on improvement efforts. See Table 4-1 for pros and cons of different gap analysis approaches.

Table 4-1 *Pros and Cons of Different Gap Analysis Approaches*

Gap Analysis Approach	Advantage	Disadvantage	Comment
Traditional Documentation Focus	Learn "gaps" if you followed documented processes	Don't gain insight into real processes followed by people	Behavior change is the most difficult process improvement

Continues

Table 4-1 *Pros and Cons of Different Gap Analysis Approaches (Continued)*

Gap Analysis Approach	Advantage	Disadvantage	Comment
Agile Interview Focus	Learn the real process the people are following	Takes more effort requiring more analysis and digging	Leads to uncovering where the most valuable process improvements lie

Let me now give you a simple example of why I stress weaknesses identified in a gap analysis are "potential weaknesses" to the business and how we determine if these "potential weaknesses" require actions to resolve in the plan to move forward.

4.5 Example of "Potential Weakness" Against CMMI in an Agile Organization

Somewhere during every interview as we are talking about how the individual executes his or her job, we get to the products they produce as part of executing that job. Eventually, I ask:

Who else looks at these products you are producing?

This discussion leads to the question about whether they conduct peer reviews on their products. Often the answer I get in Agile organizations is:

We don't do formal peer reviews on our products.

On the surface, this triggers a "potential weakness" against the CMMI model because peer reviews are a specific practice in the Verification Process Area of the CMMI model. We don't have enough time to dig into each area I identify as a potential weakness during the one-hour interview. In most areas where I find potential weaknesses, I just make a note that those areas require more investigation and probably further discussion.

As an alternative, I could just list as part of my report all the areas my client must fix to "comply" with the CMMI model. I could tell them I heard you don't do peer reviews and you need to do peer reviews because it is an expected practice within the CMMI. This is actually how I have observed the CMMI model used in many organizations. It is an example of using the model in a prescriptive way. This is not the way the model was intended to be used by its authors, nor would this approach help achieve the goal my client is looking for.

If I were to use the prescriptive approach each time I found a potential weakness against the model, I would "impose" something extra for the organization to do, and therefore add work on top of what they already do without fully understanding the value of that added work.

This approach, in my view, would be a huge mistake particularly in a successful Agile organization that is relying on their existing proven "Agile culture" to continue to bring them the success they have achieved in the past.

This approach may appear to be the most direct way to prepare the organization for a formal appraisal. It would also be the easiest thing to do as a consultant because it requires the least amount of effort.

However, from experience I know it is also the fastest way to raise the risk of driving this organization away from its Agile culture, leading it to a less efficient process than it currently has. Each time I take this approach to a potential weakness, I raise the risk of making this organization less competitive in the future.

I have observed that many process improvement professionals take this approach, and I understand why. It is natural to assume that people who developed the CMMI model are probably smarter than most process people are and the likelihood is that most organizations should be complying with whatever expected practices exist within the model.

What is frequently missed in this line of reasoning is the following *implied myth*:

> **MYTH**   The CMMI developers understood when they came up with the model all the business situations where the model might be applied.

This myth rests at the core of why we so often hear that Agile approaches conflict with the CMMI. When the model is used this way we are inappropriately utilizing the model to dictate implementation, or "how to" issues the model was never meant to address.

I will explain further how to handle these apparent conflicts as they arise, and why the vast majority turns out to be no conflict at all. First, we need to discuss the recommended plan to move forward subsequent to the gap analysis.

4.6 Running Process Improvement like a Project

At BOND, part of the plan forward was to run the process improvement effort just like any other project in the company. I worked closely with the assigned Process Improvement Lead inside the company building a project plan with a schedule, tasks, and assigned resources.[3] We used the Continuous Representation of the CMMI model and decided to prioritize process areas and attack them incrementally.

The Project Management process areas were identified as the highest priority and attacked first during the initial increment of work. To address each process area we used a tailored version of the Technical Working Groups (TWG) approach recommended by the SEI [21]. While the fundamental TWG approach is sound, there are lessons I have learned applying this approach to develop CMMI "compliant" processes that fit within an Agile culture.

4.7 TWG Approach for Agile Organizations

The purpose of a TWG is to use key subject matter experts (SMEs) in the organization to help develop, document, and deploy processes and related process support assets across an organization. In observing TWGs in the past in multiple organizations, I have found common patterns I like to avoid when implementing this approach in an Agile organization. Those patterns have led to a tailoring of the TWG approach for Agile organizations, which are described in the following paragraphs.

One of the responsibilities of a TWG is addressing any potential weaknesses against the CMMI model that might have been identified. Another is to ensure the people in the organization who must use the process and supporting process assets are trained in those processes.

> ### *Pause, Reflect, and Glance Forward*
>
> If you are experienced with Agile approaches but are new to CMMI, you might be asking at this point: "If this organization is successful using an Agile approach, why go through all this effort?"
>
> We will begin to answer this question in the next chapter where we discuss the added value the CMMI can bring to a successful Agile organization.
>
> This subject will also be addressed further in Part IV where we investigate common misapplications of agility.

---

3. Refer to appendices for an example of a template for a Project Management Plan.

The primary goal is to help the organization become more successful, or maintain its current success. However, a secondary goal is to ensure that when the formal CMMI appraisal happens, the organization is prepared to demonstrate through both objective documented evidence and interviews that they have achieved the intent of the practices in the process area.

Training and process deployment are included under the responsibilities of a TWG because often in the past, these critical efforts have fallen through the cracks in many organizational process improvement efforts.

When a new process is first developed, those who were closest to its development are best equipped to provide the rationale for key decisions and share how the processes are intended to be used.

> **LESSON 1**
>
> Hold those responsible for developing processes also responsible for training those processes at least during the pilot project and initial organizational rollout.

Some organizations operate as if the following myth is true:

> **MYTH**   If an organization is Agile, it requires less process training.

You need to communicate the rationale for your processes. There is no one better equipped to explain why things were placed in a process than those who developed them. Too often, this critical knowledge is lost after a process development working group is disbanded. It is the rationale that leads to the needed *buy-in*, which is critical to ensure the organization achieves the intended value and the people are not just "going through the motions" to comply.

When you bring CMMI process maturity to an Agile organization by maintaining the Agile culture within their documented processes, you also need more—not less—training. The reason for this is that the Agile documented processes we develop will not address every possible scenario that is likely to arise in the use of the process. These processes must be supported by *mentoring* and *on-the-job* assistance especially during the period of initial deployment.

4.8 Revisiting the Goal and Challenges on the Process Improvement Project

The goal at BOND on the process improvement project was multifold. First, it was to help the project leaders manage their projects effectively as the organization grew. Second, it was to move the organization forward toward the achievement of a formal CMMI level 3 as rapidly as possible, but without adding significant risk to their ongoing business. This meant the TWGs had to keep an eye on the CMMI model practices addressing potential weaknesses. We also had to be sensitive to the use of key people in the organization who were actively engaged, often working closely with customer counterparts on critical projects.

Third, we had been given the added challenge by Senior Management to maintain the Agile culture the owners felt was critical to the organization's success to date. To accomplish this, I added a requirement for the TWGs. If we were to add activities to the existing processes in the organization, the TWG would have to provide the rationale during the training as to why this activity added value to the organization.

This led to some interesting discussions among TWG members. Some argued that we should be able to just tell those being trained that the CMMI required it and that was sufficient rationale. I objected to this line of reasoning.

I explained to each of the TWG members that the CMMI requires you to make conscious decisions related to certain practices based on your business needs. Any decision we made based on a CMMI practice should be explained during the training from a BOND business need perspective. While this approach led to more time being required by TWG members to discuss current processes and potential weaknesses it helped the organization *reason about its own processes* and determine what the right processes were given their current business and the anticipated potential growth.

Fundamental Rule: Always Ask the Intent Question, and Then Keep Digging

The first Fundamental Rule of our Agile TWG at BOND was based on something a lead CMMI appraiser once told me:

Always ask the intent question.

What she meant was, when assessing an organization against a practice in the CMMI model, ask yourself:

What is the intent of this practice?[4]

Another phrase the lead appraiser often used was:

You don't want to create unnatural behavior in the organization.

This approach leads to another question:

Is the organization achieving the intent?

If the answer is yes, but they don't appear to be following the expected practice, the next question is:

How are they achieving the intent?

and:

What activities are they following to achieve the intent?

The approach of asking these questions fits with our goal to maintain the "Agile culture." The Agile culture is a natural culture where people follow practices that have been proven to work in getting their job done successfully. BOND had a history of success, so whatever practices they were following were, for the most part, working. This was our starting point to extract and document the right processes for this organization.

4.9 Alternative Practices and Tailored Agile TWG

The approach described may lead to an *alternative practice*. An alternative practice is defined by the CMMI guidelines as, "A practice that is a substitute for one or more generic or specific practices contained in CMMI models that achieves an equivalent effect toward satisfying the generic or specific goal associated with model practices. Alternative practices are not necessarily one-for-one replacements for the generic or specific practices." However, my experience when digging "looking-for-intent" or "equivalent effect" has been that most often, you don't arrive at an alternative practice, but rather a different implementation of an expected practice.

---

4. The informative material within the CMMI model is the best source to help in determining the intent. Caution should be used when supplying one's own intention.

> **LESSON 2**
>
> Always keep in mind that the CMMI is primarily about "what you are expected to do," not "how you do it."

The "how you do it" should always be open for discussion. By keeping Lesson 2 in mind as the TWGs dig deeper in discussion, they are opening options they might not have previously understood existed in terms of "how" a given expected practice in the CMMI model can be legitimately achieved.

Another good question to ask yourself as you are digging is:

Is there a problem in the organization because this practice as we are reading it in the CMMI model does not appear to be followed?

> **INSIGHT**   If there isn't a problem in the organization related to a given expected practice, it is likely the intent of the practice is being achieved. Keep digging and you will uncover what that technique is and probably find something worth sharing with others in your organization.

One valuable side effect of "digging deeper" is that often these TWG discussions lead subject matter experts to uncover what I refer to as a "local" practice. A "local" practice is one that works very well to achieve a given CMMI expected practice, but the practice just grew up as part of the organization's culture and wasn't even viewed by most as part of any "process."[5]

These "local" practices are often found in organizations where culture is taken for granted. I have in fact discovered many such practices during a gap analysis and then reiterated them with TWGs afterward, reminding them of what they had told me during the interviews. This kind of memory jogger has been one of the main reasons I like to sit in on client TWGs at times to help facilitate the process and remind them of their own processes.

Other common examples of powerful processes in Agile organizations often taken for granted include brainstorming sessions on white boards, maintenance of informal team task lists, and early product demonstrations with customers. These are all examples of real processes that work, can be documented, and can be shared across the organization.

---

5. Examples of "local" practices discussed later in the book include the "Undocumented super-spreadsheet" resource management process, and "Doorway" risk management process.

Questioning and digging is the major difference in how the Agile TWG operates over traditional TWGs.[6] The focus of the Agile TWG is digging to uncover the real activities that are being followed and used successfully in the organization—not to create new ones. Now let us return to the Peer Review example to learn more about how this TWG process works.

4.10 Returning to the Peer Review Example

What is the intent of the specific practices in the Verification Process Area related to performing peer reviews? The tips in the CMMI guidelines book give us good hints that can help us understand intent. In the Peer Review case, they tell us "peer reviews provide opportunities to learn and share information across the team," and "many different types of reviews might be considered." The text also tells us that the purpose of peer reviews is to:

> *Identify defects for removal and recommend other changes that are needed.*

This information leads us to ask some different questions, which we did at BOND. When I asked:

> *How do you identify defects for removal and get recommendations for other changes that are needed?*

I heard:

> *We demonstrate our products early and often to our customers.*

and:

> *We meet daily with our teammates and discuss openly the work we are doing. Our products are checked into a library every day where others can see them and are encouraged to provide feedback. And they do.*

As I listened to the answers, I realized that when they said they didn't do "formal peer reviews" they meant they didn't have a single defined time when people went into a conference room to provide feedback on a product. However, they did achieve the intent of "peer reviews" by doing continual "less formal" peer reviews throughout the development. This is a common practice in many Agile organizations.

---

6. See "Effective Techniques to Run an Agile TWG" later in this chapter, and the "Thread" Approach to Process Development and Deployment in Chapter 7, GEAR case study, for more information on running Agile TWGs.

This is an example of digging for the real process that is followed to achieve the intent of a given practice. At BOND after this discussion by the Verification Process Area TWG, it was decided that the process did need to be documented, but that it wasn't an alternate practice at all like first thought.

They were just using different "how to" techniques to "share information across the team" and "peer review" products. While this had been a concern early in preparing for the formal appraisal, it turned out there were no issues raised during the formal appraisal about peer reviews at BOND.

"Convenient, but False Arguments"

While BOND was successful, no company is perfect. Therefore, as you ask the intent question and conduct related discussions, I recommend that multiple people participate, including Agile knowledgeable and CMMI knowledgeable people, and others that might be independent of the organization to ensure the group is not creating "convenient, but false arguments." An example of a "convenient, but false argument" would be an organization that claims it does continuous team reviews on its products, and/or frequent and early product demonstrations with the customer, but doesn't follow through in a disciplined way when conducting these activities.

CAUTION
Beware of "Convenient, but False Arguments"

This situation can usually be uncovered by asking questions to determine if there is a related problem in the organization.[7]

4.11 Tailored TWG Techniques and Lessons at BOND

Let us now discuss a few more key techniques used at BOND in conducting the TWGs to document and deploy Agile processes along with a few lessons we learned to help the TWGs run more effectively. Among these techniques and lessons you will see more examples of asking questions and digging leading to more typical Agile "how-tos" that often just needed to be documented.

---

7. Another example of a "convenient, but false argument" is provided in the NANO case study in Chapter 6 related to the need for training (GP 2.5).

Some are examples where documentation and minor additional behavior changes were required.[8]

4.12 Preparation Work for Running Agile TWGs

When you are first preparing your organization to conduct Agile TWGs, you don't need to involve all the subject matter experts who will eventually be needed to help define your processes. The first few tasks to complete before the TWGs get going revolve around establishing the structure of the organizational repository and the process assets. These are discussed in the following paragraphs.

An Agile Organizational Repository Structure

The CMMI does not prescribe a structure for the organizational repository.[9] The Process Improvement Lead at BOND with my assistance established the organizational repository structure. Unless there is a good reason for a different structure (e.g., non-CMMI process requirements), I recommend establishing a repository structure that aligns with the process area categories in the CMMI model. For example, the structure could be partitioned by Engineering, Management, and Support. Process Management could have its own partition or be included under Management. This decision is ultimately up to each organization and should be made based on legacy process structure, ease of use, and organizational culture. It is recommended that the repository structure not be structured to align with a specific organizational structure since organizational structures tend to change.

4.13 Packaging of Processes

Processes do not need to align one for one with CMMI PAs. Many organizations do this, but it is not necessary. This decision is best made based on how

---

8. More significant behavior issues that needed to be addressed to achieve the full CMMI level 3 are addressed in the next chapter.

9. The discussion to follow in this book on the organizational repository structure and packaging of process assets relates to the expected practices within the Organizational Process Definition (OPD) process area of the CMMI model.

you do real work in your organization. You don't need to make the final decision for process packaging at the start of your process improvement effort. In fact, the brainstorming within TWGs may lead to the identification of processes that should be broken out separately, and processes that should be consolidated.

At BOND, the Technical Solution (TS) TWG broke out two distinct processes referred to as Design and Implementation. Verification and Validation were consolidated into one process, which is common in Agile organizations because the practices Agile organizations use for Verification and Validation tend to have significant overlap. This is because a common Agile technique is to develop complete slices of functionality in short increments, often leading to product demonstrations to the customer. As a result, Verification and Validation techniques tend to blend in such environments.

There was significant discussion over Project Planning (PP) and Project Monitor and Control (PMC) at BOND. The TWG ended up keeping these processes separate, although in other Agile organizations I have seen these consolidated. The factors to consider when making the decision to keep PP and PMC separate versus consolidating include the maturity of your organization's planning and project management activities.

In organizations where the project planning, monitoring, and control activities are sound and institutionalized, it can be more efficient to consolidate and train these processes together. This is because the expected practices under PMC align closely with those under PP and therefore can naturally be packaged and trained together. PMC expected practices revolve around monitoring and taking appropriate action associated with each of the items in your project plan. However, if your organization is just learning how to develop a project plan, it might be more effective to maintain distinct processes so each gets its proper focus.

Risk Management (RSKM) is usually broken out into its own process area, although in implementation in most Agile organizations it is frequently integrated with project planning, monitoring, and control. For example, most Agile organizations do not have distinct risk management review boards. The risk management reporting is usually integrated with project monitor, control, and reporting to Senior Management. Refer to Table 4-2 for an example of an Agile organization's eleven process descriptions and how they could provide coverage for all eighteen CMMI level 2 and 3 process areas.

Table 4-2 *Example Agile Organization Processes and CMMI Process Area Coverage*

Sample Agile Organizational Processes	CMMI Level 2 and 3 Process Area Coverage
Organizational Process Focus	OPF
Organizational Process Definition	OPD
Organizational Training	OT
Consolidated Management Process	PP, PMC, RSKM, IPM, DAR, MA
Supplier Agreement Process	SAM
Consolidated Requirements Management/Development Process	REQM, RD
Design Process	TS, DAR
Implementation Process	TS
Integration, Test, and Validation Process	VER, VAL, PI
Configuration Management Process	CM
Quality Assurance Process	QA

4.14 An Agile Organizational Process Asset Structure

The subject of organizational process asset structure has received a great deal of attention. I have heard the following myth expressed by Agile proponents:

> **MYTH**   The CMMI requires a process "superstructure."

"Superstructure" means multiple types and tiers of process assets. This myth continues to exist not because of anything the CMMI requires, but because of the way in which many large organizations have chosen to implement their process assets in the past.

As an example, it is not uncommon in many large high-tech companies to see four levels (or tiers) of process assets such as policies, processes/practices, work instructions/procedures, and enablers/templates. Policies identify the organization's expectations for establishing and maintaining the process. Processes or practices are often high-level process descriptions whereas work instructions/procedures provide more detailed steps related to the process. Enablers and templates can be any kind of process aid that helps carry out the process and can include tool guides, or templates to help build related documentation.

While the choice for a process asset structure is up to each organization, most Agile organizations I have helped have found that two tiers is sufficient. This is accomplished by consolidating a policy statement with the associated process description that encapsulates "what must be done" in carrying out the process. The second tier contains "how to" guidelines in carrying out the process and tailoring it. This level can be viewed as aids for tailoring the process, and usually includes supporting templates. I have found that in most Agile organizations, step-by-step procedures are replaced by tool guides and training/mentoring. It is worth noting here that a template, such as a Project Management Plan template, can serve as a process with the required process activities implied within the template.[10] This is a common technique I have observed for developing effective Agile process descriptions. See Figure 4-1 for a comparison of a traditional[11] and Agile organizational process asset structure.

Key Recommendation for Agile Organizations in Support of Tailoring

While decisions on process asset structure are up to each organization, there is one key related recommendation I make to Agile organizations. This recommendation was used successfully at BOND. I will state it in the form of a lesson:

> **LESSON 3**
>
> Keep your process "must dos" packaged separate from your process "guidelines."

The reason for this recommendation relates to a major concern that management and independent appraisers often hold—the fear that an Agile approach will lead to loss of project control. This ties to a popular myth:

---

10. Refer to the appendices for an example of a Project Management Plan (PMP) Template.

11. By "traditional," I mean what I have commonly observed in many large high-tech organizations.

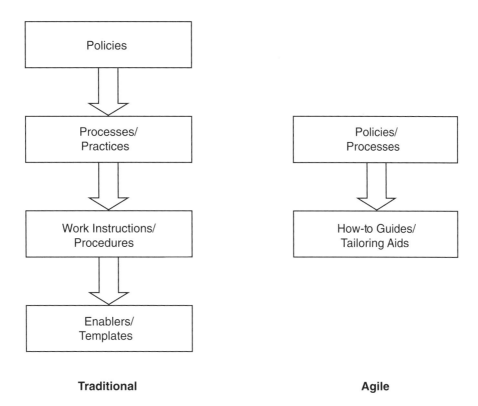

Figure 4-1 *Traditional (Sometimes) and Agile Organizational Process Asset Structure*

MYTH   Agile organizations are less disciplined than traditional organizations and do not really follow any processes.

It has been my experience that organizations that understand and implement Agile practices appropriately tend to be more disciplined[12] in their development and management practices than many traditional development organizations. This is because they believe in their practices and therefore gravitate to them in times of crisis rather than abandoning them, as many more traditional organizations who don't really embrace their practices tend to do. The evidence of this often surfaces with the fervor that can

---

12. Refer to http://www.ddj.com/architect/201804241 for a supporting article by Scott Ambler titled "The Discipline of Agile."

be sensed during the interview process when conducting a gap analysis or a more formal appraisal inside an Agile organization. In organizations in which compliance is achieved more through a "policing" approach, I have often found this same fervor and belief in the process missing.

Regardless of this observation, Agile organizations must still deal with the common perception that they don't follow sound practices, and to be honest, many organizations that claim to be Agile are in fact using the term as a smoke screen to not comply and thus add to this perception.[13]

Following the recommendation in Lesson 3 prepares the organization to deal objectively with this perception by simplifying the tailoring process and making the "must dos" clear and visible to all. A fundamental implication of Lesson 3 is that no one tailors the "must do" practices. Everyone follows them. Hopefully, the reader is starting to appreciate the importance of establishing such rules early before the TWGs develop the processes. If you follow this recommended lesson, the TWGs must carefully consider what they agree to place in the process "must do" packages because this must make sense for all projects regardless of size or scale. Refer to Figure 4-2.

When you take this approach, which works well for organizations with Agile cultures, tailoring the process is integrated with project planning. Tailoring guidelines are used during project planning to make "how to" project specific decisions, such as decisions related to the use of certain tools. Since these guidelines are packaged separately from the process "must dos," the process becomes very clear on what you are allowed to tailor and what must never be tailored.

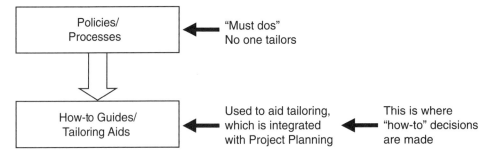

Figure 4-2 *Tailoring and Process Asset Structure*

By following this guidance, the visibility of compliance to the process becomes more evident in an Agile organization, not less. Fuzzy tailoring guidelines are now removed. It is for this reason I often make the claim that if you follow my guidance in the tailoring area when moving an organization with an Agile culture forward toward increased CMMI process maturity, you will find you have an increase in control rather than the loss of control that many falsely believe occurs in Agile organizations.

> **INSIGHT**   Many managers fear Agile will mean a loss of project control, but if you package your process assets and set up your tailoring guidelines in accordance with the guidance in this chapter, you will increase control, not lose control.

4.15 Process Asset Guidelines Used at BOND

Following are key guidelines we provided to the TWGs at BOND.[14]

- Process "must dos" are packaged separately from guidelines (hard rule).[15]
- No process is more than two pages (goal, soft rule).
- Processes do not contain "how-to" information or tool information unless you have decided to mandate this across all projects regardless of size or scale.
- Separate guidelines contain tailoring/planning options, and "how-to" information.
- Processes don't stand alone; they require mentoring and training.

4.16 Different Organizations with Different Process Asset Structures

LACM and BOND are different types of organizations in many ways. LACM is large and product-centric; BOND is small and service-centric. LACM has

---

14. Refer to the appendices for example organizational process asset guidelines.

15. Refer to the example in the appendix of the Organizational Process Definition (OPD) Process description.

decided to mandate a number of tools and standards across their organization to support more effective product-centric development and reuse. BOND has decided it makes sense to mandate few standards and few tools because their business is software service oriented, and they need to be flexible in supporting whatever tools and standards are required based on the constraints of each project.

The resulting organizational repository structures in these two organizations are very different in size and structure based on their different business strategies, but both are *"CMMI compliant"*[16] because they have been developed based on each organization's business needs.

While their organizational repository structures are different, both organizations have achieved formal advanced CMMI levels using these different structures. Contrary to popular myths, the CMMI does not mandate an organizational repository "superstructure" as I have often heard Agile proponents claim.

The CMMI does require each organization to document its processes and maintain those processes at the organizational level where they can be shared and tailored to meet the needs of each project. How you execute your tailoring is up to each organization based on its business needs. The choice is yours as to the size, structure, and agility of your process assets. Nothing in the CMMI OPD expected practices is counter to an Agile approach.

4.17 Agile TWG Roles and Responsibilities

TWGs are composed of assigned personnel who take on two distinct roles: TWG lead and TWG members. The TWG lead is the "doer," which means the lead is responsible for documenting the draft process assets according to the agreed-to process asset structure. This means the lead must clearly understand the process asset structure and guidelines. By minimizing the number of people who actually "write" the processes, we reduce the risk of extensive review cycles due to inconsistent process assets that don't follow the agreed-to rules.

The TWG members are SMEs. Members are often some of the best people in the company and their time is valuable. This approach supports the most effective use of the members' time by not requiring that they become experts

---

16. In this book, "CMMI compliant" means meeting the intent of the CMMI practices.

in the organizational process asset structure and the techniques of writing good processes.

4.18 Effective Techniques to Run an Agile TWG

One of the most effective ways to run an Agile TWG is a variant on how I conduct a gap analysis interview. You can think of an Agile TWG as the next step in "extracting" the real "as-is" process from the organization that started during the gap analysis.

To help extract the "as-is" process from TWG members I like to stand at a whiteboard and ask the TWG members to throw out words that are either activities they do as part of this process or products they produce. I tell them not to worry about creating full sentences. When you ask people to describe the process they follow, often they get wrapped up in talking about all kinds of extraneous detail. I find that it is best to let them talk this way during a gap analysis interview because it puts them at ease, allowing them to communicate more effectively. I have also found that TWGs can easily become bogged down with a great deal of nonessential discussion. This simplified guideline I have found helps to keep the working group focused on the task at hand. This is an area where the TWG lead needs to sense the group dynamics. For a small working group that has trouble getting started, it might work best to just let them talk about how they do their jobs for a period of time. However, if the leader senses the group is getting too far off task he or she might move to my simplified recommendation.

4.19 Separating the TWG Work from the Lead Offline Work

The techniques of running an Agile TWG described in the last section are intended to help keep the group at the desired level of discussion. If the discussion stays too high, the lead should ask more direct questions such as:

What aids do you use to get your job done such as guides, tools, templates?

The working group members usually do not need to discuss the packaging of the process assets into "must dos" and "guides." This is often more efficiently handled by the TWG lead after the group adjourns. It is important for the lead to take all notes such as drawings or words that were jotted down on a whiteboard. It is also important to capture the terminology used by the group members.

I have seen TWG leads who decided on their own to "translate" the terminology the group members were using in a working session into "CMMI terminology," thinking this was part of their responsibility. This is definitely a mistake and should be guarded against.

LESSON 4

Keep your processes in your organization's terminology. Don't try to translate into "CMMI terminology."

The reason for this lesson is really a variant of Lesson 2 in Chapter 2. The CMMI is not a set of dictated practices, and is not intended to dictate terminology. When we say it is a tool to help you reason about your processes, this means to reason about your terminology as well. It is therefore fine to discuss and raise potential issues about the right terminology in your organization. If a term is being used by some inappropriately, this should be discussed. Keep in mind our primary purpose is to "extract" the real process that is used first, and this includes extracting the real terminology used.

In the case when I observed a TWG lead "translating" the terms the group used, it caused a significant buy-in problem during the deployment stage of the project. This occurred because the TWG members felt the lead hadn't listened to them, and members said they didn't even recognize the process that resulted from the TWG effort as being the process they actually used and discussed in the working group. Don't let this happen to your process improvement efforts. TWG leader's responsibilities are primarily facilitation, listening, and documenting.[17]

4.20 What Do You Do When You Find a Gap?

A second gap analysis against the CMMI model is conducted offline by the TWG lead after the initial sorting out of the notes from the TWG session and creation of the initial draft Process and Guidelines documents.

When a gap is found, it usually becomes a topic for a follow-on TWG session where the group is also reviewing and commenting on the draft process and

---

17. The subject of terminology is also discussed in the NANO case study in Chapter 6.

guideline artifacts. This is where the facilitator should be in the "discovery" and "digging" mode as discussed earlier. Questions to be asking during this session include:

Is there a problem in the organization because this practice is not happening?

Usually, through this digging process if there isn't a problem in the organization, the group should be able to uncover what is being done to accomplish the intent of this practice. Once this is discovered it should be added to the process documentation so it can be shared with others in the organization during training as discussed earlier.

If the answer is "yes," the next question should be:

Do we all agree the organization should be "stretching" at this time to change its behavior to accomplish this practice?

If the group agrees the answer is "yes," they might decide to add the must-do to the process. However, each decision should be carefully considered because we are now creating some of the most difficult potential process improvement work—that is, behavior change in the organization. This will require documentation, and training with rationale as to why this new practice is needed to help the organization achieve its business goals.[18]

> **INSIGHT**   The most difficult and costly process improvements are those that involve behavior change. Ensure all initiated changes are essential to achieving business objectives.

Section II
Answers to Common Questions

4.21 Answers to Common Questions When Running an Agile TWG

Following are answers to common questions that often arise when running an Agile Technical Working Group.

---

18. In the next chapter, we talk more about the most significant gaps found at BOND and what we did to address them.

4.22 Do I Need a DAR Process?

At BOND, it was decided that a distinct Decision Analysis and Resolution (DAR) process and guidelines were not required by the organization. Following is the logic that was used to arrive at this decision, which caused no difficulty during the formal CMMI evaluation.

In the DAR TWG at BOND, the group first found itself asking the question:

What are the relevant formal decisions that arise in our organization, and how do we handle them today?

This discussion led to the recognition that formal decisions at BOND were made in two areas: Risks and Designs. The group also discussed what "formal" meant in their organization. The CMMI doesn't tell you what "formal" means, so each organization can make this decision for itself based on its own business needs. Formality at BOND (which did most things informally) was taken to mean the need to involve someone in the decision at a higher level of management. From a risk perspective, formal decisions involved the need to raise a risk to higher-level management. From a design perspective, formal decisions involved evaluating alternative design decisions that affected other groups.

In the case of a risk, the criteria to consider when deciding to raise the risk to Senior Management were included in the Risk Management guidelines that were developed as part of the Risk Management TWG. In the case of design alternatives, the criteria to use in making decisions were included in the design guidelines that were developed as part of the Technical Solution TWG. Therefore, DAR was handled through existing processes and no additional process assets were required.

4.23 Do I Need to Verify Everything I Develop?

The CMMI model does not dictate the work products that must be verified. SP 1.1 of the Verification Process Area expects each project to select the work products to be verified. Once again, as in so many areas of the CMMI model, this decision is up to you.

Often this practice is overlooked especially in organizations that have been building products for many years. A number of my client organizations are product-centric. Specific Practice 1.1 of Verification is a very good example of how the CMMI can help us reason about our processes. It helps us ask questions that can in turn help us manage our work more effectively. Often the questions that result from using the CMMI are ones we might not think to ask otherwise.

As an example, organizations that rely heavily on product reuse should also be relying heavily on reusing the end product such as the software code, and reusing requirements, test cases, and test results. In other words, if I am reusing a product that has already been verified, I should be able to reuse that verification to gain the benefits of that effort. I will still need certain levels of verification and validation in the new environment where I am reusing the product, but the potential exists to "skip" certain lower levels of verification. To help us reason about where in our processes it makes sense to allow one to "skip" certain verification steps, SP 1.3 reminds us that we should have verification criteria. This leads to the question:

> *What are the criteria we use to determine when a verification level can be skipped?*

It should be apparent that the creation of criteria can be a powerful aid to help an organization and its processes become more agile in making dynamic work-related decisions. However, criteria can only help if they have been created and personnel are trained in their use.[19]

4.24 Do I Need to Make Sure the Steps in My Processes Are in the Right Order?

> **MYTH** CMMI-compliant processes require a sequence of steps.

I have observed numerous Technical Working Groups wasting valuable time arguing about the steps in a process and the order in which those steps occur. First, the CMMI defines processes as "activities that can be recognized as implementations of practices in a CMMI model." It doesn't say the order in which those activities occur must be specified.

It has been my experience that when first developing process documentation, any order dependencies should be one of the last items we worry about. I have found that TWGs can spend incredible amounts of time discussing sequence

---

19. The power of criteria in helping an organization make more rapid real-time decisions is discussed at greater length in the GEAR case study in Chapter 7.

topics that turn out to be noncritical. I am not saying order is unimportant, just that often areas where we think we have order dependencies turn out to be "soft" order dependencies at best. Any "hard" order dependencies can always be added later.

A good example of order dependencies I refer to as "soft" is project planning. When I teach planning, I talk about the "what," "who," "when," "how," and "how much." There are certainly order dependencies here. I can't fully define the "who" (resources I need on the project) until I know the skills I need, which depends on the "what" I need to produce. I can't complete the "how much" it will cost until I have figured out all the other pieces to my plan because they all imply some level of cost. Nevertheless, I can provide a project plan template to be used as a great aid to help people plan without telling them which sections they must fill in before others. Such dependencies are best communicated through training, rather than captured through formal documented process descriptions.

4.25 Do I Need to Make Sure Process Descriptions Are Not Redundant?

Often I hear people in TWGs arguing over whether a certain activity should be included in some process document. For example, in the technical solution TWG there was considerable discussion related to whether the design process should refer to requirements development at the start of the process. I tell working groups that it is okay to include words about an activity that might be in another process if it adds to the understanding of this process. Many processes are closely connected, such as requirements and design. Because of the way most Agile teams work—iterating closely between requirement, design, implementation, and test—it makes sense to describe this process as it is executed in your organization. This is another reason why it is best not to get too hung up on order. The traditional order of requirements followed by design followed by implementation followed by test isn't the way Agile teams work. While at a high level this view still might make sense, the activities Agile teams follow during a given day might appear to jumble this order.

The bottom line is that we want to capture the activities and products produced that relate to our processes. If it helps to describe closely related activities that are also included in another process document, it doesn't hurt to say it again.

4.26 Can Requirements Be Captured in an Email or PowerPoint Slides?

This might sound like a strange question, but it is not uncommon to hear it in Agile organizations that are just starting out with a CMMI process effort. First, the CMMI does not dictate the format requirements must be captured in, so on the surface, nothing directly prohibits email or Microsoft PowerPoint slides from being used to document requirements. However, when you look more closely at related expected practices and start asking a few more questions the CMMI expected practices will raise, a different picture often results.

For example, Requirements Management PA, SP 1.3 states:

Manage changes to the requirements as they evolve…

and SP 1.4 states:

Maintain … traceability among the requirements and work products.

These expected practices lead to the following questions:

How do you manage changes to requirements as they evolve if your requirements are captured only in email or PowerPoint slides?

Are you going to update the PowerPoint presentation or email whenever changes are agreed to so the current set of accepted requirements is clear?

One of the reasons traceability is an expected practice is to ensure our testing addresses all requirements including any changes. For this reason I have always suggested to clients that, while you might not need a formal requirements management tool, you do need to have your requirements organized and managed in a way that supports the assignment of requirements identifiers to each requirement so that those identifiers can be used in a test document to ensure your testing is complete.

As you start to ask these questions that arise from using the CMMI to reason about your processes, most organizations, including those with an Agile culture, decide that email and presentation tools cannot adequately do this job. Some very small organizations, and organizations with products that have very stable requirements, might be able to survive with requirements communicated through these means, but most organizations quickly recognize the limitations of these mechanisms.

4.27 Do Requirements Need to Be Captured in Single "Shall Statements"?

This question often arises in Agile organizations that do requirements using user stories or use cases. First, there is no expected practice in the CMMI with respect to "shall statements." The same questions concerning the management of requirements through the life cycle, and traceability, need to be asked. In many Agile organizations, user stories or use cases are often found to help the developers initially understand the requirements and to develop the test cases. Once these test cases are established, the cases themselves often become the agreed-to requirements with the customers. If your customer agrees to this approach, this may suffice to achieve the intent of the requirements management specific practices related to requirements change management and traceability. This is an example where an organization needs to ask a number of "what if" questions related to future potential changes and possible consequences before making such decisions. Other good questions to ask at this time related to the way your organization currently operates include:

Is there a problem in the organization with respect to Requirements Management?

Do customers ever come back and challenge an earlier decision with respect to a requirement change?

Nothing in the CMMI says that a managed test document cannot meet the intent of managing requirements. Asking these types of questions that naturally result when using the CMMI model will often lead to very good discussions in your TWGs that help an organization understand its own processes better and where some process modifications could be of benefit.

4.28 Formalizing Informality

> **LESSON 5**
>
> You can "formalize" informality.

One of the greatest achievements with BOND was our close attention to their culture and maintaining it as they grew. As we added the necessary process formality to prepare them for both the organization's continued growth and their upcoming CMMI assessment, we monitored any changes closely to ensure we weren't damaging the Agile culture that had gotten them their rapid growth and success so far.

Key to our success at BOND was a strategy I have referred to as "formalizing informality."

If something is working well, you don't have to change it for CMMI. However, you do have to document it so it can be taught and shared with others.

It might sound odd to say this, but you can formalize informality, and we did it at BOND successfully. What I mean is if you have a process that works such as a risk management process, but it is "informal" in certain ways, you can teach what you do just like you do it, and document it just like you do it. I have found there almost always seems to be a strong tendency by process professionals to assume when working a process improvement effort, what people currently are doing must be wrong if they have no formal documented processes. This view rests at the heart of why we often find in large supposedly process mature organizations a large disconnect from what the people actually do, and what their processes say they do.

An Example of Formalizing Informality: "Doorway" Risk Management

Let me give you an example of formalizing informality. At BOND, one of the reasons the company was so successful was because risk management was an ingrained way of working. People lived risk management daily. When they had a risk they were often in the doorway of a Senior Manager's office strategizing the risk mitigation. They were doing it immediately, not waiting until a formal risk management meeting. Because of this informality, they were able to initiate risk mitigation almost instantly, thereby keeping potential risks from becoming real problems. Effective risk mitigation stood at the heart of why this organization was successful.

Rather than try to add unnecessary paperwork to this process that was already working effectively, we just described in the newly documented Risk Management Process exactly what the expectations were of how risks were identified, assessed, and categorized in the organization. We did add a small degree of documentation that wasn't going on before by adding a risk slide to the periodic senior management briefs, but we emphasized in the Risk Management training the existing culture that was expected to continue to effectively manage risks. We actually taught this informal "doorway risk management" approach.

4.29 Summary

We have shared many examples in this chapter to help illustrate what is mandated with the CMMI and what is not. "How-to" approaches are not mandated. You do need "how-to" approaches and the CMMI expects that you have them—but it doesn't mandate what they need to look like. They can look traditional or Agile. CMMI doesn't give you the answers, but it does tell you what questions you need to ask and answer for your organization and your project teams.

The focus of this chapter has been on extracting the real "as-is" process and packaging the results. However, even in very successful Agile organizations, there are practices within the CMMI where the intent is not being achieved. In these cases, often adding activities might be needed. Understanding the rationale for these added practices and how they were handled at BOND is the focus of the next chapter.

4.30 Summary: How Agile Helps CMMI

The following table provides a summary of how Agile approaches discussed in this chapter help the CMMI.

Table 4-3 *How Agile Helps CMMI*

"How-to" Approach in Agile Environment	How It Helps CMMI
"Doorway" Risk Management	Helps us implement Risk Management effectively achieving its real intent and timely risk mitigation
Customer demos early, continuous informal reviews	Helps us implement the intent of the Verification PA by identifying defects early and opportunities for improvement
Tailored Agile TWG/Gap Analysis approach	Helps us develop processes that reflect practical and proven techniques that work, and what people really do

Table 4-3 *How Agile Helps CMMI (Continued)*

"How-To" Approach in Agile Environment	How It Helps CMMI
Agile process packaging separating "must dos" from "guidelines" Agile tailoring process integrated with project planning	Supports agility and control
Agile "digging" approach when finding a gap	Helps us locate the most valuable process improvement candidates

Chapter 5

Bringing Process Maturity to Agile Organizations—Part II

Scenario: You are a small Agile organization that is implementing Agile practices effectively. You are also growing rapidly. You would like to know what more the CMMI can do for you to help your organization as you continue to grow.

5.1 What You Will Learn in This Chapter

- The added value the CMMI can bring to a previously successful Agile organization
- Common project management challenges faced by growing Agile organizations along with proven solutions
- Practical techniques to aid stakeholder involvement when the stakeholders are not under your control
- How one Agile organization established a CMMI-compliant measurement program that fit with its Agile culture

- How Senior Management reviews, and an organizational training program were successfully implemented in one Agile organization
- Issues faced in changing behavior in an Agile organization related to sharing lessons, products, and measures outside individual projects
- Techniques to reduce the risk of an unsuccessful CMMI appraisal within an Agile organization
- What you can do to mitigate the common risk of lost process improvement momentum after achieving a formal CMMI Level 3 rating

5.2 BOND Case Study Background

In the last chapter, we explained how Agile techniques can achieve the intent of many CMMI expected practices. However, as successful small Agile organizations grow, weaknesses often surface that are not handled well by Agile approaches alone. In this chapter we take another look at the same case study focusing on common weaknesses often missed when applying Agile practices, and how CMMI practices can help.

At BOND, CMMI model areas that required greater attention include:

- Project Planning (PP), Project Monitor and Control (PMC), and Risk Management (RSKM)
- Generic Practices 2.3 and 2.4, Provide Resources and Assign Responsibility
- Generic Practice 2.10, Reporting to Senior Management
- Generic Practice 2.7, Stakeholder Involvement
- Generic Practice 3.2, Feedback to the Organization
- Measurement and Analysis Process Area (MA)
- Organizational Training Process Area (OT)
- Technical Solution Process Area (TS)
- Quality Assurance Process Area (PPQA)
- Organizational Process Focus (OPF) and Organizational Process Definition (OPD)

Organizational Process Focus (OPF) and Organizational Process Definition (OPD) were covered in the last chapter. Before discussing the other areas listed, I want to establish the context for this chapter by revisiting a key strategy I recommend when using the CMMI model in an Agile organization.

Adding New Process Activities Should Always Be the Least Preferred Choice

Adding new process activities should always be your least preferred choice when developing new process assets, or improving existing ones. This point was made in the previous chapter through the focus placed on "always asking the intent question," and *digging* for the "real existing practice" that is achieving that intent when there isn't a clearly related problem in the organization.

But why is it so important to find these "real existing practices," if they exist, rather than just add an activity that is known to meet the practice and has been proven to work in other organizations?

The reason—simply put—is that changing human behavior is the hardest and most costly part of process improvement. Furthermore, if the change isn't solving a real problem associated with your business needs, it is likely you are *degrading* your organizational performance with this change.

Therefore, making such changes should in almost all cases—and I'll address some exceptions in this chapter—add clear value to the effort in the eyes of the process improvement team and those who are asked to use the process.

Now, some might object by saying that those who must follow the process do not need to see the value. They might say, if it has been determined that the value exists, those who execute the process just need to follow the rules. While there are a few cases where this line of reasoning might be true, in general, if you force process activities on people where the value of those activities is not clear, experience has shown that the intended value will not be achieved.

A previous example of this was forcing formal peer review meetings in an organization that was already removing defects effectively by less formal techniques. Other examples might include forcing meeting minutes or action items at the wrong time or in the wrong way. This is not to say meeting minutes and action items are not necessary—they are, even in Agile organizations—but there is an appropriate time and technique to handle such activities, which we will explain in this chapter.

By not being sensitive to the existing culture, including what is working and what isn't in your organization, you might inadvertently initiate what I refer to as "creeping non-value-added effort." This will take your organization away from what works best. That is not the intent of process improvement.

For this reason, at BOND I pushed the organization to provide a clear *rationale* in training for any new activities added. This forced the process improvement team not to merely document processes, but to determine the right processes for this organization.

I wanted to ensure we had irrefutable evidence as to why any new activity was being added to the existing processes. I made it clear to the process working groups that using the argument that the CMMI required it was an unacceptable argument. This did result in added effort on the part of the working groups—but it also mitigated the risk of damaging the existing successful culture in the company, which was a requirement from Senior Management.

Pause, Reflect, and Glance Forward

It is not uncommon to see a gap analysis conducted solely against the process descriptions in an organization, rather than against the real behavior. While this type of gap analysis can make sense in certain situations, as we move forward we will see why real sustained improvement results primarily from actions taken based on insights learned from observing how the organization really operates. We will also see that the most valuable observations are those found when the organization is operating during times of stress.

I find that I must constantly remind those on process improvement teams that the model was always intended to be used as a tool to help us *reason* about our processes, not as a list of mandated practices. Unfortunately, the mandated approach is the way too many organizations use the model today.

Why do we continually add something new? I believe it is often easier to just write down an activity in the documented process and be done with it when we feel the goal is to get processes defined and deployed that comply with the CMMI. Talking to the people in the organization who will be asked to use that process and digging deeper to uncover a potentially more effective implementation of the practice takes time. However, this effort can be the most valuable time spent by process improvement teams.

This is not to say that there won't be cases where new practices are required along with behavior changes. We found this to be the case at BOND. As successful as this organization was, by digging and finding the real processes a major side benefit of this activity was also realized. We uncovered the *real process weaknesses* that needed to be addressed to benefit the organization.

Examples of such real process weaknesses common to many Agile organizations are the subject of this chapter. If you work in an organization with an Agile culture I recommend you use the experiences at BOND discussed here as a starting point for your own discussions. But keep in mind that each organization is unique, and must be understood within its own business context and constraints. Let us start with project management at BOND.

Section I
Project Management

5.3 Project Management at BOND

Small organizations often start out as the brain-child of just a few individuals who often maintain a great deal of information about how things are done in those organizations in just one place—inside their heads. This was the case at BOND. In the early years, the majority of the project management activities were carried out by just a few individuals. Because they were small, the same person often held multiple roles simplifying communication. But in 2003, the organization was growing rapidly, and it was clear that project management activities needed to be delegated.

In that same year when I conducted the CMMI gap analysis, this delegation initiative had already begun. I observed during my interviews in 2003, confusion and concern in the organization with respect to responsibilities. A number of the next-tier leaders below the owners were being asked to pick up project management responsibilities. They were unsure exactly what those responsibilities were. Furthermore, they were unsure how to carry them out, and particularly concerned because they weren't being relieved of their previous responsibilities.

Examples of new project management activities included the development of a project plan, monitoring the project in accordance with the plan, and knowing when to raise risks to Senior Management.

One specific concern I heard during my gap analysis from multiple potential new project managers was not just how to develop a plan, but how to scale a plan appropriately to project-specific conditions. This was important because many of the projects in the organization at the time were very small. This even raised the question of what constituted a "project" in this organization. What kinds of efforts required a documented plan at all? Table 5-1 provides sample criteria similar to what was eventually developed and used to aid management decisions on when a Project Management Plan (PMP) was required.[1]

Table 5-1 *Criteria to Aid Management Decision for Requiring a PMP*

Length of Project Schedule
Project Budget
Senior Management Visibility
Customer Visibility
Risk

Although the organization was successful, it was clear that the processes they were using would not continue to meet the organization's needs due to its rapid growth. A high-priority finding from that gap analysis was the need to document and train Project Management processes. These findings were directly related to three CMMI process areas—Project Planning, Project Monitor and Control, and Risk Management. Because the most critical issue at the time related to delegation and the communication of responsibilities, my recommendation was to start by defining roles and responsibilities in the organization. Defining and documenting organizational roles and responsibilities is not a typical Agile practice.

5.4 Starting with Roles and Responsibilities at BOND

The CMMI doesn't explicitly have a practice related to defining and documenting roles and responsibilities, but its need can be derived from the generic practice, GP 2.3, which states:

> *Provide adequate resources for performing the [fill in process area], developing the work products, and providing the services of the process.*

---

1. Refer to the appendices for a sample PMP template similar to what was developed and used to help train project managers at BOND.

and GP 2.4, which states:

Assign responsibility and authority for performing the process, developing the work products, and providing the services of the [fill in process area].

One of the reasons the delegation of responsibilities was difficult at BOND was because initially the organization did not have defined roles and responsibilities. Many project management activities that needed to be done were just done by a handful of key people in the small organization.

As we extracted the project management practices from the heads of the organization's leaders, we also began the process of documenting standard organizational roles and responsibilities. This effort would be revisited and refined multiple times during the multi-year effort of moving the organization to CMMI Level 3. This was partly because the responsibilities associated with roles *evolved* as the organization and capabilities of the people grew. As the responsibilities of a project leader became increasingly understood, training was instituted to help communicate these responsibilities in a consistent way across the multiple on-going projects in the organization.[2] For an example of standard organizational roles and responsibilities similar to what we developed at BOND, refer to Table 5-2.

Table 5-2 *Example Standard Organizational Roles and Responsibilities*

Project Manager
Support bid and proposal
Provide project level direction and oversight
Estimate project resources and tasks
Plan project and maintain project plan per project planning process
Ensure project level roles are assigned and tasks are completed
Report status to Senior Management

Continues

---

2. Defining roles and responsibilities, and maintaining a close alignment of those roles and responsibilities with documented processes in an Agile organization is covered further in the next chapter on the NANO Case Study.

Table 5-2 *Example Standard Organizational Roles and Responsibilities (Continued)*

Senior Project Manager
Assist with business development
Provide project-level direction and oversight
Estimate project-level resources
Provide mentoring to project managers

Technical Lead
Review project estimates, schedule, tasks, and reconcile with actual resources
Identify and communicate engineering tasks
Perform requirements analysis
Elicit and communicate risks, issues, lessons, and best practices

5.5 Growing Project Leaders from the Inside

The strategy at BOND to help maintain the existing successful culture was to grow project managers from within the organization, rather than hire from the outside.

To facilitate this growth as the Project Management processes were extracted, and documented, along with roles and responsibilities, project leadership workshops were conducted.

In support of the Agile culture in the organization these workshops highlighted Agile project management practices[3] [22], which were also captured within the defined project planning, project monitor and control, and risk management processes.

The workshop trained the project leaders in "how-to" techniques, some of which were already prevalent in the organization, in carrying out the now

---

3. In an article appearing in *Crosstalk* (see reference), key differences between Agile project management and traditional project management practices are highlighted and compared. There is also a table later in this chapter summarizing key Agile project management aids.

defined and documented project management processes. Some of the practices within these processes required new behaviors that the working groups agreed necessary.

These workshops were highly interactive focusing on typical scenarios occurring on real projects. Acceptable options leaders had in addressing various project conditions and constraints in carrying out the company's processes were included. Any new behaviors the project leaders were being asked to follow were referred to as "stretch points" and highlighted in the workshop.

I have mentioned the importance we placed on *rationale* when asking the people in the organization to change their behavior or "stretch." In moving the organization toward CMMI Level 3 project management practices, there were a number of areas we did push behavior changes. This did not happen quickly. It took time for these new practices to be employed in a manner where the organization could see the tangible benefits and achieve buy-in to the new expected behaviors.

I now want to share some of the specific practices added as "stretch points," and the rationale provided to the project leaders during training for these additions.

5.6 Example Stretch Point: Adding a Project Management Plan per Agreed Template

Initially a project management plan (PMP) document was not being produced, reviewed, and approved at the start of projects. This is not to say that project planning was not occurring at BOND. It was happening, as it does in many small Agile organizations. Often, the rationale for decisions, and the specifics of the plan, are communicated verbally, and never find their way into a documented planning artifact that provides an overall vision, scope, and plan for the project that can be reviewed and approved by higher-level management and other key stakeholders in the organization.

LESSON 1

When an organization is small, formal documented plans and rationale for decisions might be unnecessary. As organizations grow, documenting overall plans and related decisions in a consistent way begins to have greater value.

This is because as the organization grows, people get busy and can no longer maintain all the key facts and agreements with respect to a project in their heads. Documenting project plans in a consistent way under these conditions now begins to have more value to the organization. The consistency side of the plan has value to stakeholders who must review and agree to the plan, those who are tasked with developing the plan, and those who must follow the plan.

To aid the institutionalization of project planning at BOND, a Project Management Plan (PMP) template was developed and used during the Project Lead Workshop to help train leaders in what was expected in each section of the plan.

At BOND, we used the CMMI Project Planning (PP) process area as a starting point, reducing the fourteen practices in this process area down to five steps based on proven Agile Project Management best practices [22]. The five steps are referred to in the following paragraphs as "the What," "the Who," "the When," "the How," and "the How Much."

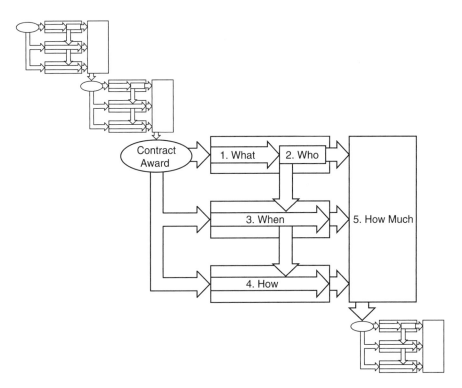

Figure 5-1 *Five-Step Agile Project Management Planning Process*

This is not to say that all fourteen specific practices in the CMMI model are not important, but we found that by focusing on the five simplified steps, project planning maturity at BOND could evolve and still be consistent with the organization's culture and business needs.

Refer to Figure 5-1. The repetition in the figure of the five-step symbol before contract award, and after the completion of step five, is intended to indicate that planning isn't something that occurs only once, but rather is a continuous process that we go through multiple times when using an Agile approach.

The five steps are each discussed further in the following section. Refer to the appendices for an example of a Project Management Plan template. Table 5-3 provides a mapping between the five steps discussed in this chapter and the major sections of the template in the appendix.

Table 5-3 *Mapping Five Planning Steps to Project Plan Template*

Planning Step	Project Plan Template Section
"What"	1. Scope and System Overview
"Who"	2. Organization and Staffing
"When"	3. Life Cycle and Schedule
"How"	4. Project Monitor and Control
"How Much"	5. Metrics

5.7 "The What"—Scoping the Effort

In the front of the plan we requested a brief paragraph about the product or service that was being provided, and a related diagram. This was intended to be very high level, not to indicate design information, or requirements. Its intent was to give the reader a high-level perspective, and a visual aid as to the scope of the effort. The rationale provided was that experience has shown you can't generate a useful plan if you don't have a good sense of the scope of the effort you are planning. During the training, I explained that even a simple diagram of what was being provided often stimulated valuable discussions as to what is inside the scope and what is outside the scope of the project. The organization was already doing this type of brainstorming up front and the diagram we were looking for was usually being produced. However, often it had never found its way past a white board and into a more formal tool where it could be maintained. The only change in behavior in this area was to have someone capture the diagram in a tool such as Power-Point or Visio and then place it with a few related words in the appropriate PMP section.

Another part of the rationale used for capturing this diagram related to how planning is different on Agile projects. Because we don't do as much detailed planning up front on Agile efforts, it becomes more important to know that we have adequately scoped the work. This is because we might be opening ourselves up for scope issues later.[4] In the CMMI model Project Planning process area, SP 1.1 states:

> Establish…work breakdown structure to estimate the scope….

This specific practice reminds us that even for incremental and Agile efforts it is important to get our arms around all the planning work as early as possible (even if we don't detail it out). BOND didn't actually have a traditional-looking work breakdown structure document, but the *intent* of this practice was met through a combination of the *diagram*, which did show the "work breakdown" and the *high-level schedule.* The schedule will be discussed further under the section titled, "The When." For more information on Agile methods and requirements development, refer to [23].

5.8 "The Who"—Managing Your Resource and Skill Needs

Many books on Agile methods seem to assume that personnel have already been assigned and have the skills to do the job. Providing resources and ensuring those people have the skills needed to do the job is critical to the success of a project. Practices related to providing resources (GP 2.3) to projects, assigning responsibilities (GP 2.4), and ensuring those people who are assigned have been trained in the skills they need (GP 2.5) are all key practices we are *reminded* of through the generic practices within the CMMI model.[5]

---

4. Managing scope is also discussed later in the book in the DART case study.

5. Addressing adequate skill needs is also discussed later in the book in the DART case study.

In the PMP template was a section that identified required roles, names of people assigned to roles, and skills required. During the development of the template, and in the ensuing training, there was discussion as to the need to list skills required. In small Agile organizations often the allocation of people to projects and the assurance those people have appropriate skills happen informally and are often not written down. But as organizations grow and multiple projects are executing in parallel, it is not uncommon for some of these projects to run into unanticipated difficulties, leading Senior Management to make priority staffing decisions that modify the initial planned staffing. This often leads to key personnel on one project being reassigned to support a different project.

As organizations grow, leaders can easily forget the rationale for the initial selection of an individual to a given project, which often includes specific skill needs or experience specifically related to that project. Even the people on the project could forget why the original decision was made. Further, as the project evolves there might be changes in the requirements that can affect skill needs. This provides a good rationale for writing down the skill needs of people, providing backup information related to why they were selected for the project.

Some objected during the initial workshops to defining roles in the organization, based on a fear that people would be pigeonholed. One of the reasons many people enjoy working in small organizations is because they get to do a range of tasks that often are not available in larger organizations where personnel are hired into individual departments with a limited charter of responsibilities.

I explained that our intent in defining roles was not to change the culture of the organization that encouraged and supported individuals helping others and taking on additional assignments. The value in defining roles was to raise the awareness of work that had to be done. A person could take on multiple roles and that was fine. By defining roles with a list of responsibilities, management would have better visibility of the resource needs of the organization. It can be a very good thing for people to take on multiple roles within an organization, but it is also important to have visibility to ensure we understand when individuals might be taking on too much work, risking the overall goals of the organization.[6]

---

6. Roles and responsibilities are also discussed later in the book in the DART case study. Another reason defining roles and responsibilities in an Agile organization is important is because key support roles can easily be missed. By support, I mean the roles of Quality Assurance and Configuration Management. The subject of Quality Assurance is addressed in Chapter 7 in the GEAR case study.

> **LESSON 2**
>
> As organizations grow, the value of defined roles and responsibilities increases as an aid for human resource management.

5.9 Common "Undocumented-Super-Spreadsheet" Resource Management Process

At BOND, Senior Management maintained a "Super-Spreadsheet" that contained all the personnel in the company and showed their allocation to projects. Senior Management met weekly to discuss current staffing needs of projects, specifying changes needed to address ongoing issues.

Often, such spreadsheets are used at meetings in both Agile and traditional organizations, but this resource management process is frequently not documented, or thought of as a formal process in the company. The criticality of documenting such a process is not as high since only a few people need to know about it and use it. Moreover, such processes are not under great risk of getting lost. This example demonstrates the relationship between the need for process documentation, the number of people affected by a given process, and the state of institutionalization of that process. While the priority of documenting this process was not as high as other processes, it still needed to be documented and trained in support of future company growth.

5.10 "The When"

Often, Agile organizations don't develop and maintain traditional detailed project schedules, with critical paths. Under the Project Planning process area, expected practice SP 2.1 states:

Establish…the project's budget and schedule.

The degree of detail in the schedule, and when that detail is created, is a decision left to each organization and project to decide based on the organization's business needs. Scheduling guidelines are recommended to be provided along with training for responsible project personnel.

While Agile projects do plan, they tend to produce a higher-level plan early[7] [4], and then detailed planning in short increments. At the end of each increment, they use the additional knowledge gained during the increment to make the most effective plan for the next increment. The schedule evolves with the evolving incremental plan.

One of the common pitfalls when executing incrementally is to push off work, thinking it is lower priority because people think it will be easy to do. The key to success is balancing the focus on the high-priority work that needs to be done now, while keeping an eye on the big picture and reducing risk of unknown areas where analysis has not yet been completed.[8] In the BOND workshop, we used typical scenarios to help train project leaders in the ramification of incremental and evolutionary development.

At BOND, we required a complete, high-level project schedule indicating major milestones at the start of each project. This schedule would be maintained. Recognizing that the current real work was being managed through the day-to-day *standup meetings* and *visible task lists* that were institutionalized in the organization,[9] we explained that we did not encourage great detail in the master schedule.

> **LESSON 3**
>
> A common pitfall in both Agile and traditional development organizations is building schedules early with too much detail too far out, leading to inconsistencies with real on-going work.

The purpose of the master schedule was to ensure that all stakeholders, including the customer and senior management, understood the big picture. This schedule was used as a *reminder* of major commitments to ensure we weren't adding unacceptable risk by pushing off work that should be addressed earlier. We trained project leaders in the specific scheduling guidelines that had been agreed to relative to the master schedule, the level of detail, and which details should and shouldn't be included to keep the master schedule current without unnecessary effort. Refer to Table 5-4 for an example of schedule guidelines similar to what was used at BOND.

---

7. Reference "Coarse Grain Planning" described in *Crystal Clear*. See the reference for more information.

8. In the DART case study later in the book, this common pitfall is discussed along with a practical approach to help avoid it.

9. Most projects used Scrum practices at BOND. Daily "standup" meetings and visible task lists are common Agile practices. These practices are discussed further in the DART case study.

Table 5-4 *Example Agile Scheduling Guidelines*

Include customer milestones and deliverables
Include major external dependencies
Include all work of all project people
Ensure correlation with daily task list, but not redundant detail
Periodically update in accordance with project management plan

This training helped to keep the project management artifacts (e.g., master project schedule) aligned with the work produced by the development teams. A pitfall in many organizations—Agile and traditional—is building detailed critical path schedules that go too far into the future, and then finding they are unmaintainable and inconsistent with what development teams are doing.

The CMMI Project Planning process area expects a schedule to be established and maintained. It doesn't tell you when you need to create it, or what level of detail needs to be in it. Schedules can be maintained at a high level in a master schedule with detailed schedules maintained by workers in the task lists as many Agile teams do. There is nothing inconsistent between the CMMI expected practices related to scheduling and managing work and how Agile teams schedule and manage their work. But what the CMMI provides beyond what BOND was already doing was the *reminder* that we needed to capture the process so we could train others.

By teaching project leaders *"how-to"* techniques with respect to project management that fit with an organization's Agile culture, we avoided the common pitfall I often see in other organizations that are trying to increase their agility—the development of project management artifacts that are not aligned with the real engineering work effort.

5.11 Life Cycle—It's Your Choice

Specific Practice (SP) 1.3 in the Project Planning process area states:

Define the project life cycle…

This practice doesn't tell you what life cycle you have to use. You can use Waterfall, Incremental, Spiral, or your own hybrid defined life cycle. This decision is up to you and should be made based on agreed-to and documented life cycles that make sense within your organization.[10] For more information on Agile life cycles, refer to [24].

If you are an Agile organization, you might wonder why you should care about the life cycle. Often, small Agile organizations don't worry about defining their life cycle. However, a defined life cycle becomes increasingly important as your organization grows. When you start to have more project artifacts being developed on both the management and engineering side, having a consistent life-cycle view can help your project keep its management and engineering sides communicating more effectively.

This is why once you decide on a life cycle, you want to train people in all parts of the organization how to align their work with that life cycle. This includes both engineering work such as task lists maintained by development team members, and project management artifacts, such as a master schedule. This is an example why project leaders need to be aware of decisions to use an Agile approach. Engineering artifacts and project management artifacts must both align with the life cycle chosen.[11] The CMMI model helps us by bringing this important practice to light.

> **LESSON 4**
>
> By keeping people on the project aware of the purpose of a life cycle, we can help improve communication across the project. This is an area where the CMMI can help an Agile organization as it grows.

At BOND, training the project managers in Agile management fundamentals avoided a scenario I have observed in many large organizations where engineering has decided to go Agile (maybe "stealth Agile"), but project management is unaware or doesn't realize the consequences of this decision.

A symptom of this scenario is the "5000-line detailed master schedule" developed up front on the project management side of the house, and an engineering organization that says it plans to use Agile techniques.

---

10. Refer to Specific Practice 1.2 of the OPD Process Area, which states: "Establish Life Cycle Model Descriptions."

11. Consequences of misalignment of management artifacts with engineering work and what you can do about it are discussed further in the GEAR case study in Chapter 7.

5.12 "The How"—Team Meetings, Task Monitoring, and Course Correction

Another area where the CMMI can help Agile organizations as they grow relates to team meetings. When I do gap analysis interviews in Agile organizations, I often hear great "how-to" techniques that are often not written down. Examples include the *daily standup meetings* for daily task management, and Agile team practices related to task course correction. These are good proven "how-to" techniques that meet the intent of specific practices found in the Project Monitor and Control process area.

In the BOND case, I suggested that they describe in their Project Management Plan (PMP) the daily standup meeting and how these meetings are conducted. This serves a number of purposes. When new people come on the project, they can come up to speed quickly by first reading the PMP. This document captures the planned project vision.

Agile practices, while effective, don't lead to documenting this kind of information. The CMMI project management practices lead you in this direction, which can help Agile organizations share expectations across the organization. This becomes increasingly important as organizations grow and new people are brought in, especially those who might not have been previously exposed to Agile techniques.

As just described, simply writing down what the teams were already doing was often all that was needed. In other cases, the CMMI stimulated discussions that led people at BOND to realize they did need some new management reporting behaviors. One of those areas that needed change was reporting up the chain to Senior Management.

5.13 Senior Management Briefings: An Area in Which the CMMI Can Help Agile

> **LESSON 5**
>
> Looking out for the overall welfare of the company is a necessary practice we are reminded of by CMMI Generic Practice 2.10: "Review the activities, status, and results...with higher-level management and resolve issues."

An example of behavior changes needed at BOND is the Senior Management briefs. Agile practices focus on the project. They don't give us much help with respect to reporting status to Senior Management. This is an area where we had to *stretch* the current behavior of the BOND organization. When I initially did my gap analysis in 2003, there was no required format for senior management briefs, nor did they occur on a regular schedule. GP 2.10 of the CMMI states:

> *Review the activities, status, and results ... with higher level management...*

This isn't a typical practice of an Agile team, but it becomes increasingly important as an organization grows. Senior Management must take on a different perspective from project personnel, as they are looking out for the overall welfare of the company. Sometimes they have to make decisions that might not be in the best interests of a single project (e.g., reassigning a key person). This can be caused by an issue on a different project that might have a higher priority from an overall business perspective.

To best help the company in these situations, Senior Management must have the best status possible on all projects. GP 2.10 doesn't dictate how this is achieved, but many organizations use periodic Senior Management briefings to do so. To support effective communication, a Senior Management brief template is often developed and standardized so that all projects report in a consistent way using consistent terminology. This helps ensure communication is accurate up the chain.

The overall intent is to ensure higher-level management, who has interest in the organization beyond individual day-to-day project activities, has appropriate visibility to help make better decisions for the organization. When you don't have a set format of information to present, it is easy to just get caught up in focusing on what you might think are the key issues from your immediate perspective, and miss others that Senior Management needs to hear about given their different set of responsibilities.

5.14 Example of Senior Brief Evolution: Backup Slides for Efficient Use of Time

The Senior Management brief template became a set format at BOND. It evolved based on feedback from Senior Managers and Project Leaders. Initially there were complaints from Senior Management that the brief contained too much nonessential information.

Senior Management personnel wanted to make sure the package contained only the pertinent critical data that could affect a decision they might have to make in the near future. Cost, staffing, schedule, and risk were clearly priority topics all agreed with. This led to a question:

> What about other areas that are covered by the CMMI model?

GP 2.10 crosses all process areas, and therefore it is expected that activities, status, and results are addressed that cover all areas. For some process areas, this was covered in a Management Steering Group (MSG) brief that was held periodically, addressing the Process Improvement Project status. However, these meetings often didn't delve into process issues specific to individual projects. To address this potential need, and keep the Senior Management brief focused on priority issues, backup slides were included in the brief. This allowed management to scan lower-priority information and raise any issues or concerns they might have had.

5.15 "The How Much"—Don't Force the Team to Perform "Unnatural Acts"

Within the CMMI Project Planning process area, SP 1.2 states:

> Establish...estimates of the attributes of the work products and tasks.

This practice generated considerable discussion at BOND and demonstrates the value of always asking the intent question. At BOND even though the organization developed software as one of its primary services, they did not maintain or use common attributes of software such as line of code counts in their estimation process.

We asked:

> What is the intent of this practice?

Part of the intent was to facilitate consistent assessment of the project's effort, cost, and schedule. BOND had a history of consistently meeting fixed schedules with high-level startup requirements. Projects succeeded because project leaders had close working relationships with their customers. They worked together *collaboratively*[12] to establish what functionality was possible given schedule and cost constraints. As new information arose,

---

12. Customer collaboration is a common Agile practice. This practice is discussed further in the DART case study later in this book.

priorities were often reevaluated in the light of what the team felt could be achieved based on its *specific experience with that specific project.*

Given this business model, the next question was: "What attributes of work products and tasks are actually used to consistently meet customer expectations?" The answer that most team members at BOND felt was right was that they worked to the constraints the customer gave them with respect to Cost and Schedule targets.

Effectively they backed into the answers from the customer input in terms of cost and schedule. While this is not the approach in many traditional development organizations, because BOND personnel had close working relationships with their customers, this approach worked effectively. This example demonstrates how some traditional estimation methods might be affected when working in a collaborative relationship with your customer.

As a result of this discussion, we did not force the team to conduct an *unnatural act* related to estimating work product and task attributes. We simply documented the process "as-is" and shared this approach as the model that has helped the organization succeed to date. This was the process encouraged on future projects.

It is important to note here that this is an example of an Agile practice that is highly dependent on customer relationship. It should be discussed with the lead appraiser early to avoid surprises during an appraisal. We also trained personnel to become aware of the dependency this practice has on a *collaborative customer.* It could easily backfire in a noncollaborative nontrusting environment. This point was emphasized during the training of project leaders at BOND. It is also important to note here that a key objective related to being disciplined, whether Agile or traditional, is developing a capability to assess size or velocity to know how much you can commit to get done. For more information on estimating when using Agile methods, refer to [25].

Section II
Lessons and Answers to Common Questions

5.16 Lessons from Formalizing Planning at BOND

We did add a degree of formality to the project planning activity at BOND. Requiring a PMP document was a change to the organization's culture. At first, this caused push-back from project personnel. The immediate reaction was that developing such a document would take too long and negatively affect project performance. I emphasized that project personnel were already doing this work except for documenting results (e.g., capturing a white board diagram, or writing down agreed-to rationale for a decision that had been verbally discussed).

We explained the value of documenting was to help project personnel and that most PMPs could be written in ten pages or less taking no more than eight hours. Some project leaders objected, saying it took them closer to forty hours to develop a PMP. When pressed, most of that forty hours was spent on analysis necessary to validate their plan whether they documented it or not. This included gaining concurrence of real schedule milestones with stakeholders, and the names of people who would be assigned to key roles on projects, plus scheduling team meetings.

By training the organization how to develop a PMP and requiring the PMP on all projects, we were able to institutionalize project planning at BOND. Guidelines were also created using criteria distinguishing between projects that required a PMP and "tasks" that only required budget authorization.

The added visibility of project planning through the PMP and improved communication up the chain through the Senior Management brief resulted in measurable improvements in the consistency of project performance observed by both Senior Management and customer personnel. BOND was successful prior to these changes, but successful projects can always improve their performance. Refer to Table 5-5 for a summary of key Agile Project Management Practices Aids. For more information on Agile Project Management, refer to [26, 27, 28, 29].

Table 5-5 *Summary of Key Agile Project Management Practice Aids[13]*

Integrated Project Management Plan (PMP) Template
Agile Action Item Guidelines
Agile Schedule Guidelines
Documentation of Team meetings and related rules
Documentation of real risk management expected practices (e.g., Doorway Risk Management)

---

13. Many of these aids are addressed later in this chapter.

Table 5-5 *Summary of Key Agile Project Management Practice Aids (Continued)*

Defined roles and responsibilities

Stakeholder matrix

Measurements based on real process followed (e.g., estimates)

Measurements used each day to make decisions

Agile Senior Management brief template

5.17 The Plan as a Living Document at BOND

At BOND, we observed the greatest value of the PMP was getting the project started with a common vision for the team. It initiated new personnel quickly to the project.

Specific Practice 3.2 of the CMMI Project Planning process area states:

Reconcile the project plan…

At BOND, this reconciliation was taught and occurred daily through the next level of detail plans at the team task list level and through the flow of issues to project leads and Senior Management during periodic briefings. The "reconciled" plan was viewed as a set of *living artifacts* rather than the original PMP document. Those reconciled planning artifacts included team task lists, personnel currently assigned, and standard agreed-to measures periodically reported through Senior Management briefs. These artifacts became the "real" current plan. The PMP document was updated less frequently. How the standard measures were arrived at in the organization is discussed next.

5.18 The Power of Templates

Templates, such as Project Management and Senior Management Brief templates, turned out to be extremely powerful process aids in helping to communicate process expectations and institutionalizing processes at BOND. They were also powerful as aids to gather objective evidence in preparing for a formal CMMI appraisal. To gain the full benefits of templates at BOND, we had to institute a few related rules.

As part of the tailoring process at BOND, one key rule was that sections of templates were never deleted. If a section was not applicable on a project, the tailoring rules required you to state *NA* in that section. However, we developed most templates at BOND with the goal of providing the "minimum" that all projects would need. This meant there should rarely be sections that were not applicable. The "minimum" strategy was not intended to imply we expected projects to only provide the minimum, but rather to help clarify the lower bound of tailoring.

To achieve this, template content and process definitions were developed within the Technical Working Groups. The groups were asked to think about the issues involved with scaling when developing these templates.

By creating templates as "minimums," tailoring became *tailor up*, not tailor down activity. This simplifies tailoring for the small projects. Too often in large organizations, tailor down approaches are used. This is least efficient, creating the greatest amount of work on smaller projects that have the greatest resource constraints.

When templates are developed from the "minimum must do" perspective aligning with the "as-is" processes, and the thinking that has gone on through a CMMI gap analysis, they become powerful aids in creating clear expectations for the executing team, and any external group that might need to assess on-going activities.

In July 2007 when we conducted the formal CMMI appraisal at BOND striving for a CMMI level 3 rating over 18 Process Areas, it was estimated that this appraisal included over 4000 objective pieces of evidence to back up our results. Hundreds of these objective evidence points were found in single documents developed using well-defined templates. The total number of actual physical artifacts needed to acquire those 4000 points therefore turned out to be less than 400. That is the power of using templates![14]

An example of how the development of a plan by using a Project Management Plan (PMP) template and then following that plan, can result in the generation of multiple pieces of evidence that meet CMMI specific and generic practices can be found in Table 5-6.[15]

---

14. Tailoring is discussed at greater length in Chapter 7 in the GEAR case study.

15. Refer to annotated PMP template in the appendices for more information.

Table 5-6 *Example CMMI Evidence Generated Using a PMP Template*

Training Guidance	PMP Template Section[16]	CMMI Practice Achieved
The "What"—High Level Scope of Work	1. Scope and System Overview	PP SP 1.1 Estimate Scope of Project
The "Who"—Identify Roles and People Assigned	2. Organization and Staffing	GP 2.3 Provide Resources, GP 2.4 Assign Responsibility
The "When"—Identify High Level Schedule with Major Milestones	3. Life Cycle and Schedule	PP SP 1.3 Define Project Life Cycle, PP SP 2.1 Establish Schedule
The "How"—Identify Team Meetings, When They Occur, Rules for Meetings	4. Project Monitor and Control	PMC SP 1.1 Monitor Project Planning Parameters, PMC SP 1.6 Conduct Progress Reviews, PMC SP 2.1 Analyze Issues, PMC SP 2.2 Take Corrective Action, PMC SP 2.3 Manage Corrective Action
The "How"—Identify Measures Collected, Where Placed, Who Sent to, How Used	5. Metrics	MA SP 1.2 Specify Measures, MA SP 2.1 Collect Measurement Data, SP 2.3 Store Data, SP 2.4 Communicate Results
The "How"—Identify Risks, Risk Attributes, Where Placed, Risk Status	4. Project Monitor and Control	RSKM SP 1.2 Define Risk Parameters, SP 2.1 Identify Risks, SP 3.1 Develop Risk Mitigation Plans, SP 3.2 Implement Risk Mitigation Plans

Continues

---

16. Refer to example of Annotated Project Management Plan (PMP) Template in the appendices.

Table 5-6 *Example CMMI Evidence Generated Using a PMP Template (Continued)*

Training Guidance	PMP Template Section	CMMI Practice Achieved
The "How"—Identify What Audited, Frequency of Audits, Where Results Maintained, Who Results Sent to	4. Project Monitor and Control	PPQA SP 1.1 Objectively Evaluate, PPQA SP 2.1 Communicate & Ensure Resolution, SP 2.2 Establish Records
The "How"—Identify Controlled Artifacts, Where Managed	5. Project Monitor and Control	CM SP 1.1 Identify Configuration Items, CM SP 1.2 Establish CM System, CM SP 1.3 Create or Release Baselines

Can a Template Meet the Intent of a Process?

The CMMI defines process as:

> *Activities that can be recognized as implementations of practices in a CMMI model.*

A template identifies required activities to gather information and document the results implied within its structure. A process does not need to be a strict sequence of activities. When dependencies do exist, they can be captured by notes in the template or fields on a form that are not accessible until other pre-requisite fields are completed.

Templates have practical value conveying the real intent of a process. They often avoid the ambiguities commonly found in "wordy" process documents. Templates, like other Agile process artifacts, should not stand alone, but be deployed along with training material including rationale.

5.19 Do I Need to Write Down Meeting Minutes and Action Items?

This question often surfaces in Agile organizations. The CMMI does not explicitly state that it expects written meeting minutes or documented action items. The Project Monitor and Control Process Area, SP 2.1 states:

Collect and analyze the issues…

SP 2.2 states:

Take corrective action…

SP 2.3 states:

Manage corrective actions…

Agile teams commonly use daily standup meetings where the team lead listens during a go round of team members. The role of the team lead is to help remove obstacles.

To force formal minutes and formal written action items on these brief daily standup meeting would likely undo the value of these meetings. People would be less likely to speak up because of the added burden of documenting the issues raised. At the same time, we do need feedback that these meetings are achieving their intent and that issues are adequately being addressed. This is an area where the CMMI helps us ask good questions, ensuring the team meetings are achieving their intent. At BOND, I recommended and they complied with the following:

> *Daily standup meetings are to focus on the real work going on, and meeting minutes are captured in any updates to the task list. This is keeping with Agile practices and the intent. With respect to action items, I proposed a **criterion** as follows:*
>
> *If an action coming out of a daily standup can be resolved before the next daily standup, it does not need to be documented. However, the issue needs to be raised again at the following standup to ensure it has been closed. Any issue or action raised that cannot be closed within one day, or affects a stakeholder outside the immediate group, should be written and captured in an action item system.*

Some companies have formal Action Item tools. Some Agile teams just place actions on the work list like any other piece of work. How action items are captured is up to each organization. I recommended that any action that only affects the team to be handled through the team's task list only, and should not require more formal documentation.

This is an area where some creativity is possible. Today with web tools such as Wikis, many Agile organizations keep meeting minutes and task lists in a very succinct open access form.

Busy leaders might take notes on Blackberries, in notebooks, or even on scraps of paper, filtering and then capturing relevant issues in document form at a later point in the week.

This can be a good time for the leaders to "debrief" themselves on how the week went, allowing for a period of "stepping back" reflecting on any possible plan refinements that might be needed.

Work out a system that makes sense for your culture, keeping in mind the intent is to ensure the real issues being raised are followed up on in a timely fashion, and closed. If there are no issues with this in your organization, don't create extra work just for the CMMI. Be honest in assessing how your organization runs. Ask yourself:

> When projects are driving toward a critical milestone, do people get busy and do actions fall through cracks?

If so, this is a legitimate weakness that needs some attention. Agile organizations are just as susceptible to these problems as traditional organizations are. Therefore, practices are required in both traditional and Agile organizations to ensure key actions that could burn us downstream aren't being dropped. Refer to Table 5-7 for a sample Action Item form.

Table 5-7 *Sample Action Item Form*

Action Item No.	Action Item Description	Person Responsible	Status	Date Assigned	Date Due	Date Closed	Comments

5.20 Involving Relevant Stakeholders

CMMI Generic Practice 2.7 states:

> … Involve Relevant Stakeholders.

A relevant stakeholder as defined in the CMMI is a stakeholder that is identified for involvement in specified activities and is included in a plan. In small Agile organizations where most everyone interacts daily in a face-to-face environment, involving relevant stakeholders is not difficult. However, as organizations grow, and projects get larger, sometimes all team members might not be located in the same physical space. As we become busier and projects become more complex, it becomes easier for the "ball to be dropped" and for relevant stakeholders to get missed.

One of the best techniques I have observed in traditional and Agile organizations to address this situation is the development of a *relevant stakeholder matrix*. This matrix of stakeholders identifies key roles within the company and what activities they need to be involved in. Such a matrix can be used both for initial project planning and as a *reminder* during project execution.[17] Refer to Table 5-8 for an example of a relevant stakeholder matrix (partial matrix).

Table 5-8 *Example Relevant Stakeholder Matrix*

Product	Producer	Reviewer	Approver	Notify on Change
System Requirements Specification	System Engineer	Chief Engineer	Functional Leads, Program Manager	Team Leads, Chief Engineer, Program Manager
Concept of Operation	System Engineer	Chief Engineer, Customer Rep	Chief Engineer	Customer Rep, Chief Engineer
Software Design Document	Software Engineer	Chief Engineer, Software Functional Lead	Chief Engineer, Software Functional Lead	All Functional Leads, Chief Engineer
Test Procedures	System Engineer	Chief Engineer	Functional Leads, Test Director	Chief Engineer, Test Director

5.21 Involving Relevant Stakeholders —Additional Help Sometimes Needed

The CMMI focuses on expected practices related to "what," not "how." This doesn't mean you don't have to make sure your "how" is effective. It means it is up to you to figure out the "right how" for your organization.

---

17. The use of a stakeholder matrix to address key weaknesses in an organization is discussed further in Chapters 6 and 7 on the NANO and GEAR case studies.

At BOND, many of the projects are often made up of teams from multiple organizations that are physically distributed. Agile practices such as collaborating with customer personnel and daily standup meetings help us involve relevant stakeholders by supporting more effective direct communication. During a project lead workshop at BOND, the difficulties that often arise in facilitating the involvement of relevant stakeholders when team members are not physically collocated—and might even be from external organizations with differing cultures from BOND—arose.

Typically, objective evidence employed in a CMMI appraisal to indicate that stakeholder involvement is being achieved are things such as meeting invitation lists. I have heard comments such as:

> As long as you have invited them, that is all you need to do.

However, showing that you invited someone to a meeting doesn't demonstrate whether that person was really *involved*. What do you do if you invite people, but they don't respond?

Because this is a common issue at BOND, we have made it a specific training topic within the workshop by presenting scenarios and asking the group to share options to handling each. Example scenarios that have been discussed include:

> What do you do when the person responsible for the initial project plan is in another organization and you can't control that person?

People at BOND have become successful with this type of challenge through proactive efforts. In workshops, we have heard stories of team members who have started a draft project plan for an external team member and then emailed it to them. They followed up with a phone call discussing the value of developing such a plan. Such proactive techniques have proven effective in helping projects that are trying to use an Agile approach, but might have team members who are not yet up to speed.

5.22 Sharing Across the Organization

Agile techniques focus on the project. CMMI is concerned about projects, but also about the organization. When we focus on projects, personnel can become isolated, missing valuable experiences on other projects. Sharing experiences and lessons across projects is one benefit of interactive workshops. Workshops encourage participants to share techniques they have discovered addressing common project challenges. The CMMI raises our awareness of the need to share best practices across the organization. This is the intent of GP 3.2, which states:

> *Collect work products, measures, measurement results, and improvement information…to support the future use and improvement of the organization's processes and process assets.*

While training workshops are one mechanism to share experiences, it is also desirable to share products as "best examples," such as a plan or design document.

The Exceptions to the "Don't Add Anything to the Process"

There are exceptions to the "don't add anything to the process unless the workers see the value" rule. When we ask people to do things and they don't see the value, sometimes it might be because the value is there, but isn't immediately recognizable to them. This might be caused by people not fully understanding their job responsibilities. Often, this occurs with respect to tasks that help the organization.

At BOND, we explained in the training that there will be things you have to do for a bigger reason. Some argued we had to do it because of the CMMI, but the things that felt like they were for the CMMI were usually for the long-term benefit of the organization.[18]

When an individual leaves a company, that person takes with him or her learned personal skills. Many of the practices we are putting in place when using the CMMI, while they support individual growth, extend beyond the individual supporting the overall organization.

Some have argued the CMMI is primarily about helping the organization, rather than the individual.

MYTH   The CMMI places greater focus on the organization than on its people.

---

18. If it was only for the CMMI and we couldn't find the rationale that by doing a practice it would help the organization, then our rule was we wouldn't do it. We previously saw an example of this in the section titled "Don't Force the Team to Perform Unnatural Acts" with respect to SP 1.2 of the Project Planning Process Area.

The CMMI does not say one should focus more on GP 3.2 (Collect improvement information … to support the future use and improvement of the organization's processes and process assets), than on GP 2.5 (Train the people … as needed).

This myth results from perceptions based on how organizations have chosen to implement the model, rather than what the model actually contains.[19]

Exception 1 Example: Feedback to the Organizational Level

Placing project developed assets in an organizational repository to share with other projects is an example where personnel might feel the effort is intrusive and is not helping them get their job done. In these cases, it is important to communicate to workers the full scope of their responsibilities, which should include this feedback to the organization. At BOND when we defined roles and responsibilities we included responsibilities related to the organization. When personnel are reviewed and given a performance appraisal, all responsibilities associated with their job should be considered so they understand the full scope and expectations of their job.

Exception 2 Example: Do You Understand the Full Scope of Your Task?

Do your workers know the expectations of your organization with respect to completing a task? Do they know what *done* means? If you are a programmer, is it just getting the code written and tested? Does *done* include reviews and documentation? Does *done* include ensuring all dependent parties have been notified and appropriately involved?

Sometimes people view involving others as an obstacle to getting their job done.[20] When an organization knows it has weaknesses in areas of task responsibilities, it is often a good indication that adding some "beef" to the process definitions and supporting training materials related to task completion criteria is a good idea.

---

19. People issues and the CMMI are covered in greater detail later in the DART case study in Chapter 8.

20. Later in the GEAR case study, addressing such organizational weaknesses through compliance checks will be discussed further.

5.23 A Measurement and Analysis Process That Fits an Agile Organization

SP 1.1 of the Measurement and Analysis Process Area states:

> Establish … measurement objectives that are derived from … needs and objectives.

I told a Senior Manager at BOND that I have starting point process templates, but you have to go to the next step to achieve your objectives. Part of that next step was having the working groups extract the real processes that worked in the company. In some cases, those working groups required us to engage senior managers. An example was Measurement and Analysis (MA).

I had developed a simple "Agile" Measurement and Analysis Process template that could help an organization just starting its CMMI effort. To use it, we needed to make some key management related decisions. I told them that before we decide what to measure, we needed to discuss the objectives of the measurement program. The first question I asked was:

> What is the objective of your measurement program?

After some discussion, the leaders agreed that the main objective of the measurement program should be to help the project leaders be successful in managing their projects. The first statement we placed in the Measurement and Analysis Process was the agreed-to measurement objectives:

> Provide accurate information to aide the project engineer's decision-making process in effectively executing the project management plan.

It was also agreed that this was a starting point objective for the measurement program and we would revisit it regularly. Later this objective was expanded as we began to institutionalize the Senior Management reviews to include the statement:

> Provide objective oversight/insight for senior project management.[21]

We next discussed the measures to support these objectives. We brought in a number of experienced project leads to participate in this discussion, asking

---

21. The CMMI doesn't tell you what your measurement objectives need to be. You are supposed to decide, and it is fine to evolve your objectives as your organization grows. The CMMI doesn't say you need a "boatload" of metrics.

them to talk about what information was necessary to support them in carrying out their responsibilities. Based on this brainstorming, a set of six core metrics were established that initially included Requirements, Size, Cost, Schedule, Staffing, and Project Resources.

Size Measures in an Agile Organization

There was considerable discussion around the size measure and it was eventually decided to remove this measure for the initial release of the process.[22] This was because while this measure could have benefit, it wasn't currently viewed as useful given the way BOND was operating. Size was not used in estimating work or progress in the company, and project leaders were unsure of its value. Therefore, we agreed not to require it.

In the initial MA process, we added a "must do" activity to document within the plan how the measures were collected, frequency of collection, and how they were distributed to the stakeholders who needed them. The company decided not to dictate this level of process definition, but leave it up to each project leader to decide and report this in his or her project plan. There was a template developed for project planning that provided a section for measures that became a "reminder" to each project leader to answer these questions when he or she planned the project.

By comparison, if you recall, at LACM it was decided to specify at the "must do" level what the measures were, and the data collection, frequency of reporting, and who received them. The advantage at LACM was that all projects handled measures the same way.

As the measurement program at BOND evolved—to keep things simple— the measures were collected directly in the Senior Management briefs. We then added to the training that these reports were not just for Senior Management and therefore they needed to be developed periodically even if a Senior Management brief for some reason was cancelled. This was because these measures needed to be used by the project leaders to help them make more effective *decisions.* In other words, the same measurement data reported to Senior Management was used by project personnel to manage the project.[23]

---

22. Size was originally included in the core metrics because some of those in the brainstorming thought it would be a good metric even though the organization was not currently using it.

23. There were also lower-level measures (e.g., team task list data) that rolled up in support of the measures in the senior management briefs.

What Form Must a Measurement Repository Take?

At BOND, the measurement repository became the collection of Management briefs across the projects. During the formal appraisal there was an issue raised about the adequacy of this measurement repository because it was distributed and wasn't actually a "database." One of the interviewed project personnel responded to this issue by stating in his words:

It works better for us this way because we carry the measures forward.

This response I believe hit right at the main issue on how measures were actually used in the organization to meet the stated objectives.

His point was they were using the measures to make *decisions* every day that tied back to the objectives as stated in the process. This included *decisions* that could affect the immediate performance of the project, and *decisions* to improve the processes currently in use on the project, as well as to help Senior Management with bigger company-wide *decisions*.

This practical and effective approach can be contrasted to the Measurement Repository described in the LACM case study in Chapter 3 where the data collected was disconnected from the real work and therefore not used to help in making real *decisions* in the organization.

Nothing in the CMMI says your measurement data can't be distributed, nor does it say what format it needs to take. This is a *decision* each organization needs to make given its business situation. You can pick the standard measures you want all projects to report and you can dictate how they are collected and stored on all projects, or leave some of these *decisions* up to the project.

In many Agile organizations, I find these decisions are often left up to the project teams, but as organizations grow, there is benefit in specifying more common measures and approaches across the projects as LACM did. This also helps management see consistent data at Senior Management reviews. As BOND matured, the Senior Managers realized this and increased standardization of measures across projects.

Agile approaches help us gain more accurate *project-specific measures* because they involve the team that understands how real projects work. Experience has shown this can be of great benefit in validating higher-level schedule and progress assessments. Agile techniques also help in getting the needed commitment from those who must execute the plan. Measures that flow up from an Agile team tend to be more accurate because they take into consideration more project-specific information including the capabilities of the people currently assigned to the project. These Agile techniques can help a CMMI effort. For example, refer to the Project Planning Process Area, SP 3.3, which states:

> *Obtain commitment from relevant stakeholders....*

Agile approaches help to gain commitment of those who must perform, and help us measure real work on projects more accurately. However, they don't tend to provide much help when it comes to stepping back to ensure we have the right measures across the organization and ensuring those measures are aligned with measurement objectives derived from the organization's business needs.

These are the strengths the CMMI Measurement and Analysis Process Area can bring to help an Agile organization. The primary strength of Agile techniques is at the project level. The CMMI ensures we are thinking about the needs of the organization as well.

It is worth pointing out that you can evolve your measurement program as BOND did. You can start with just a few focused measurement objectives and a few key measures, and expand or modify them later as your business needs evolve and change.

5.24 Training All Project Personnel in the Organization

When I say that the CMMI cares about the "what" and not the "how," this is not intended to imply you don't need effective "how-to" guidance. It means that the CMMI is not dictating to organizations the *decisions* those organizations need to make related to the "how-to" practices. If the "how-to" processes that work best in your organization are Agile, they will work for the CMMI.

At BOND we recognized we needed "how-to" processes. We instituted a next level of training at the technical leader level that discussed in greater detail the Engineering Processes and the best "how-to" practices that were being employed in the organization. Most of this information had been captured in engineering guidelines process assets. While they were the best practices currently encouraged in the organization, projects were always encouraged to consider new best practices and share their experiences with the organization.

In our engineering workshops, management practices were also stressed and how these practices, including measurements, *flowed down* to the engineering level. This helped to ensure measurements that were used at the lower level, and flowed back up to the Senior Management briefs, were aligned with real work tasks.

The engineering workshops were run in an interactive style similar to the process development working groups and the project management leadership workshops. These engineering workshops served to train project members and provide a level of *validation* in the real processes used in the organization. Feedback was captured from the workshops and used in future process updates.

Other forms of training employed at BOND included less formal brown-bag lunch training sessions. Focused sustainment training sessions were used to bring attention to areas where quality audits were indicating weakness trends. On-the-job mentoring was continually encouraged and employed.

In discussing the technical lead role with a number of technical leaders in the organization, it became evident that this role was understood as a helper to the project leader, but also as a mentor to developers. Technical leaders were grown in the organization from the developer ranks. Project leaders were grown from the technical leader ranks. Mentoring was everyone's responsibility and expected at all levels of the organization.

The CMMI Organizational Training (OT) Process Area and the Generic Practice 2.5 helped us institutionalize training at BOND by continually *reminding* us of the importance of training for all project personnel. Agile techniques alone would not have been sufficient to motivate the training program we put in place to ensure we could continue to provide personnel with the right skills to support the successful culture at BOND.

5.25 Technical Solution in an Agile Organization

At BOND, the technical solution working group decided they needed two distinct processes referred to as the Design Process and the Implementation Process. Along with the Design process, a design document template was developed with the "minimum must do's." This was a similar approach to what we did in the Project Planning Process Area where the Project Management Plan template contained the "minimum must do's."

An example of a "must do" section in the design document template was "Design Alternatives and Rationale for Decisions."

Like most Agile organizations, good technical discussions were taking place at white board sessions, but too often the *rationale behind decisions* was being lost. Under the Technical Solution (TS) Process Area, SP 1.1 states:

> *Develop alternative solutions and selection criteria.*

A question arises here:

> *Did the TS Working group at BOND require this section in the design template just to satisfy this specific practice of the CMMI?*

Hopefully, the answer is now evident to you that the CMMI was used to help us ask a question with respect to what the organization felt was important, and the conclusion was unanimous by the working group team that we should capture our design decisions.

I have never run into an organization that didn't agree this was important, but most often until organizations put this level of template and documented process requirements in place, the personal discipline isn't there across the organization to make this happen consistently.

I usually find examples where individuals are doing it already, but that is because of their *personal process discipline* they brought to the job. As a result, across the organization, consistency in this regard rarely exists prior to a serious CMMI process improvement effort. It is through aids such as design templates that *CMMI helps Agile* organizations sustain their valued practices through the stressful times.

5.26 Product and Process Quality Assurance

The purpose of Quality Assurance is frequently misunderstood. Because "quality" is the responsibility of engineering, some believe additional practices addressing quality are not required. Others believe that the "quality check" is where they are assured the product meets the requirements before it goes out the door. Both these views miss the real purpose of the PPQA process area in the CMMI model, which is to provide *objective insight*.

Organizations have multiple options in *how to* implement an effective PPQA organization. BOND implemented one of the most unique and effective approaches I have seen by continually rotating some of the best people in the organization through the PPQA group.[24]

5.27 Mitigating the Risk of Your CMMI Appraisal in an Agile Organization

In this section, I provide three practical techniques used at BOND to mitigate the risk associated with the CMMI appraisal.

> **TECHNIQUE**
>
> Select a CMMI lead appraiser who has knowledge or openness to learn about Agile approaches.

One of the best mitigations is to have a lead appraiser who is already Agile knowledgeable or at least demonstrates an openness to Agile approaches with a willingness to learn.

> **TECHNIQUE**
>
> Frequent phone calls to lead appraiser.

The next step is to brief the lead appraiser on your culture and your brand of agility, including sharing terminology and discussing early potential controversial practices your organization follows. We did this at BOND through regular phone calls with the lead appraiser conducted during the six months prior to the first appraisal.

> **TECHNIQUE**
>
> Consider an incremental appraisal approach using the continuous representation of the model.

There are a number of advantages to using an incremental approach and the Continuous Representation of the model. We conducted a formal SCAMPI[25]

---

24. Advantages and disadvantages of this approach are discussed in Chapter 7 where we look in greater detail at PPQA.

25. SCAMPI stands for Standard CMMI Appraisal Method for Process Improvement.

with eight Process Areas in 2005. We also conducted a formal SCAMPI with the full eighteen Process Areas in 2007. By doing the early appraisal in 2005, we significantly reduced risk for the second appraisal. This provided risk abatement because we used many of the same team members during the second appraisal. They knew each other and had previously been trained by the lead appraiser.

5.28 Lost Momentum Risk After Reaching Your CMMI Goal

It is not uncommon for organizations to lose process improvement momentum after achieving a major milestone such as achieving a formal CMMI level 3 rating. What we have learned might help you reduce this risk in your organization.

> **LESSON 6**
>
> Communicate to the decision makers that you must improve, not just maintain a CMMI level.

Experience has shown you can't just maintain a CMMI level without expending effort. If you really want to maintain a level of process maturity, you must continuously expend effort to improve. This is because project conditions and people keep changing. This means you need to keep training new people just to hold your level. As you train new people and as new projects end, maintenance of processes implies responding to the new issues that arise. If no one is listening and responding, you are falling behind. To maintain requires effort.

> **LESSON 7**
>
> CMMI level 3 is the point where you face your greatest potential opportunity for improvement. It isn't a good place to stay.

Level 3 is actually a point where you have some consistency, but are not necessarily performing at the efficiency level you desire. Levels 4 and 5 bring practices where you can initiate improvement optimizations based on objective data. Communicate this important lesson to those who can make a difference in the process improvement decisions in your organiza-tion.[26]

The following true story should be motivation to pay some attention to this risk.

5.29 Party Time! We're Level 3! The Meeting a Year Later with Ethan

I happened to be at the BOND facility to attend a meeting with another client a year after the organization had achieved its formal CMMI level 3 rating. When I stopped by to talk to Ethan (one of the co-founders of BOND), I learned that this organization—which had been growing at a 30 percent per year rate reaching over 150 people at the time of the 2007 appraisal—was now down to 90 people just one year later. When I asked Ethan about it, he replied:

I don't think they understand what they bought. They got us completely turned around heading in the other direction.

I had a discussion earlier with a leader of the corporation that acquired BOND and I was trying to explain how the CMMI could help an organiza-tion achieve its goals. He replied:

Sounds like the CMMI can help us. Our goal is to reduce overhead.

I told Ethan whenever I hear this I never have a good answer. Ethan replied:

This view comes from people who have never had an opportunity or been trained to build an organization with a future—one that will grow and have greater value tomorrow than today. The problem in these large organi-zations is that they put people in senior positions who all their life have been given budgets and they think the goal is just to get to the end when the bud-get runs out—they think the end is when the budget is zero and there is nothing more. They think that is the goal. The problem is, when you think this way you get exactly what you are focusing on. You are driving toward a goal where at the end there is nothing. And that is where we are headed here. They just don't understand what it takes to grow a business. They don't understand the real goal.

---

26. For more information on the value of level 4 and 5 practices, refer back to Chapter 3, and ahead to Chapters 9 and 10.

Multiple factors contributed to the decline at BOND. Prior to the acquisition, it was rare for people to leave the company because most employees felt that Ethan and his partner cared about the people in the organization.

When an organization stops investing in its people, it is not uncommon for attrition to rise. It is not just an organization's documented process descriptions that support the maintenance of a CMMI process maturity level. It also requires adequately trained people to execute those processes. When your trained people start leaving, you are losing the critical assets needed to maintain your CMMI maturity.

> **INSIGHT**   You have to look beyond short-term goals if you want your organization to have a future.

When I think about what is happening at BOND now, I am reminded of what is happening at LACM where the VP is continually driving improvements from the business need side, and grassroots efforts are driving improvements from the project side. This type of activity, which might be viewed by some as a "nice-to-have," is actually the best path to survival.

5.30 Summary

In this chapter and the previous chapter, I presented the case for doing everything possible not to add new process activities. Our focus has been on extracting the real *as-is* process that works in your organization. Often I have found even in organizations that are operating chaotically there are "best practices" being applied somewhere in the organization. These can be used as an effective model to share across a wider group of projects in the organization. A proven best way to improve your organization is to start with what works in your organization and build on it.

The BOND case was based on an organization that understands Agile methods and has a sound implementation. Many organizations that call themselves "Agile" don't fit this model. In the next two case studies, we look at organizations that refer to themselves as Agile, and use the term to try to explain some of their behaviors, but are missing key "Agile" fundamentals. Through these case studies, we will explore techniques to identify misapplications of agility, and what to do if you recognize similar patterns in your organization.

5.31 Summary: How CMMI Helps Agile

The following table provides a summary of how CMMI areas discussed in this chapter help Agile.

Table 5-9 *How CMMI Helps Agile*

CMMI Area and Associated Agile-Supporting Artifacts	How They Help Agile
Project Planning PA, Agile Integrated Project Management Plan (PMP) Template	Helps capture planning decisions, including rationale that can facilitate project integration for new and future employees.
Project Monitor and Control PA, Agile Action Item Guidelines, Agile Schedule Guidelines, Documentation of Team Meetings	Helps capture and track to closure actions items that can fall through the cracks, especially as organizations grow and project pressures increase. Helps to develop maintainable schedules. Helps to train new people.
Risk Management PA, Documentation of Real Expected Practice (Doorway Risk Management)	Helps people understand the real process expected and used in the organization.
GP 2.3, Provide Resources, GP 2.4, Assign Responsibilities Defined Roles and Responsibilities	Increases understanding of real work and expectations in the organization and supports fulfillment of the same.
GP 2.7, Involve Stakeholders Agile Stakeholder Involvement Training Agile Stakeholder Matrix	Helps the team learn techniques to involve remote teammates. Provides a reminder aid to involve the right people at the right time.
GP 3.2 Collect Improvement Information, Best Case Examples	Helps Agile organizations share what works on projects with others in the organization.

Continues

Table 5-9 *How CMMI Helps Agile (Continued)*

CMMI Area and Associated Agile-Supporting Artifacts	How They Help Agile
Process and Product Quality Assurance, Agile PPQA Mentor/Helper Approach	Helps us provide an environment where we know we can trust our people, and leverage collaboration culture by providing "objective insight" into where people need help.
Measurement and Analysis PA, Agile Measurement Repository	Helps "carry the measures forward" using measures every day to make better decisions.
GP 2.10 Review Status with Higher-Level Management, Agile Senior Management Brief Guidelines	Helps ensure individual Agile projects are provided with the support needed considering the overall welfare of the company by giving Senior Management the most accurate picture of project status.
Organizational Training PA	Reminds us of need to train all people.
Technical Solution PA	Reminds us of the need to capture our designs, and alternatives considered.

PART IV

CMMI Helping Address Agile Misapplications

Not all those organizations who call themselves "Agile" implement Agile approaches appropriately. In Chapters 6 and 7, we examine two organizations that run into trouble by misapplying Agile approaches. We learn through these stories about common areas where Agile practices are susceptible to breakdown.

These case studies demonstrate how the CMMI can help organizations that are running into difficulties by providing reminders of practices that are key to success, but often get lost when organizations are growing rapidly and projects are struggling under schedule and technical pressures.

In Chapter 8, we take a closer look at the challenges faced on the people side when moving toward increased agility.

The stories in this part of the book should be of particular interest to Agile experts who want to learn more about where Agile approaches often start to break down due to common real-world constraints especially in high-tech industries. They also provide good examples of where the CMMI can help Agile organizations with challenges commonly faced due to rapid growth.

Chapter 6

Common Misunderstandings of Defined Processes and Agility

Scenario: *Your successful small organization is growing as the result of the heroic efforts of your people. You would like to initiate a process improvement effort to help your organization attain a more sustainable workload. Unfortunately, Senior Management doesn't see the need. They only see the result, not the toll each heroic project is taking on the overall organization. You know you can't continue this way and survive. You also fear the potential effect change might have on current projects. What should you do? What options do you have?*

Sometimes we can learn the most by taking a close look at our greatest weaknesses. In this chapter, you will learn about NANO, a successful growing organization with satisfied customers. From the outside, things look good inside NANO, but internally the organization has recognized that the way it operates today is not sustainable in the future.

To address its known weaknesses NANO has started a CMMI initiative, but as we look deeper into this organization, we learn how key process misunderstandings have hindered improvement efforts. NANO is a good example of an organization where the CMMI could help maintain its agility and sustain increased growth, but due to key mistakes NANO has made in implementing its processes, it is currently failing to reap the potential benefits of its CMMI initiative.

Still, all is not bad at NANO. In this organization, we also learn about some nontraditional techniques that can achieve the intent of key CMMI practices while helping organizations with critical business challenges.

6.1 What You Will Learn in This Chapter

- Characteristics of CMMI level 3 processes key to long-term organizational success, often missed by " Agile-like"[1] organizations
- Techniques to evolve deficient legacy processes toward CMMI level 3 compliance
- A common myth held in many "Agile-like" organizations with respect to training
- How to support an Agile culture by using measures less formally for better decisions
- An Agile perspective on measurement
- Techniques to effectively manage risk during a process improvement effort
- Techniques supported by CMMI practices to help move a traditional hierarchical command and control organization toward increased distribution of authority and responsibility
- An alternate approach to capture roles and responsibilities supporting effective use of people
- An alternate and efficient approach to tailoring that is CMMI compliant
- An example of planning with uncertainty that is consistent with both Agile and CMMI

This chapter provides a case study of a successful "Agile-like" organization in trouble. The organization lost its true agility because of business growth, internal organizational political pressures, and process misunderstandings, and then turned to the CMMI for help.

---

1. Reminder: When I use the phrase "Agile-like" or "wannabe Agile," I mean organizations that are trying to use an Agile approach, but are missing key ingredients of true agility.

Section I
Process Misunderstandings

6.2 NANO Case Study Background and Problem Faced

NANO is an organization that began with about 25 people in 2004 and had grown to over 80 people by the end of 2007. Continued rapid growth was projected. They had been very successful, which was part of why they were growing rapidly. Their customer, the U.S. Department of Defense, liked their product and kept coming back with more work—but NANO had a problem.

NANO is part of a much larger organization. A competing group with a CMMI level 5 claimed this work fell within their defined charter. As this other group positioned itself to take business away from NANO, politics and in-fighting became an issue.

On the surface, it appears NANO's future is doomed except for one thing. Whenever the customer sent work to the CMMI level 5 group, they took three times as long to get the work done and cost twice as much as NANO.

In 2008, I conducted a gap analysis against the CMMI model for NANO. While they were very good at what they did, in 2007 they had no written processes. NANO was an "Agile-like" organization that existed in the middle of a non-Agile world and was fighting for its survival. A CMMI level 3 would go a long way to secure its future by substantiating the argument that they possessed the credentials necessary to be successful as they grew. They contracted my services originally in 2007 to help them initiate a CMMI process improvement effort.

6.3 How NANO Achieved Success and Then Got in Trouble

When I conducted the gap analysis at NANO, one of the first persons I interviewed was the Director of the organization. I asked him what he really wanted to come out of this effort. He replied:

> *I know the way we are currently operating is not sustainable with our planned growth. We need to do some things differently.*

That was good to hear. The Director was telling me he wasn't doing this only to say he was CMMI level 3, although he did know that was important for his future. I had heard before interviewing him that the Director at NANO was a control-oriented leader many people refused to work with. I found him to be different from expected. He clearly understood his customers' needs having spent much of his career as one of them, and I quickly began to understand why this organization had been as successful as it was and the issues it faced.

The Director was in the middle of every decision—and I mean every one of them. He had the big picture. He did the risk assessments and made the risk mitigation decisions. Any question about work scope went through him. He sat on the configuration control board. He even approved bug fixes in the software!

When there were only 25 people in the organization this worked fairly well. Now the organization had over 80 employees with almost 50 of them doing software. While they were still successful, it was now clear to me why the Director knew that the way they were operating was not sustainable.

While doing my gap analysis I heard from some that the organization was understaffed. I found some people were very busy—mostly those directly reporting to the Director. However, others often found themselves with nothing to do while they waited for someone else to make a decision. I also heard when interviewing one of the people who reported directly to the Director:

> *I wish just once I could come to work and not have my priorities change between 9 AM and 11 AM.*

6.4 The Positive Side of NANO's Agility

The picture was becoming clear. The Director was extremely sensitive and responsive to his customers' needs and requests and was keeping his immediate staff focused on the top-priority issues of the day (or hour) to keep customers happy.

6.5 Where NANO's Agile Approach Broke Down

This model had worked well when the organization was small. Now—at least partly due to the growth in their organization—they were experiencing a number of negative side effects. From the gap analysis, I learned how communication occurred at NANO. They had a strong customer-focused top-level requirements process. When a new project kicked off, they held meetings with the customer and agreed on requirements, which were flowed down to the engineering group. Any changes to those requirements had to be approved by the Director.

To support rapid customer response, requirements change approvals often occurred verbally with the Director communicating those changes directly to his immediate staff. They in turn communicated the approvals down the chain within the organization. When the organization was small this direct *human-to-human* communication mechanism worked well, but as the organization grew and changes to requirements began to occur more frequently, miscommunication became more prevalent. From the gap analysis interviews, I began to understand what was happening. I heard comments such as:

> *Because there is a lot of informal communication we often talk past each other,*

and

> *Often the requirements changes become what we think we heard and sometimes it turns out what we think we heard was wrong.*

6.6 Complicating Factors at NANO

My immediate thought was that the organization needed a more clearly defined requirements change and approval process. Not all of those I interviewed expressed agreement. Some, in fact, defended the way the organization operated and told me that a major reason this organization was still successful and growing was due to the rapid response they demonstrated with respect to customer changes. They also felt that if that process began to bog down with more time-consuming bureaucratic approvals, the future of their organization would be placed at risk by the cut-throat politics within the larger organization.

6.7 Preparing for the Gap Analysis at NANO

I had spoken with NANO about getting a CMMI effort going over a year before they finally called me to actually conduct the gap analysis early in

2008. I explained to them early in 2007 the fundamentals of what CMMI level 3 meant and the importance of documenting their processes.

One of the first tasks I recommended was to capture the organization's current "as-is" process before attempting to make any changes. I like to be able to guide the "as-is" process capture effort so I can remind those writing the "as-is" processes what they should be thinking about and including in the process descriptions. In the case of NANO, the Director had directed each group within his organization to document their own processes. He felt each group that reported to him needed to be responsible for its own processes.

6.8 Gap Analysis Findings at NANO

Early in 2008 when I was called in to conduct the gap analysis, I found that the processes they had written the previous year were deficient with respect to key CMMI level 3 process characteristics. The best way to explain this deficiency is to start with a discussion of the CMMI Generic Practices. Generic Practices in the CMMI often don't get the attention they deserve, and are commonly misunderstood. Let us start this discussion with a commonly held myth.

A Commonly Held Myth about the CMMI Generic Practices

> **MYTH**   The Generic Practices in the CMMI are not Specific, which means there is nothing Specific we need to do to achieve them.

This philosophy was reflected in how NANO had written their processes, and how those processes had been executed. As the organization grew, those same processes began to break down.

6.9 Example of a Generic Practice

As an example, Generic Practice 2.7 states:

Identify and involve relevant stakeholders of the [fill in relevant process area] process as planned.

The term "relevant stakeholder" when used in the CMMI means:

A stakeholder that is identified for involvement in specified activities and is included in a plan.

Now, let us look closer at the effect on the organization of the way NANO viewed this generic practice, along with a key characteristic of many specific practices.

6.10 How Some View Process in Agile Organizations

During the gap analysis at NANO it became clear that many people in the organization were good at what they did, and knew who they needed to interact with to successfully carry out their jobs. However, when I reviewed their written processes I found them lacking in key essentials found using Generic Practices, such as the identification of *relevant stakeholders to involve*. I also found them lacking in *criteria* for consideration when *decisions* needed to be made. Refer to Table 6-1.

Table 6-1 *CMMI Level 3 Essentials Missed in "Agile-like" Organizations*

Involving relevant stakeholders
Use of criteria to aid decisions

The recommendation to include *criteria* within process descriptions can be found in many of the Specific Practices throughout the CMMI model. Examples include:

Technical Solution, Specific Practice 1.1 Develop Alternative Solutions and Selection Criteria

Decision Analysis and Resolution, Specific Practice 1.2 Establish Evaluation Criteria

Verification, Specific Practice 1.3 Establish Verification Procedures and Criteria.

Although many people understood the daily issues they faced, who they needed to involve, and what criteria to use when making key decisions, they had written their processes as if *no one else* ever needed to be *involved* and *no decisions* ever needed to be made once the process was under way.

They had in effect written their processes only for the case when everything went according to the original plan, nothing ever went wrong, and all *decisions* that needed to be made had been made before the process was initiated.

As I dug deeper, I began to understand why they had written their processes this way. I discovered that some mistakenly believed that process was relevant only to well-defined tasks that never went off track. As a result, they had written processes that read like "cookie-cutter" steps. Next, we examine the consequences of writing processes this way on the organization.

6.11 An Example of Process Misunderstanding

I discovered from talking to key experienced people that many in the organization knew who the relevant stakeholders were, and when to involve them. However, let me give you a real example of what was happening in this organization due to its rapid growth.

One of the common project types in this organization was referred to as an "install." An install involved the installation of a pre-defined hardware capability at a specific site. There were different levels of installs possible, with varying hardware packages, and environmental site requirements.

While interviewing personnel responsible for conducting an install I heard about a problem that occurred. It seemed workers had arrived at a site on the day specified for the install to find that the required site preparations had not all occurred. In one case, a circuit breaker was required prior to the install. When that worker got to the site the work had not been performed.

It seems obvious that it would be normal procedure to contact the site before a visit to ensure the preparation work had been completed. An experienced installer said he always did this and that it was important to contact the site to ensure all the *preparation* work had been completed. However, when I reviewed the install process description it specified the steps to do the install once on site with no reference to contacting site personnel ahead of time to ensure the site was prepared for the installation.

As the organization grew so did the number of installs and they were now conducting more installs and using new personnel in carrying out the installs. Often the new personnel were brought in without all the necessary *training.* Because the documented process failed to mention calling the site ahead of time, the organization was experiencing more failures in a process that had previously been carried out with few reported problems.

6.12 Another Example of Process Misunderstanding

One of the more senior engineers I spoke with at NANO told me he believed in process, but felt much of the work he did wasn't relevant to a defined process. I asked him if he would explain what he meant. He said he often had to work out a design approach that was new. He said this was a very *creative and dynamic process.* Often the Director would call him up on short notice with a problem that needed a solution. After analyzing and developing a solution that might solve the problem, he would call the Director and they would brainstorm it over the phone. If the Director liked the idea, he might ask that the approach be documented in a white paper. The white paper would be emailed to others on the Director's staff so they could provide their comments. If they liked the idea the next step was to take it into a lab environment to prototype it for proof it would work before making any final *decisions* about using it. At the end he said that he thought what he had described should make it clear why he could not follow a process in doing such work.

What became clear to me while listening was his belief that any kind of activity that involved thinking, brainstorming, and learning was outside the bounds of process definition. He seemed to believe that until he could give someone exact "cookie cutter" steps to follow that required *no further decisions*, any associated work should not fall within the realm of a defined process.

At the conclusion of the interview, I told him that while he didn't think he followed a process, he actually did follow a very sound process. He had described it to me, including the stakeholders who get involved (reviewers) and the products produced (white paper).

I also shared with him that just because he didn't know where the effort would lead when he started was no reason to think he could not follow a documented process. By writing down exactly what he had shared with me, others could learn and follow the same process. I suggested that it would also be beneficial to examine all the roles of the people who were sent the white paper for review to ensure all key people who should review it ahead of time were being included.

> **LESSON 1**
>
> It is a misunderstanding to think "good CMMI-compliant" processes are only meant to help you when you know the answer ahead of time, and when things go according to a plan. When a process is written well using the CMMI as a guide, its greatest value is in helping to know what to do when things go wrong and uncertainty exists.

Why Processes Often Don't Get Used When They Are Needed Most

If processes aren't written to address the real issues—including the tough issues—they won't be used. Unfortunately, what I learned through the gap analysis at NANO was that when things happened in the organization that were different from the plan, they tossed away the process because the way the processes were written couldn't help when help was needed most. And needing help was a common everyday occurrence at NANO.

6.13 The Good and Not So Good Sides of Distributed Process Ownership

I was glad the Director was holding those who reported to him responsible for their own processes. However, there are good and not so good sides to distributed process ownership in an organization.

The good side is that we have a better chance of developing the right processes to help people do their job when those who must use processes own their processes. The not so good side is that not everyone knows how to write good processes.

> **MYTH** Processes are easy to write, and anyone who is responsible to do work can write a good process describing how he or she should do that work.

6.14 Priority Recommendations at NANO

I was now faced with the challenge of making a recommendation on how to best move this organization forward given the current situation. They had written some processes that were accurate as far as they went, but were incomplete. Another positive attribute of the current processes was that they did reflect to a point how the organization was currently running. To leverage the value of the existing work I recommended that we develop guidance and rules to improve the processes and raise them up to where they needed to be for a CMMI level 3 organization. Refer to Table 6-2 for techniques to evolve deficient legacy processes. These recommendations are discussed in the following paragraphs.

Table 6-2 *Techniques to Evolve Deficient Legacy Processes*

Use an incremental approach.
Start with OPD/OPF: Develop guidance and rules for developing, reviewing, and approving process assets.
Consider using the CMMI framework as a roadmap.
Address key weaknesses at the organizational level (e.g., stakeholder matrix).

6.15 Develop an OPF and OPD Process at NANO

I recommended starting the process improvement effort within the Organizational Process Focus (OPF) and Organizational Process Definition (OPD) process areas. At NANO, they had already moved forward with an effort to document their processes, but no organizational level of guidance had been provided to help them understand what should be included in those processes or how to organize them. Furthermore, there was no clear process on how process assets should be reviewed, approved, released, and updated within the organizational process asset library.[2] I assisted NANO in developing these processes by providing guidance similar to guidance I had given at BOND.

One of my first observations of NANO's processes was that they didn't have a common format. There was no cover page with approval information, and no revision information. My first step was to develop guidelines defining what their processes should look like, what "minimum content" should be in each, and how they should be structured.[3]

---

2. An example of an Organizational Process Asset Review and Approval Process is provided in the appendices.

3. Example guidelines for process assets and examples of an OPF and OPD process are provided in the appendices.

6.16 Using the CMMI Framework as a Process Roadmap at NANO

In developing this guidance, I was sensitive to the work they had already done and the existing political risks. I advised them not to update all their processes all at once. If existing process assets met the intent of certain CMMI practices, we would leave the asset in its legacy form and location and create additional documentation clearly identifying its purpose. I referred to this additional documentation as a process "roadmap" that could help new people understand the existing process assets at NANO.

CAUTION

Beware of efforts that could lead to just copying CMMI practices, rather than developing your own.

NANO decided to use the CMMI framework as the roadmap for their process assets. At first I resisted this approach for fear it could be perceived that we were just copying practices from the CMMI model. I didn't want people at NANO to get the wrong impression, thinking we were forcing everyone in the organization to learn the CMMI model. However, given where this organization was I eventually agreed because I felt the advantages of this approach outweighed the disadvantages.

The advantages of using the CMMI Process Areas and practices as a top-level structure were that it made it easier for us to track our progress in moving toward CMMI level 3. It would also be beneficial when explaining processes at NANO to a formal CMMI appraisal team.

I did, however, caution NANO personnel that by taking this approach we would need to teach the people in the organization that the CMMI was merely a framework to define and help manage the NANO processes. We were not using the CMMI practices as NANO's practices.

This distinction is important and fundamental to the CMMI model. That is, the CMMI is not a set of dictated practices. It is a model from which we reason about our processes. At NANO, we used the CMMI to *reason* about their processes, and to *help manage* and evolve the process assets.

An example of using the CMMI model as a roadmap to help organizations with existing legacy process assets is provided here.

6.17 Example of Using CMMI Framework as a Roadmap

Generic Practice 2.1 states:

> *Establish and maintain an organizational policy for planning and perform-ing the [fill in the relevant process area].*

At NANO while they didn't have specific policy statements written for each process, they did have a set of approved Enterprise Plans. Those plans pro-vided a well thought-out vision for the entire organization and included the organizational expectations of Senior Management with respect to process.

A policy from Senior Management doesn't need to bear the name "policy" to achieve the intent of a CMMI policy. In this case, it was contained in a document referred to as a plan. Nonetheless, it achieved the intent of CMMI GP 2.1. Therefore, within NANO's Process "Roadmap" framework we had a GP 2.1 entry where we placed a pointer to the appropriate section of the Enterprise Plan achieving the intent of the policy.

6.18 Addressing the Stakeholder Weakness at NANO

GP 2.7 (identifying and involving relevant stakeholders) had been com-pletely missed by NANO in developing most of their processes. Rather than require changes to every legacy process by forcing them to add a stakeholder section, I recommended we address this practice at the organizational level.

> **LESSON 2**
>
> While distributed process ownership aids buy-in, coordinating and training key practices at the organizational level can aid efficient and effective process deployment.

Specifically my recommendation was to develop at the organizational level a *stakeholder matrix* that identified relevant stakeholders needing to be involved in various activities across all of the process areas.

This approach provided a number of advantages. It didn't require us to update every single legacy process that had been previously developed. And since this area had already been identified as a weakness in the organization, I felt we needed to raise the visibility of its importance by managing it at the organizational level.

By identifying relevant stakeholders for activities that crossed all of the CMMI Process Areas through a single matrix, we were able to bring a needed focus to this area of weakness. We used the matrix to train people in the expectations with respect to relevant stakeholder involvement. An example of a relevant stakeholder matrix can be found in Chapter 5. A relevant stakeholder matrix could be invoked through a common organizational process that is used to remind project personnel to use the matrix in determining who to involve in various project activities.

Why Do I Need Training If I Hire Good People?

The purpose of the Organizational Training (OT) process area in the CMMI model is to:

> *Develop the skills and knowledge of people so they can perform their roles effectively and efficiently.*

In most of the Agile organizations I am asked to help—and this was true at NANO—there is usually very little formal training prior to a CMMI effort. At NANO, one of the senior leaders told me they were very careful about the people they brought into the organization and didn't hire people if they didn't already have the skills needed to do the job.

Often I find leaders in small growing Agile organizations believe if they are careful whom they hire, an internal training program is not necessary. This topic is discussed further in the following paragraphs.

6.19 Maintaining a Successful Agile Culture as You Grow Requires Training

What is missed with the "I hire people with the skills needed" approach is that people can't bring with them how things work inside your organization when you hire them from outside your organization. This includes how people are expected to carry out the processes they are responsible to follow, which includes who they need to involve and when they need to involve them. This type of training is *unique* to each organization.

> **MYTH**   If I make sure I hire people with the right skills, I don't need to provide additional training.

I have observed in the organizations I've gone to certain people who appear to be particularly effective at getting work done. This kind of information is a powerful side benefit of doing gap analysis interviews. Through the interviews, I capture in the words of the successful people key techniques related to how they do their job. I then share these techniques with others within the organization by translating them into documented job *scenarios* that can be employed as training aids. When I do this I am always careful to maintain the *terminology* people use inside the organization.

This is the kind of training that best benefits an organization, and is used by both new and experienced people. This kind of training can't possibly be brought to a job from the outside. I have found this type of training to be one of the most valuable techniques in maintaining a successful Agile organization's culture while the organization grows. We share through job scenarios how things are done, including those done informally such as the "doorway risk management" discussed in the BOND case study. Refer to Figure 6-1.

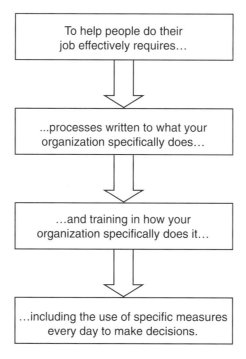

Figure 6-1 *Supporting an Agile Culture Through Informal Decision Training*

6.20 You Can't Just Use Another Organization's Processes and Get the Intended Value

When processes are developed as described in this book, the real intended value is achieved. However, the related consequences must be understood. While I was helping GEAR (discussed later in the book), the VP of Engineering said that he was also responsible for another group the parent company had acquired. He wanted them to use the processes we were developing for GEAR so they could get to CMMI level 3 as well. The other group produced a different product from GEAR and was located in a different part of the country.

The problem is effective processes have value because they reflect how work is actually done in a *specific* organization. What gives the *stakeholder matrix* value is that it provides specific guidance related to who needs to be involved and in what activities, such as who needs to review and approve a design document. This kind of information is *unique* to each organization. Refer to the example relevant stakeholder matrix provided in Chapter 5. The more specific you can make this matrix with respect to the roles and products in your organization, the more effective it becomes at clarifying process expectations for your people.

I have seen large organizations raise up the process documentation so it can be reused across different groups by eliminating a level of detail. This leads to processes looking more like policies. While they become more reusable across a wider range of groups in the organization, they also become less valuable. This is one of the reasons we often hear from workers in the trenches at large high-tech companies say their company processes are too high level to add value to the work they really do. This is why you can't just pick up another organization's processes and gain the intended value.

6.21 Another Example of Formalizing Informality

In the following paragraphs, another example of formalizing informality is provided.

Measurement Flow Down

In the BOND case study I provided an example of how an Agile organization can "formalize informality" through the "Doorway" Risk Management example. Another example of an "informal" process in Agile organizations is measurement flow down.

Not all measures have to be "formal" in the traditional sense of the word formal (e.g., written). Some of the most valuable measures leaders use every day in making *decisions* are employed "less formally." I have used the following scenarios to help Agile organizations "formalize" and train an Agile Measurement Program.

To demonstrate how measures are used less formally, consider the developer who brings a concern to his project leader regarding a teammate named Joe, who has missed a team meeting. The project leader makes a quick assessment and decides that no action is required. He knows Joe and he knows Joe is normally reliable. This is the first time he has heard of any potential problem and therefore decides no action is needed at this time. In a second scenario, another developer raises to the project lead a situation where Tom, another team member, has missed the last three team meetings. In this case, the project leader decides he needs to talk to Tom to find out what is happening.

After presenting the two scenarios, I then ask the class if they think the project leader used any measures in carrying out his job in either of the scenarios. Often the immediate reaction is that measures are not used here, but this turns out to be false.

An Agile Perspective on Measurement

Agile Perspective on Measurement: A measure is a *standard* used for *comparison* to *reduce uncertainty* when making a *decision*.[4]

In both cases, the project lead uses a standard, which is the expectation that people attend team meetings almost all the time, and sometimes things happen causing people to miss meetings (e.g., sick, doctor appointment...). When someone misses three meetings in a row, this is a signal that action should be taken. This situation is outside the expected standard. The point of this discussion in training is to communicate the fact that we use measures constantly in our job and that both formal and less formal measures have value. Such scenarios also help people understand the culture that exists within an organization and the expectations in doing a job in that organization whether it is traditional or *Agile*.

---

4. Definition based on *American College Dictionary*.

Why Should We Care about Formalizing Informality?

One might question the value of training the use of *informal (or less formal) measures* such as the scenario just described. If these measures are intended to remain informal, why should we care to discuss them and bring them to our attention in training?

The reason we should care is because even though they are *informal* they are affecting our real *decisions,* and therefore affecting our business. Think about the number of informal decisions made every day in your business. This means at times there is value in stepping back to consider how the informal measures we use affect our *decisions.*

This could be viewed as a periodic alignment of the *criteria* used to make decisions. After discussing the results with others in your organization, you might decide to *document* and train certain *less formal criteria* used to guide decisions. This is one more example of *formalizing informality* in an Agile organization. It is also an example of why your training needs to be specific to your organization and culture.

Measurement Flow Down Too Often Missed in Large Organizations

Process flow down common in Agile organizations that employ small teams often is missing in many large organizations—especially when the processes are maintained at a high abstract level. Small team leaders in large organizations are too often unaware of how the company processes relate to what they do. In small Agile organizations, everyone is aware of the Agile processes and shares them openly.

Too often in the larger organizations, the only agility is "stealth" agility. Too often inside large companies the company processes are abstract and disconnected from what people really do. This is why I have claimed that many small Agile organizations are actually achieving the intent of the CMMI more effectively than many large organizations. This is another example that demonstrates how *Agile can help the CMMI.*

6.22 Addressing Risk in the Process Improvement Plan at NANO

At NANO, we had to address the issue related to the effective use of people. We also needed to be sensitive to the concern of the potential loss of their business to another group in the organization. The Director knew he needed to start making changes related to delegation, involving more of the organization in the *decision-making process*. He understood the ramifications to organizational productivity when people often found themselves *waiting* on others to make a decision. He knew he was at least partially responsible for this situation. But he wasn't prepared to tackle what he viewed as *unacceptable risk* to ongoing projects.

This is an area where too often process improvement efforts fall short of leveraging some of the best opportunities for real value within an organization. NANO did exhibit a number of "Agile" characteristics that had helped them achieve their success. At this point, they were continuing to survive because of those reasons. However, they were beginning to fail more frequently due to weaknesses in the scalability of those processes. The Director knew it. And he knew those failures would continue to increase if action wasn't initiated quickly.

If NANO tried to make too many changes too fast, it was certain to set their performance back while people adjusted to the new expectations. This, in turn, would increase the risk of losing their business due to the cut-throat internal politics.

On the other hand, the Director also knew that if he didn't start making changes now, his project troubles were certain to grow. Eventually he would lose his business to dissatisfied customers. We had to put a plan in place that could move the organization forward, managing both of these risks.

Too often, I see process improvement initiatives too far removed from this level of thinking and collaboration on real project issues. If you are not *thinking through* the plan at this level including potential consequences, you are not managing.

When the real risks to projects are not adequately considered, project managers steer clear—and rightly so—of ongoing process improvement initiatives, rather than gravitate toward them. As a result, real process improvement opportunities that could benefit projects and organizations too often get missed.

LESSON 3

When planning process improvement initiatives, think through the full set of issues including process deployment risks to on-going projects.

6.23 The NANO Process Improvement Plan

Recognizing the risks to the organization, I proposed an *incremental priority-based* process improvement plan. This plan included focused *scenario* training to support *risk mitigation.*

By rolling out improvements in an incremental fashion, we limited the risk associated with any single roll out. By supplementing the rollout with very specific scenario training, we *mitigated* the risk of *miscommunication* of expectations.

6.24 Priority-Based Incremental Deployment Supported by Scenario Training

The top priority improvements identified included the flow down of requirements and change management, along with the alignment of related engineering work. These improvements specifically addressed weaknesses identified in the gap analysis in the Requirement Management, Technical Solution, and Verification Process Areas. Along with these process changes, the first release of our organizational stakeholder matrix was scheduled. Because the strategy was incremental, we were "incrementally" addressing the stakeholder involvement weakness across the organization as well.

Role-based scenarios were developed and provided through *just-in-time* training. This helped us deploy a streamlined requirements change process supporting rapid response, and address the involvement of key stakeholders.

All affected parties were provided with the role-based scenario training to help them understand how their role was affected by the change prior to the incremental release and deployment of the new process.[5] Early releases of the stakeholder matrix focused on ensuring the right people up and down the chain were involved in reviewing and approving requirements changes before new work was initiated.

---

5. This is another example where GP 2.5 Train the People reminds us not to forget the importance of training when rolling out new processes in an organization—Agile or traditional. This is an example where CMMI helps Agile.

6.25 More on GP 2.7 and Clarifying Roles and Responsibilities at NANO

The intent of GP 2.7 is to establish and maintain the involvement of relevant stakeholders. The tendency in many organizations is to think first of customers and managers who must sign off on products and product changes as relevant stakeholders.

Each organization tends to have its own *unique* set of strengths and weaknesses with respect to GP 2.7. The weaknesses most often can best be observed in times of crisis.

At NANO, the senior staff immediately became engaged and involved in times of crisis. Those in the trenches were left in the dark, and often experienced lost productivity due to loss of needed guidance. This is where we could begin to provide value-added help to the organization, but change had to be carefully *thought through*.

The recommendations I had made because of the gap analysis were to review and document the roles and responsibilities in the organization.

Pause, Reflect, and Glance Forward

Can you observe the repeating pattern at NANO? Can you also see common conditions where we might be able to detect ahead of time when this repeating pattern is likely to occur?

Think about your own organization. Where are the repeating patterns that most frequently occur, and hinder your people from achieving their goals?

Later in the book when we explore more deeply the concept of repeating specific weaknesses, we also examine how the use of strategically selected "checkpoints" can help an organization keep its repeating weaknesses from coming back.

This could be a powerful vehicle aiding the Director in clarifying the decisions he expected those deeper in the organization to make without his immediate involvement. If done correctly, the result could substantially diminish the productivity drain that so often occurred when senior personnel were distracted and unable to provide the needed *day-to-day* guidance. The Director immediately agreed and called an off-site full-day meeting with his immediate staff and me to focus on roles and responsibilities.

6.26 The NANO Roles and Responsibilities Off-Site Meeting

I found the NANO roles and responsibilities off-site meeting to be extremely beneficial for multiple reasons. Toward the beginning of the meeting the Director displayed a slide containing a large circle with a number of smaller overlapping circles within it. He referred to the larger circle as his organization and the overlapping circles inside as the pieces of his organization many of the leaders in the room were responsible for. He made the comment that he did not plan to explicitly fill the "white space" within the larger circle—the area that was part of the big organization, but outside the responsibility of specific subgroups. Refer to Figure 6-2. He said:

> *Funding the last 10 percent of an organization is disproportionately high. Those things can be more effectively filled by direction, priority, and management.*

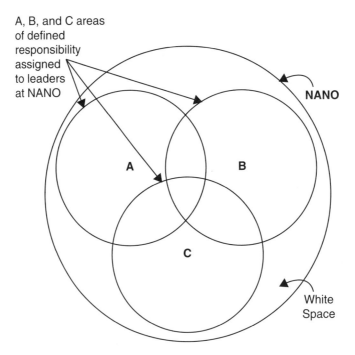

Figure 6-2 *"White Space" Tasks*

Nothing in the CMMI says you can't use "direction, priority, and management" to determine how certain responsibilities are assigned. Under Decision Analysis and Resolution (DAR) it does recommend that *criteria* be established (SP 1.2) to help with *decision making*. When I hear that certain decisions are being left up to "direction, priority, and management," I often recommend that a criterion be documented as DAR suggests to help guide these decisions in a consistent way that makes sense for that organization.

LESSON 4

If you are having difficulty with delegation in your organization, drive discussions of criteria for making and raising decisions. Then document and train the results.

6.27 "White Space" Tasks

I found this discussion very interesting because as we moved through the day discussing each person's roles and responsibilities, I noticed that no one was identifying him or herself as being responsible for processes and process management.

A few months earlier at the out-brief of the gap analysis the Director made it very clear to me that he viewed each of his leaders as responsible for his or her own processes—including documentation, management, and training. He also told me one of the hardest things he had to do was to get his people to write things down. I raised the issue:

Why are people not identifying process responsibilities?

One person responded:

That is in the white space.

But I retorted:

It's too big for white space. In the past when you have tried to do process as a white space task it didn't get done because it didn't get the priority.

I had identified these findings at the out-brief of the gap analysis. I had talked to this organization over a year earlier and they had tried to write their own processes. However, the processes were not CMMI level 3 "compliant," and many were never even completed. The increased recognition of process needs resulting from this off-site meeting led to an increased organizational focus on process that was clearly needed.

LESSON 5

Forcing a discussion of roles and responsibilities can be the catalyst for discussions related to when people feel they have responsibility and authority to make decisions and when they feel they need to raise the decision up. This can lead to capturing and documenting valuable criteria that might then be used to train others in the organization.

How the CMMI Can Help with Delegation and Effective Use of People

Many of the practices within the CMMI model relate to providing *criteria* to use and identifying who to involve (e.g., key *stakeholders)* in the decision-making process when you don't have all the answers. The CMMI does not tell you what the criteria need to be, or who needs to be involved. This is left up to each organization to determine based on its own business needs.

Some believe the CMMI is prescriptive.

MYTH   The CMMI is prescriptive; unless by prescriptive one means it prescribes each organization must think and decide for itself how decisions are made in that organization.

It also doesn't prescribe when an organization or a project needs to make certain decisions.

INSIGHT   To be Agile and not compromise the quality of products requires decisions based on sound criteria. The CMMI encourages the use of such criteria throughout the model. It doesn't specify what the criteria should be, but it does expect an organization to share its own criteria with its people, helping them make better decisions.

This approach to decision making is consistent with Agile approaches. Agile approaches do favor making decisions as late as possible when the information is most accurate. Nothing in the CMMI says that an organization cannot provide such guidance within its criteria. The *criteria* encouraged throughout the *CMMI can help an Agile* (or traditional) organization make more effective decisions (formal or informal).

Section II
CMMI Practice Alternatives

Refer to Table 6-3 for CMMI practice alternatives. These are discussed in the following paragraphs.

Table 6-3 *CMMI Practice Alternatives*

Consider starting with the talents of your people when refining roles and responsibilities.
Consider "pre-tailoring" for common project types.

6.28 An Alternative Approach to Defining Roles and Responsibilities

As I sat listening to the discussion at the NANO off-site, I realized they were using a different method than what I had observed in many organizations in defining their roles and responsibilities. Most organizations I have observed first identify general roles such as Project Manager, or Lead Systems Engineer, and then brainstorm a list of responsibilities they view as associated with each role without considering the strengths and weaknesses of the currently available personnel.

Rather than take this tact, the NANO Director asked all of his direct reports to provide the group a list of all their individual responsibilities as they each perceived them. Discussions resulted in some modifications of each person's list primarily with the Director reassigning certain responsibilities.

At one point, I raised an issue about the use of the term "Project Lead" that was being floated about by leaders of two different groups in the organization. I asked:

When you each say "Project Lead," do you both mean the same thing?

In unison, one replied "Yes!" and the other "No!" A discussion ensued leading to the recognition that the expectations of a "Project Lead" were different under the two managers. This led to one person stating:

We need to define Project Lead consistently across the organization.

The Director immediately responded:

No, we don't. What we need to do is change the word.

He then said:

I don't want you to change what your people do as "Project Leads," but we do need to use another word to describe it.

One can easily argue the advantages and disadvantages of arriving at roles and responsibilities in an organization using the method just described. I share this story first to point out that the CMMI model does not dictate what roles and responsibilities an organization defines, how they are defined, or how or when you go about tailoring them.

6.29 An Alternative Approach to Tailoring at NANO

The approach the Director at NANO took was in my judgment the most effective to gain the best use of his current resources. He was in effect tailoring the roles and responsibilities in his organization according to the unique strengths and weaknesses of his people.

It has been my experience that taking this level of care in assigning responsibilities to people can bring great benefits to an organization. On the other hand, I have heard some argue against this type of approach because it tends to lead away from organizational consistency, which is a key characteristic of CMMI level 3 organizations.

If you read the tip under Organizational Process Focus Specific Practice 1.3 Establish Tailoring Criteria and Guidelines, it states:

The challenge is to provide guidance that has sufficient flexibility to meet the unique needs of each project, but at the same time ensure meaningful consistency.

At NANO this type of tailoring of roles and responsibilities was conducted periodically based on changes at the organization level rather than on individual project starts, which is the common method observed in most organizations.[6]

NANO had also found a way to tailor their processes more efficiently. NANO observed that they had three repeating types of projects and the tailoring required by each project type was almost identical. Rather than have each project at startup repeat this same tailoring, they created *pre-tailored templates* for each of the project types, simplifying the tailoring process at each project startup. This made sense at NANO because of the repeating nature of these three project types. This might or might not make sense for other organizations.

Nothing in the CMMI says when you need to do your tailoring and what process assets you need to tailor. If you have repeating project types like NANO, consider using the pre-tailoring approach to save time and effort for each of your projects. Also, it is worth giving thought to when it might make sense to tailor your roles and responsibilities given the nature of the projects you have in your organization and the changing skills of your people.

> **CAUTION**
>
> Don't let pre-tailoring replace important planning that needs to take place at the start of each project.[7]

6.30 Planning with Uncertainty Using an Agile and CMMI-Compliant Approach

At NANO, all the leaders who directly reported to the Director had not bought into the whole CMMI idea. Since the Director had initiated the off-site on roles and responsibilities and because process-related actions came out of this, I used this effort to gain momentum by aligning the CMMI plan with the already agreed-to process-related actions out of the meeting.

The Project Planning (PP) Process Area of the CMMI model has fourteen specific practices. The CMMI doesn't tell you when or how to conduct these practices. It doesn't say you can't plan incrementally. Furthermore, Project

---

6. The topic of balancing uniqueness and consistency is discussed at greater length in Chapters 9 and 10.

7. Tailoring is covered in greater detail in the following chapter on the GEAR case study.

Monitor and Control (PMC), another CMMI Process Area, could be interpreted as providing best practices to continuously adjust the plan to keep it current, which is what Agile approaches recommend.

On the NANO process improvement project, I put together a simple nine-page project plan using the CMMI Project Planning Process Area as a guide to make sure I was hitting the right issues and as an on-the-job teaching aid for my client.

One of the difficulties often faced is how to handle uncertainty in planning. Frequently, Agile approaches appear to conflict with traditional approaches in this area. The traditional approach has been to solidify as many *decisions* as one can up front, so the related cost and schedule can also be solidified. The rationale for this approach has been to better *estimate* work and reduce the risk of scope creep.

Agile advocates take the position that we gain greater value by *continuous refinement* of the plan based on the latest information and on-going *collaboration* with the customer.

One of the tough issues I faced when planning the Process Improvement effort for NANO was estimating effort and schedule. I was unsure how long it would take this team to accomplish many of the process-related tasks because of my lack of knowledge of their process-related skills.

I believed it was good that the leaders in the organization were owning process responsibility because I felt this would address the issue where the people who use processes don't feel the processes reflect what they really do on the job. It would be up to those who use the process to tell us what should be in the process.

However, the problem was to figure out a way to communicate to my client the kinds of things that should be included in CMMI level 3 processes and help them develop those processes. The trick was to do this without telling them what they needed to put in each of their processes, or what processes they needed to develop.

It was crucial that I get them involved in defining their own processes. However, now I was struggling with completing certain sections of the plan because there were unknowns created by this approach. As I reviewed the plan, I knew that some of those who were being asked to commit to it would resist because it didn't address how much time would be required by them and their people. I thought to myself:

Would I commit to a plan that didn't specify how much time I was signing up for?

This was a real dilemma for me. Therefore, I went back and created a section of the plan that talked about exactly how we would determine and agree to the resources and effort. We were using an *incremental* approach. We had a *criterion* to make *decisions* about work we would do in each increment. We would look at each potential piece of work on a case-by-case basis, considering *priority* of the work, *personnel availability*, *effort estimates*, and *skill level of those assigned*. This way no one would be forced to sign up for something without knowing the consequences ahead of time. I wouldn't have to guess about how much time each task would take before I even knew who might be assigned.

LESSON 6

When planning, if you don't know the answer, don't guess. Explain in your plan exactly what you are going to do to get the answer. Then, when more information is available, update the plan.

I found people resisted this plan at first, but eventually bought in. It was exactly what we planned to do. But why did people resist originally? I believe at first they wanted a plan that just called out the answer, but we didn't have the full answer. Why don't they like this? The answer is because it isn't easy. It means you have to participate throughout the project to make *decisions* about each task as sufficient information becomes available.[8]

I told one of the leaders of NANO that my role was to guide this effort and give him helpful hints along the way, and he quickly responded by saying:

I don't want hints; just tell me what the CMMI says I have to do.

I then explained that the CMMI does not dictate things you have to do. It is a reference model to help you ask key questions about your processes so you can figure out what the right processes are for your organization. That client was clearly a bit frustrated with my answer. I could tell he wanted me to just write his processes for him since he viewed me as the expert. I also explained that he knew his business and his organization's culture far better than I did and the goal was to develop processes that fit his work and helped his people do their job.

---

8. Reference Agile Manifesto Principle 4: Business people and developers must work together daily throughout the project.

This was the right thing to do, but it meant more effort and involvement and decisions along the road for the leaders involved and the workers deeper in the organization. They didn't like it, but eventually they reluctantly agreed. Often the right answer requires more *involvement of people* and more *decisions* along the way.[9]

> **CAUTION**
>
> This approach to continuous planning requires collaboration, which takes time and commitment.[10]

6.31 CMMI Project Planning Consistent with Agile Planning

The CMMI Project Planning (PP) Process Area provides an interesting insight applicable to this effort. There exists a Specific Practice 1.4 in this process area that says:

> *Determine estimates of effort and cost.*

It doesn't say when you need to do this. Some argued that without the details the plan was not complete. I argued the plan was accurate, and yes, there would be more planning to come. The plan reflected how we would arrive at those effort estimates. I wanted to describe in the plan exactly what we were going to do and how we were going to do it. I didn't want to make up things to make people feel we had more answers than we did.

> **LESSON 7**
>
> The CMMI doesn't require you to do things in a certain order or at a certain time. It does expect you to say in your plan what you are going to do, and then follow your plan. When the plan changes, update the plan. This is consistent with both Agile concepts and the CMMI.

---

9. Refer to the appendices for a template for a Project Management Plan (PMP).

10. Collaboration is discussed at greater length in the DART case study in Chapter 8.

6.32 Summary: How CMMI Helps Agile

The following table provides a summary of how CMMI areas discussed in this chapter help Agile.

CMMI Area	How It Helps Agile
GP 2.3 Provide Resources, GP 2.4 Assign Responsibility, Defined Roles and Responsibilities.	Helps to spread authority and responsibility appropriately throughout the organization.
Generic Practice 2.7 Identify and Involve Relevant Stakeholders Organizational Stakeholder Matrix	As Agile organizations grow, using informal means alone to ensure all stakeholders are notified can begin to break down (e.g., site people involved with installs).
Generic Practice 2.5 Train the People, Train people specifically in how to do their jobs	Helps us to provide an environment that gives our people the support they need, training them specifically in how to make better decisions in the organization.
Measurement and Analysis Levels of Measure Formality	Helps us use measures in everyday decisions more effectively.
Project Planning Plans reflect what actually do	Helps establish more accurate estimates by considering project-specific factors.

6.33 Summary: How Agile Helps CMMI

The following table provides a summary of how Agile approaches discussed in this chapter help the CMMI.

Agile Approach	How It Helps CMMI
Defining roles and responsibilities based on unique talents of the current workforce	Helps organizations assign responsibilities (GP 2.4) to people maximizing effectiveness of the workforce
Pre-tailored project types	Helps project perform tailoring (GP 3.1) effectively and efficiently
Continual collaboration on the plan	Helps us achieve the most effective plans based on the most accurate knowledge
Processes owned by those who execute them	Helps achieve buy-in to processes and the most accurate and useful processes
Flow down of management responsibility to small teams	Helps achieve more effective Project Monitor and Control (PMC) and more accurate progress assessments
Flow down and training on the use of informal measures in daily decisions	Helps people at all levels of the organization make better decisions

Chapter 7

Bringing Process Maturity to an R&D Culture

Scenario and Real Case Study Facts: In this chapter, you will learn about GEAR, an R&D organization that had succeeded based largely on the skills and talents of its people, and its ability to respond rapidly to changing customer needs. But today, GEAR is facing new challenges brought on by this success. GEAR is moving out of the R&D world, and into a much larger world of fixed cost and schedule programs. Its success has led to rapid growth and new opportunities, but its parent company is concerned that GEAR's agility—which in large part brought its current success—is now more of a risk than an asset to the organization.

7.1 What You Will Learn in This Chapter

- Practical and proven techniques to help an organization with the hardest part of process improvement—process deployment and compliance
- A proven process tailoring technique to help you deploy processes more effectively and efficiently

- Three optimizations supporting more efficient and effective process development and deployment
- A powerful technique rarely taken advantage of, but encouraged within the CMMI framework that can facilitate disciplined agility

This chapter is divided into three sections. In Section I, you will hear lessons similar to those at BOND and NANO. However, our solutions differed. In Section II, you will learn what we did differently at GEAR to aid more efficient and effective process development and deployment. In Section III, you will learn about options and recommendations related to tailoring, process compliance, and the use of criteria to aid both effective CMMI implementations and agility. *Those who don't need reinforcement of previous material can skip Section I, or just scan the lessons and paragraph titles for topics of interest.*

Section I
Common Lessons

7.2 GEAR Case Study Background

GEAR is a small growing organization that for many years was involved in Research and Development (R&D) of a critical cutting-edge U.S. defense technology. A few years ago, GEAR was acquired by a large U.S. defense company. Prior to the acquisition most of GEAR's projects were small proof of concept efforts worked closely with customer personnel.

In 2008, the organization found itself on the verge of winning a large fixed-price full-scale development project with several similar opportunities on the near horizon. A concern of the parent organization was the ability of GEAR to manage an effort of this magnitude given their R&D history, which included a track record of frequent cost and schedule overruns. In response, GEAR initiated a CMMI process improvement effort. I was asked to conduct a gap analysis for GEAR against the CMMI model and help them develop a plan to move the organization to a full staged CMMI level 3 with future plans to move to CMMI level 5.

Often when doing a gap analysis against the CMMI model in small Agile organizations, common patterns emerge, along with unique strengths and weaknesses. To create the most effective plan for each organization, these unique conditions must be carefully observed and considered. My analysis and recommendations to GEAR were based on this approach.

7.3 Common Patterns at GEAR

When I was asked to help GEAR, it wasn't their first attempt at process improvement. GEAR had previously instituted a Process Management Steering Group (MSG). Like NANO, GEAR had embarked on a distributed process responsibility approach encouraging each department in the organization to document its own processes.

7.4 The Common Pattern of Unclear Process Asset Requirements

Each department at GEAR had been working for over a year to document its own processes when I conducted the gap analysis. I observed inconsistent format and structure for the process assets I reviewed. There also was no clearly defined process for review, approval, and release of process assets. Some process assets were maintained in a folder referred to as "released." When I questioned MSG members, I found different opinions of who was responsible for approving the content of processes in the organization and who had approved the processes that had been placed in the released folder.

> **LESSON 1**
>
> The first step to an effective process improvement effort is to clearly establish the rules for your process assets, and the rules for review, approval, release, and changes to process assets.

The CMMI doesn't tell you what your process asset rules need to be. It *reminds* us of the importance of these rules through its specific practices within the Organizational Process Definition (OPD) Process Area. When I say "rules for your process assets," I include where you maintain your process assets and how you package them.

This might sound obvious, but it is not uncommon in small Agile organizations just starting a process improvement effort for these issues to be missed, especially when a distributed process responsibility approach is taken.

At GEAR, I learned that the MSG were supposed to be the final approval, but not the subject matter experts on every process. The intent was for each department to conduct its own process content review before submitting processes to the MSG for final approval. I asked people in individual departments what they were looking for when they were asked to review process assets. The responses I received were varied.

> **LESSON 2**
>
> Ensure the content requirements for process assets—specifically minimums—are clear, and communicate those requirements to those assigned to develop and review processes.

The CMMI doesn't dictate answers. It does give us good *reminders* of things to consider through its practices. The reason I stress defining "minimums" is not to drive organizations to only produce the minimum, but rather to know where the boundaries are so we know when we are not ready to proceed. This is particularly important for Agile-like organizations at times of project stress.

Lessons 1 and 2 are similar to those learned in the NANO case study. Recall the common myth exposed at NANO with respect to the belief that it is easy to write good processes. When I assessed the processes written at GEAR, I found they were reasonably accurate to the level they were written. The processes, however, lacked the needed depth to be effective. They were missing key ingredients, findings quite similar to those at NANO.

To explain what I mean by "lacked the needed depth to be effective" let us revisit my recommended process asset structure described in the case study at BOND. I recommended in that case study that one always package the "what you must do" separate from the "how you do it." This simplifies the "what you must do" process documentation, but does not imply you don't need significant content in the "how you do it."

The recommendation to package these separately is made for multiple reasons. One is to clarify what needs to be done as part of your tailoring and planning activities on each project and what should not be considered because we have already agreed that everyone does it.

7.5 Criteria and Product Content Templates

An example of what GEAR was lacking was the "how you do it" guidance for product content requirements. Their "must do" process documentation was reasonably good to the level they had defined it. For example, in the Technical Solution area it stated that a design artifact must be developed, and reviewed. However, as I examined their artifacts in greater depth I found no specification as to what content needed to be in that design artifact. Without this information, any person assigned to develop or review a design artifact would not know what to place in the document or what to review it for. What GEAR needed were improvements in the area of *criteria*, and *product templates*.

I discovered a number of templates that had been developed within the software organization at GEAR. However, I found few of them actually being used. I asked questions to the workers at GEAR such as:

- Are these templates required?
- Is each project allowed to tailor the templates, and if so, who approves the tailoring?
- Is there a minimum that each design artifact must contain that cannot be tailored out?

The answers I received to these questions were inconsistent and weren't written down or agreed to across the organization.

7.6 Writing Processes for People in "My Department"

At GEAR, I observed patterns similar to the "cookie cutter" processes at NANO. However, the reason it occurred at GEAR was different. At NANO, many held the misguided view of process as relevant only for work that had no uncertainty associated with it. At GEAR I observed a lack of stakeholder identification (similar to NANO), but in this case it appeared to be the result of a desire within each department to ensure they could control the activities in the process within just their own department.

GEAR was a small organization structured like many large organizations with distinct software, systems, hardware, and test departments. When the MSG asked these departments to define their processes, each primarily looked inside their department ("my department") and didn't adequately consider interfaces and dependencies with the other departments.

I observed this in the way they wrote their processes, and how they executed them. One senior systems person said it was not uncommon to go to a hardware design review and find only hardware people even though the software runs on their hardware. When he would ask them why no one from the software department was attending the review, the response was that no one thought software people needed to be at a hardware review. He told me he had to constantly explain that software does have dependencies on hardware design decisions.

7.7 Stakeholder Matrix and Product Template Recommendations

At GEAR, I recommended the development of a *stakeholder matrix* managed at the organizational level to bring visibility to the missing stakeholders from outside departments. This required close attention because it would affect process descriptions, and behavior and culture within the organization. I also recommended the development of templates with clear minimums that could not be tailored out. These became two high-priority areas for early process working group focus.

7.8 OPF and OPD for Agile Organizations

I recommended GEAR start with their OPF and OPD processes.[1] This might seem odd to some since both of these process areas are at the CMMI Staged level 3. However, for Agile organizations—in particular those that have effective processes, but just need to document them, or add a few ingredients—if you don't start with OPF and OPD you will end up reworking your processes. Working OPF and OPD first just simplifies the overall effort.

Another reason for establishing the organizational process asset rules early is that they are critical to your tailoring approach. Tailoring is an extremely powerful mechanism for Agile organizations that wish to maintain their agility or for high maturity organizations seeking to increase their agility.[2] Establishing the organizational process asset rules early was also critical at GEAR because of a key weakness identified in the gap analysis—Compliance.[3]

---

1. OPF stands for Organizational Process Focus, and OPD stands for Organizational Process Definition. Refer to the appendices for examples of OPD and OPF processes, and organizational process asset rules.

2. Tailoring and its relationship to agility are discussed at greater length later in this chapter.

3. When I use the term "compliance," I mean compliance with the defined project processes.

7.9 At GEAR, "No One Has a Hammer"

When I explained to people at GEAR my recommendations for process asset guidance including keeping the "what you must do" separate from the "how you do it," I motivated this process packaging through a specific weakness I had identified during the gap analysis.

This weakness can best be expressed by a phrase used by one of the people I interviewed: "No one has a hammer." This relates to a culture at GEAR not uncommon in R&D environments. GEAR was driven by its exceptionally gifted engineering organization, which included brilliant engineers who were motivated to build the best product possible.

When project pressures mount, I find each organization tends to have a unique survival response. At NANO, Senior Management would take charge and drive a solution from the management side. At GEAR, the engineering side of the organization most often rose to meet a challenge and drove the solution from the technical side. This had proven effective in the past and was a large part of why they had achieved such technical success. However, it had also contributed to their past cost and schedule overrun problems.

GEAR had no quality organization, and effectively no checks and balances. Part of my rationale for driving a clearly defined process asset structure with rules and templates was to force clear criteria for product reviews, and compliance checks. I knew they needed a quality group, but there was no sense starting quality checks until we could give the quality organization clear rules to check on. I explained to Senior Management at the gap analysis outbrief that one of the top priorities in my recommendations was to establish a clear minimum criterion to check against so everyone would know when it was time to say:

NO, YOU ARE NOT READY TO PROCEED.

7.10 Another Advantage to Keeping the "How-to" Guidance Separate

GEAR liked the approach of separating "how-to" guidance, pointing out an advantage I hadn't previously considered. Because there were many highly skilled technical people in the organization with strong opinions about "how" they did their job, one of the major problems they had previously encountered when trying to document their processes was agreeing on "how-to" details.

By separating the "what you must do" from the "how to do it," GEAR management felt the organization would move forward and reach consensus more easily on process definitions since we were essentially raising the discussion above where most conflicts had arisen in the past.

7.11 Aligning Engineering and Project Management at GEAR

In the CMMI Project Planning Process Area, Specific Practice 1.3 states:

Define the project lifecycle phases on which to scope the planning effort.

The results of defining a project life-cycle should create a framework for estimating and managing project work. The life cycle documentation I reviewed at GEAR indicated they used a waterfall development approach. However, when I listened to people talk about how they did their job, the actual work described sounded more like an incremental and evolutionary approach.

When I raised this as a potential issue, some in engineering responded that they didn't see the significance of the issue I was raising. Their comment was:

We just look at what we do as a series of waterfalls when we don't have all the requirements up front. What difference does it make how we define the life cycle?

The problem I saw and explained to them, was that this appeared to occur on most projects, and affected the real work that was going on. I understood why they worked the way they did, but they were planning as if they were going to conduct a single pass through each of their waterfall phases. That was how management had set up the project master schedule and allocated budgets.

Because they didn't work this way, a misalignment between the planned and budgeted work and what work they actually did resulted. Frequent cost and schedule overruns were the serious consequence. This discussion led to greater awareness in the organization of the purpose of a life cycle as an aid to keep finance and engineering aligned.

CMMI Project Planning Process Area SP 1.3, Define Project Life Cycle, can help "Agile-like" organizations that exhibit cost and schedule management problems by improving *communication* among engineering, management, and finance.

7.12 At GEAR, "It Depends on Who Shows Up"

In the gap analysis interviews, I heard about a number of effective project monitor and control activities. One was a regular Monday meeting between project managers and functional managers that used a staffing spreadsheet to facilitate discussions of current project priority staffing needs.

I also heard about an "institutionalized"[4] Thursday meeting with Senior Management and project leaders. The Thursday meeting was a project-specific Senior Management review using a standard chart, referred to as the quad chart, which contained key measures related to the cost, schedule, risk, and performance health of each project.

While I heard about these meetings in my interviews, I found nothing written that described the purpose of these meetings or the existence of the artifacts they used to support them (i.e., staffing chart, quad chart).

During the gap analysis out-brief at GEAR, I explained the important distinction the CMMI model makes between "do it" (e.g., "perform it") and "do it" as an institutionalized "managed" or "defined" process. I explained the importance of this distinction using words from a technical leader's response to a question about the effectiveness of key meetings at GEAR:

> *It depends on who shows up.*

What I found at GEAR was that the Monday and Thursday meetings were very effective. Other meetings, such as Project Kickoff meetings, or Project Weekly schedule status meetings could not be counted on to be effective. The value of meetings at GEAR was driven by the people who believed those meetings had value.

---

4. By "institutionalized" here I mean only that it was done with great regularity in the organization. It is worth noting that this does not meet the intent of "institutionalization" in the CMMI sense of being "managed" or "defined."

This was a key finding in the gap analysis. There were many good management and engineering practices happening at GEAR—but they weren't happening because of any particular *policy, planned process,* or *training* in the organization.

I don't mean to downplay the importance of influential people driving effective process execution. This is essential. It was clear many highly motivated and skilled people were critical to the success GEAR had achieved. While explaining this during my gap analysis out-brief, I emphasized that the organization was at risk in a number of critical areas because they were heavily dependent on key individuals to make certain activities occur.

This is why a recommendation for GEAR, like BOND and NANO, was to extract valuable practices and document them for the benefit of others in the organization. This is another replay from BOND.

LESSON 3

Process improvement doesn't always mean behavior change.

Many of the most important process improvements in Agile organizations[5] involve capturing what already works and sharing it with others so it will continue to work even if key people unexpectedly change roles, or leave the organization.

7.13 Does the Written and Trained Process Match the Real Process?

On the Engineering side where the requirements development process and flow down had been written down, we had a different challenge. In this case, engineering had a written requirements development and management process, but the process reflected a very strict waterfall approach to development. This was not the way most of the projects were working.

In this case, I specified the reasons why it was important to reflect how the organization really worked in written processes. This would help train new people in how to work, and others in how to plan work so the schedule and budget authorizations would align with on-going real work in the organization. This was a case where we had a real problem with cost overruns. We needed to make changes in GEAR's practices for improvement to take hold.

---

5. This is not intended to imply that being "Agile-like" is satisfactory. Only that capturing what works is important, but might not be sufficient.

Because of the collaborative working relationship between engineering personnel and customer personnel, it was not unusual for changes in requirements to flow in during a design review. I knew that the organization didn't want to overly restrict this process because this rapid response to customer needs had become instrumental in building a rapport with the customer. This was a large part of why this organization was expanding and positioned to win a number of new large jobs.

I understood this point. I explained to GEAR that they could still have a process that allowed for very rapid approval of requirements changes, but it was essential those requirements were analyzed for impact and approved before work was initiated in order to manage their cost and schedule more effectively.

7.14 Requirements Change Approval Alignment with Real Work

Requirements change approval that meant flow down to engineering work became a high-priority area during the early process improvement effort.

This was because of its criticality in helping GEAR prepare to manage a large complex effort to a fixed cost and schedule.

It was evident from observing this organization how they had gotten into cost and schedule difficulties in the past frequently agreeing to more work than they had estimated in their pricing. This occurred because they wanted to give their customer the best product possible. However, they were failing to raise the risk they were taking in engineering at the project management level.

Engineering had a history of making decisions on technical work without returning to program management for approval. Without proper analysis

> ### *Pause, Reflect, and Glance Forward*
>
> Can you observe the repeating pattern at GEAR? GEAR's repeating specific weaknesses are different from what we saw at NANO, but it is worth noting how repeating specific weaknesses can oftentimes best be observed in times of crisis.
>
> This fact also provides insight we can use in helping us know when to be on the lookout for our own repeating specific weaknesses…
>
> …And, as we will see later in Part V, it can help us identify the most useful "checkpoints" to help us move our organization forward toward real sustainable performance improvement.

of the impact, they would take on too much work. Once this realization set in, and they found themselves under pressure to stay on schedule, they often resorted to cutting corners, such as paring down design reviews or testing. Since "no one had a hammer" in this organization, the process would frequently lead to long integrations—the consequence of not doing an adequate job up front.

7.15 Asking the Intent Question Leads to Behavior Change

I have previously discussed the importance of always asking the intent question when evaluating an organization's current processes against certain CMMI practices. At GEAR, I found they did do planning, but a large part of the results of their project planning efforts was kept in a PowerPoint brief. In the gap analysis out-brief, I referenced Specific Practice 2.7 of the Project Planning Process Area, which states:

> *Establish and maintain the overall project plan content.*

The phrase "establish and maintain" means document[6] and use, which implies the need to keep the plan current. Again, nothing in the CMMI requires their plan to be in any particular format. However, in my experience, most organizations do not go back to update PowerPoint briefs when a plan changes.

They agreed that this artifact had worked well for them to kick off a project, but when things changed they never went back to update the slides. As a result, when new people came on the project it was difficult to get them up to speed on the current project plan.

By continually asking the intent question about a specific practice—in this case, *What is the intent of "establishing and maintaining the plan"?*—you often realize you do need to change your behavior for the good of the overall project and organization.

---

6. The word "document" here does not mean an actual document (noun sense), but rather in the verb sense that there are "bread crumbs" of some sort...documentary, or historical clues. .

Section II
Process Optimizations

7.16 Process Development and Deployment Optimizations at GEAR

While many of the issues faced at GEAR were similar to those at BOND and NANO, my recommendations differed at GEAR based on lessons I had learned in similar process improvement efforts. I would now like to share three optimizations where we took different approaches at GEAR.

Optimization A: Managing Staffing on the Process Improvement Project

The first recommendation I hit hard with GEAR was the need to run the process improvement project like any other project in the company. I had made the same recommendation at BOND and NANO. At BOND, it worked well because the Senior Management took this recommendation seriously. At NANO, because of political issues and priority conflicts, progress was constantly interrupted by loss of key people.

I explained at GEAR the lessons I had learned at NANO when a process working group was derailed because a key subject matter expert was unavailable for several scheduled process brainstorming sessions. This eventually pushed a release months behind schedule.

My initial thinking was to run the process working groups at GEAR the way we had run them at BOND, with the process improvement lead playing both the role of process improvement project manager and technical lead. After listening to my lesson learned from the NANO case, a VP at GEAR suggested an alternative model. He recommended that we assign both a project manager and a technical lead (different people). He felt this was important because of the culture at GEAR and because of what I had said about the importance of taking resource assignments seriously.

He believed that for the project to succeed, it was important to have a project manager focused on the management side. He went on to say this included attending the Monday meeting with the functional managers because that was the meeting where you fight for your people every week.

This was part of the culture of the organization at GEAR. The VP had listened to me. He knew the way this organization ran and what needed to be done for a project to succeed at GEAR. He knew what I didn't know because I hadn't worked in this environment. This turned out to be one of the most important decisions making the process improvement project at GEAR a success.

Optimization B: Facilitating a Process Writing Working Group Effectively

BOND was one of the first organizations to use the tailored TWG approach for Agile organizations. The tailoring was based on a streamlining I developed largely from participating in process working groups in more traditional development organizations. If you don't have experience facilitating a process writing working group, you can quickly find yourself in trouble. While we avoided a number of the traditional problems, new lessons always emerge.

One of my biggest frustrations—and this continued at BOND to a degree—is the amount of thrashing and rehashing of information that is only tangentially relevant to the goals of a process writing working group. I find that exorbitant amounts of time are often spent in areas that contain little payback associated with the goals of the effort. We solved some of this at BOND, but I still felt greater efficiency gains could be made if we had set the context and the goal for the group more effectively up front.

A significant efficiency was gained at BOND through the roles of SME and "Doer."[7] This helped us minimize the time required by valuable SMEs. However, the way we extracted process information at BOND produced a great deal of extraneous discussion and data that still needed to be filtered off-line. Feedback from participants indicated that they didn't feel their time in the group was always well spent. They felt much of the project-specific discussions weren't relevant to them.

Part of this was caused by the way the task was laid out to the group in starting the working group brainstorming discussions. The discussion was open to all to describe what they do on their project with respect to the relevant process area. The process improvement leader at BOND and I had a discussion about this off-line. She had felt it was fine for all to listen to this project-specific information because it provided some cross-training. My

---

7. Refer to Chapter 4 for more about "SME" and "Doer" roles in an Agile Technical Working Group.

feeling was that it was not part of our charter to cross-train. I viewed this as *scope creep* to our task.

CAUTION
Don't use a process writing working group to learn about what goes on with other projects in the organization.

At the time, I was uncertain how I would have run the group differently. Later when I was training these processes, I realized a more efficient approach. In the training I began by asking questions of the group to see how much of the process they could discover before we actually looked at the process descriptions. I went to a white pad and said to the group:

> *We are now going to talk about the Design Process. Before we look at the Design Process documented description, let's make a list of artifacts you produce and activities you conduct when you are involved in design work.*

When they would have trouble, I gave them hints such as:

> *Does anyone else ever look at the design artifacts you produce?*

This would remind them about reviews. I then might say:

> *Are there other things you do to ensure you have developed the right product?*

This would remind them about demonstrations with a customer, and so on.

My questions helped to focus them on the things they should be thinking about in writing or following a process. It usually would take less than 10 minutes to do this brainstorming in the training for a given process. We would then open the actual process description, examining it to see how close we came. In almost every case, we would have captured in 10 minutes the essence of what was in a process that might have taken months to develop with multiple two-hour process writing sessions.

Why could the people in the training group create almost the same processes in much shorter time than the original process writing group? I believe the answer was the way I asked the question in the training versus the way we had conducted the original process writing working group. The working group was too open ended. The training was very focused and kept people on task.

I decided, if this worked so well in the training, couldn't we potentially save a great deal of time developing processes by using this same technique in the process writing workshops?

We did this at GEAR and had varied results with different groups. However, in every case the result provided a significant improvement over the more open brainstorming approach used at BOND. The new approach is much more efficient for an organization that fundamentally understands its processes, but might just need to document them better.

For an organization that is less mature and needs more help with the fundamentals, additional time might be required when initially developing processes. I have the following caution and related insight for the reader to consider in deciding the right process writing working group strategy for your organization.

> **CAUTION**
> Be careful when you are facilitating a process writing working group that you are not overly restricting needed discussions driving the wrong process description for the organization.

On the other hand, the following insight can help an organization derive processes efficiently.

> **INSIGHT**   The ability to rapidly sense when the discussion is drifting away from the goal and re-vector the group to the task at hand is essential to the effective facilitation of a process writing working group.

Techniques I use to keep process writing groups focused include: First, focus on "what," not "how." When the group starts with "how," write down an action and come back to it. Once you have made a cut at the "what you must do," have a focused discussion on the "how-to" options.

Optimization C: The "Thread" Approach to Process Development and Deployment

At BOND, the TWGs were based on the CMMI Process Areas. This meant scheduling and working through eighteen technical working groups. I observed significant overlap of discussions. The Process Areas within the CMMI model are each distinct, but not independent, and some have significant coupling and even what appears to be overlap. At GEAR, we modified this approach.

Project Planning includes Risk Identification. Therefore, in the Project Planning working group it is natural to get into Risk Management, which has its own Process Area. Project Planning Specific Practice 3.2 states:

Reconcile the project plan to reflect available and estimated resources.

Related discussions often lead to actions taken to keep the plan current, which in turn leads to practices within the Project Monitor and Control Process Area.

One of the challenges of managing an aggressive CMMI Process Improvement schedule is getting the right people together at the right time to talk about practices. The right Subject Matter Experts for Project Planning, Project Monitor and Control, and Risk Management are often the same people. It is natural to perform these management functions in an integrated way in many organizations; therefore, it is natural and efficient to discuss these practices together.

Another benefit of working closely coupled process areas together is that process descriptions emerge fitting in a more *integrated* and efficient way. Nothing in the CMMI model says you need to package your processes as the CMMI model has packaged its process areas.

Because of this I recommended that the working groups at GEAR be organized around natural "threads" of work that were closely coupled, rather than around the CMMI Process Areas. We made sure we hit all the specific practices. However, using this approach helped address each area more efficiently.

Another advantage to this approach related to a comment the VP of Engineering at GEAR made. He wanted to make sure the organization knew that we were taking the process improvement project seriously. He wanted everyone in the organization to know we were committed to its success, and understand that if they were assigned a task on the process improvement project that it held the same high priority just as any task they would get with a project that had an external customer. This remark, I believe, he made in response to my comments about NANO where the process improvement project priority always seemed to be on the bottom of the list. A process improvement effort only works if people in the organization assigned to process tasks self-manage their time and meet their assigned process task commitments.

When I was making my recommendation for running the working groups as *threads* through multiple CMMI Process Areas, I pointed out how this approach supported the VP's desire to let the organization know we were serious. Using this approach, each working group would have *multiple releases* of its processes and training. The initial release would hit a subset of specific practices in each of Project Planning (PP), Project Monitor and Control (PMC), and Risk Management (RSKM). The advantage was we didn't have to get it all done in any particular PA to get an initial deployment of processes. The group could focus on areas they felt were most important and commit to get valuable product out based on business needs and what *opportunities* existed to *pilot* the processes.

Time-boxing is an important scheduling mechanism with Agile methods. This is an example where we used time-boxing at GEAR on the process improvement project. Time-boxing means committing to a schedule and releasing the product on schedule. We might have to reduce functionality. In this case, the functionality might be the number of CMMI Specific Practices we were able to address in each CMMI Process Area within a given release.

The advantage is the organization is getting training earlier, and in smaller chunks and more often. They are aware that process improvement is happening. The people in the organization are our customers, and we listen and use their feedback as we factor in the priorities for our next release.

This provided good risk abatement to ensure the processes we were releasing were the right processes for the company, as we were getting continuous *validation feedback* from the process users (our customers). This approach also allowed us to release "stretch points" gradually, which provided time for people to learn the changes in behavior that were expected without overwhelming them with too many behavior change requests at once.

This same approach was used for the Engineering Process Areas at GEAR. It was decided to work Engineering improvements in parallel with Management. The initial thread through Engineering included Requirements Management, Requirements Development, and Technical Solution. This approach also made sense given how this organization really worked, which was based more on an incremental/evolutionary life cycle than their documented waterfall view.

7.17 Advantages and Disadvantages to the "Thread" Approach

The "thread" approach to process development and deployment is really an *Agile approach*. Advantages to this approach include more efficient use of subject matter expert's time. Another advantage is more *integrated* process definitions that fit the way people really work in the organization. Yet another is better communication of the issues between departments in the organization. Communication between departments had been identified as a weakness during the GEAR gap analysis. Refer to Table 7-1.

Table 7-1 *Advantages to Thread Approach to Process Development and Deployment*

More effective use of key people's time
More integrated processes that fit with the way people work
Improved communication between departments
Improved support for rapid process deployment
Earlier training
Earlier process validation

Disadvantages include sometimes needing to have more people in a working group than is desirable. Too many people can slow progress. When you are talking about issues that cross from requirements, development, and into test, and your organization has distinct departments for each of these traditional functions, more people might need to be involved in the discussions than is sometimes desirable.

Another potential disadvantage is the difficulty in planning a working group in a way that effectively uses the time of all the working group members. Because you don't always know ahead of time when using the *thread* approach where a given meeting's discussions might lead, some people might end up feeling their participation was not of value.

I wouldn't recommend the thread approach in an organization that hadn't previously given their processes considerable thought. You need to be at a level of maturity to discuss and develop *integrated processes*. However, if the organization is mature, this is a more efficient and effective approach to process development and deployment than isolating working group discussions based on the CMMI model Process Areas.

Section III
Tailoring, Process Compliance, and Criteria

We next discuss in more detail, Process Tailoring, Compliance, and the Use of Criteria to Aid Process Agility.

7.18 Process Tailoring

When I interviewed people at GEAR who were involved in project planning, the subject of tailoring usually came up. I heard multiple times about the three categories of projects—large, medium, and small—and about the spreadsheet that each project developed identifying the artifacts they planned to produce based on their project category.

7.19 Strengths and Weaknesses of Tailoring at GEAR

Tailoring was important at GEAR because there were many small efforts. When I dug deeper trying to discover exactly what was required for each of the three project categories, I found the documented guidance lacking. The written guidance just said: "Choose whichever are appropriate" from a long list and provided no additional guidance or criteria to determine what was "appropriate." A strength at GEAR was that they understood the importance and intent of tailoring. Their weakness was they were not gaining the full potential benefits of tailoring due to lack of criteria to aid decisions.

7.20 Tailoring Recommendations at GEAR

My first recommendation at GEAR was for them to clearly define their "must do's." This is a critical starting point for effective tailoring. The next step is to use a "tailor up" strategy.

7.21 Agile Process Tailoring Guidance: Always Tailor Up

Process tailoring is one of most misunderstood and misused areas of the CMMI model. There continues to be a common misbelief about the CMMI and tailoring.

> **MYTH**   The CMMI requires a tailoring down approach.

In 2009, I continued to hear this myth being propagated even by some CMMI Lead appraisers. It is true that to achieve CMMI level 3 you do need *tailoring guidelines* and you do need to follow those guidelines to tailor the *organizational standard processes* to address the *unique* needs of each project. The CMMI Organizational Process Definition (OPD) Process Area SP 1.3 does expect each organization to:

> *Establish and maintain the tailoring criteria and guidelines for the organization's set of standard processes.*

However, the CMMI does not dictate what an organization needs to put into its own tailoring guidelines. You can decide to tailor up, or tailor down. This is up to each organization to decide based on its own business needs. You just need to state your approach in your guidelines and then follow it. While it is up to each organization to decide, I do have a strong recommendation on which approach is best especially for Agile organizations, or organizations that would like to increase their agility.

> **LESSON 4**
>
> Always tailor up if you want to increase control on your project, simplify your planning/ tailoring process, and run projects with appropriate agility, efficiency, and discipline.

My tailoring recommendations make sense for organizations that want to increase their agility or maintain their current agility. When we make projects tailor down, we are starting from the supposition that most projects need everything. This assumes large and complex as the starting point and puts the greatest onus of effort on small projects to explicitly tailor out. I believe this is backward, especially for organizations using an Agile approach. We should define the *minimum* everyone *must do*, and then tailor up as necessary.

7.22 Tailoring Down—The Wrong Approach but Used in Many Organizations

What I see in most large "high maturity organizations" today is a tailor down approach. This approach requires people to expend effort explaining why something is not needed.

This adds the greatest amount of work for the simplest programs, which is not an Agile-friendly approach.

7.23 Why Tailoring Up Makes Sense

When you tailor down, how far can you go? Is there a minimum defined? I have found this is often a gray area in many large organizations, and allows large projects to get in trouble through abuse. If you start at a *minimum* set where the minimum set is what everyone "must do," you *eliminate the risk* of "tailoring out" a "must do." This is why I say that starting with the "must do's" helps you control your project.

LESSON 5

A tailoring up approach is consistent with Agile approaches, and completely CMMI compliant.

7.24 Will Tailoring Up[8] Solve All Your Tailoring Issues?

At GEAR, I heard complaints that during the planning/tailoring phase on some projects, agreements had been reached to produce certain artifacts that no one used. These artifacts were placed in the artifact spreadsheet using a tailoring up approach.

So I asked:

How do you decide what artifacts to produce on a given project when you are tailoring up?

---

8. The goal of the Agile Scaling Model (ASM), https://www.ibm.com/developerworks/mydeveloperworks/blogs/ambler/?lang=en, is to help people understand the context in which they are applying Agile approaches. If you don't understand the context, you have little hope of tailoring effectively.

People explained to me about the three categories of projects, but there didn't exist clear written guidance or *criteria* on how to decide which artifacts made sense for each of the three project categories. When I asked how people decided, I heard from one senior leader in the company:

> *We just give them the big list to pick from and tell them to pick what they need, but we don't tell them how to make that decision.*

And then he added:

> *I think it would be hard to tell them what to include without knowing more about their project.*

7.25 The Purpose of Criteria and How They Can Help Tailoring

This brings us to the subject of *criteria*. It does take time to develop good criteria. It requires you to *think* about and discuss the *factors* you want your people to consider during their project planning. When you don't take the time to provide this criteria to help guide people in their planning phase, it becomes too easy for them to select things without really *thinking through* why they are doing it.

What I found at GEAR was that even though they did "tailor up," they often tailored up too much because they didn't ask themselves the *right questions* when creating the artifact list. Think about how much more work you could be causing your company by simply not placing adequate attention on this activity early on your project. An example of *simple criteria* to help people ask the right questions when tailoring up could be:

1. Is it a required deliverable?
2. Does someone need this information to do his or her job either inside this company or a dependent contractor?"

LESSON 6

Without criteria to help, you can tailor up too much.

7.26 Process Compliance Issues at GEAR—The Problem

At GEAR, there were few checks and balances in the organization. Each department had been delegated the responsibility for much of its own support needs, including quality checks. This is not uncommon in R&D organizations where the priority is usually rapid development and demonstration of capability. I had heard in my gap analysis interviews that "minimum" process requirements did exist for key development activities such as design and testing. However, these minimums as far as I could tell existed only in the heads of a few functional leaders, and no one else was checking to ensure they happened.

I also found that when you looked closely at their processes, those "minimums" were a bit fuzzy, allowing for loose interpretations in many situations. What I mean is their processes were not supported by clearly defined *artifacts* with *templates* that made it clear what *content* should be included, which *reviews* needed to be conducted, and which *stakeholders* needed to be included in those reviews.

I have found that this is common in organizations that are given responsibility for their own process definitions. In these cases, there is often a tendency to focus process on the things that are easiest to control rather than on those that are most important for the end product.

An example discussed earlier is the tendency to invite people to a review from your own department, and forget to invite dependent groups. This speeds progress prior to integration, but often hides difficulties until integration. Long integrations were, in fact, a common occurrence at GEAR.

When I brought these issues to the attention of Senior Management at GEAR, they were not surprised. They knew that a more effective quality program was needed. They had put this decision off for fear it would slow the organization just when they needed rapid response to demonstrate capabilities that could win the larger programs they had been seeking. However, there was a catch-22 here since one of their key customers had already expressed concern about their ability to handle a large full-scale development effort without quality checks in place.

7.27 Process Compliance from a CMMI Model Perspective

In the CMMI model, I focus on two areas when I observe process compliance issues. These areas include the Product and Process Quality Assurance (PPQA) Process Area, and Generic Practice (GP) 2.8[9] "Monitor and Control the [fill in relevant process area] against the plan for performing the process and take appropriate corrective action."

7.28 Product and Process Quality Assurance (PPQA)

The purpose of the PPQA process area is:

To provide staff and management with objective insight into processes and associated work products.

This process area is sometimes confused with the Verification Process Area. When I hear a leader complain about the quality organization because too many bugs are being found in products being delivered to customers, this is an indication there might be a confusion of responsibilities in the organization.

The purpose of the Verification process area is to:

Ensure that selected work products meet their specified requirements.

Testing and peer reviews are examples of "how-to" techniques used to meet the intent of this process area. PPQA techniques employed should be providing "objective insight," but its purpose is not to ensure products have been adequately verified. In most organizations, PPQA practices are implemented using some form of a "sampling" to gain the required objective insight because it is not cost-effective to conduct a more comprehensive check. This is one reason why these practices should not be relied on for Verification. Verification of work products is the responsibility of the engineering organization, and when excessive bugs are being reported, an organization should first look closely at the effectiveness of their Verification approaches, not their Quality processes.

---

9. I don't mention GP 2.9 here because the "independence/objective" aspect of GP 2.9 is already covered by PPQA.

7.29 GP 2.8 Monitor and Control the Process

The key distinction between GP 2.8 and PPQA is that GP 2.8 is intended for a group to monitor itself to ensure it is performing its own process as intended and taking corrective action where appropriate, whereas PPQA is intended to be more of an objective, or independent, check.

7.30 Options to Achieve GP 2.8

So how much "monitoring and controlling" do you need for your processes, and who should be doing it? The answer to these questions depends on the culture in your organization. There isn't a single prescribed best approach provided within the CMMI model.

In some Agile organizations, the team actually monitors itself, and this works because when they catch themselves not following the process, team members speak up and initiate immediate corrective action. This is often done through what is referred to as *daily standup meetings*.

However, some organizations are not this disciplined when it comes to monitoring themselves and therefore need extra help. This often occurs in organizations where the culture is out of balance. This is what I had observed at GEAR where the tendency was for Engineering to take over and sometimes fail to involve Project Management in key decisions. In the case of NANO, I observed the reverse tendency where Management took over, and often failed to involve Engineering appropriately.

7.31 Keeping an Organization "Balanced" Versus Shifting a Culture

When organizations know they are out of balance, some try to fix the problem with *Quality Control* checks. My experience has been that this is not the most effective vehicle because its purpose is different. A quality program tends to work well at keeping a fundamentally balanced organization balanced. It does this through sampling and reporting process variances. However, when you are trying to *shift a culture*, you need a more powerful mechanism. One of the most effective mechanisms I have observed is referred to in many organizations as *Gates*.

7.32 An Option to Help Achieve GP 2.8 Through Gates

At GEAR, I heard that the Project Kickoff process was very good, but that sometimes it didn't happen. I also heard that how good the Project Kickoff was when it did happen depended on "who happened to show up."

One technique I have observed organizations using to address these kinds of issues is referred to as *Gates*. Gates are key *checkpoints* on a project that are usually instituted *outside* each specific Engineering department, but *inside* Engineering and Project Management and Support Operations as a whole. There is an important distinction between *Gates* and what a *Quality* organization does. Gates are a mechanism for an organization to *monitor and control itself* by having a level of checks inside its own organization without relying on the *sampling checks* from an independent Quality Group.

Gates are usually instituted in a *collaborative* way by Engineering and Project Management working together to ensure all project requirements to proceed from a given project milestone have been met. They have a *cross-functional focus* to counter the natural tendency of functional groups to focus inward. Gates are not required by the CMMI. They are a proven "how-to" mechanism that can assist achieving the intent of GP 2.8. Depending on the culture in your organization, it is also possible to integrate Gates with Quality Compliance Checks.

7.33 "How to" Options to Implement PPQA

Organizations have available to them multiple options to achieve the intent of the PPQA Process Area. Most often, the intent is achieved through a distinct group that reports to Senior Management independent of engineering. Often the culture that results from such an "independent" group is one of an external "police force" whose job it is to "enforce" process compliance.

I have observed an *alternative* implementation that resulted in the growth of an effective quality culture within an Agile organization, and provided some unanticipated side benefits. This occurred at BOND.

The CMMI process improvement project lead who I worked with at BOND was also given the responsibility to initiate a quality program in the company. At BOND, one of the objectives the owners of the company gave the CMMI team was to maintain the successful Agile culture in the organization. One of the benefits to this culture was the *team approach* that everyone brought to all challenges faced. To maintain this culture at BOND, rather than create the "police force" quality group, we created a quality role with clearly defined responsibilities. We instituted a program where developers in the organization would *cycle through* the quality organization, each taking turns taking on a quality role. The organization already had a culture where individuals enjoyed and were encouraged to wear multiple hats by taking on *multiple roles* and helping each other, so we just extended that culture as we built the quality organization.

There were very clear responsibilities associated with the quality role on a project at BOND. A quality plan had to be written. This was actually a section of the Project Management Plan. The plan clarified which products and processes would be checked. A checklist was created, and used by the quality engineer to ensure the project was following its processes and building its products in accordance with their own plan, and agreed-to templates.

An unanticipated benefit that resulted was a strong *mentoring culture* that became one of the main themes of the quality organization. Rather than being viewed as the "police force," they became viewed as mentors who shared their experiences, and provided assistance to less experienced personnel.

Quality audits became opportunities for people to share knowledge across projects. An individual taking on the "quality role" on one project was often actually a developer on another project. This implementation of PPQA enhanced a mentoring and sharing culture within the organization.

One disadvantage to this PPQA model observed at BOND was the difficulty those in the quality role had when it came to *raising a deficiency* to senior management. The purpose of PPQA is *objective insight*, which means when deficiencies are not being corrected in a timely manner, they need to be raised to Senior Management and actions need to be taken. Because those in the quality role viewed themselves as "helpers" and "mentors," rather than as the "police," they found it difficult to raise issues of compliance in a timely way. As you decide how to create your PPQA culture, both sides of this issue should be seriously considered.

7.34 Recommendations at GEAR: First Step Is, Define the Rules

Before you can put an effective quality compliance program in place, you need to know what you have to comply with. At GEAR, I recommended clarifying rules first, which included the process *"must do's,"* and the template *minimums*. Without these items, a PPQA group doesn't know what to look at to determine compliance. The process rules must precede an effective PPQA implementation.

7.35 Recommendations at GEAR: Second Step Is, Compliance Checks

One of the principles of the Agile Manifesto states:

> *Build projects around motivated individuals. Give them the environment and support they need, and trust them to get the job done.*[10]

Part of the solution to noncompliance issues at BOND was to establish a very clear set of checklist items where one could easily say yes or no for each item. While the PPQA audits had a mentoring/helping feel, we taught the PPQA team that it was still their responsibility to complete the checklist, and if there was noncompliance, dates had to be set and agreed to for correction. It was the responsibility of the person taking on the quality role to do follow-up checks.

When issues weren't resolved in a timely fashion, a report to Senior Management was required. Regardless of the culture created through your PPQA group (mentor, police officer, or combination), there needs to be a well-defined checklist of items, documentation of the results, and communication of issues to higher management. These are expected practices within the CMMI PPQA Process Area.

As the maturity of your organization grows, so should the items the PPQA group audits for. The PPQA checklists should always be *aligned* with the processes that have currently been deployed. In other words, both at BOND and GEAR, as we *incrementally* rolled out new or improved processes and

---

10. Reference Appendix A, *Principles Behind the Agile Manifesto*.

training, we also *incrementally* modified the PPQA checklist to align with the process and product template expectations.

Because of the culture at GEAR, a degree of the "policeman" role was required, but as the organization matures, its quality culture can also evolve an appropriate balance of the mentor/helper perspective.

> **INSIGHT**   We all want to trust people. However, even the best people have weaknesses, and therefore we need mechanisms on both traditional and Agile projects to ensure trust is warranted.

7.36 The Power of Criteria to Aid Agility

There exists a powerful *Agility-Enhancing* mechanism that is sprinkled throughout the CMMI model. Unfortunately, far too often this mechanism is underused. Let us set the context for this discussion with a few common scenarios.

During my interviews at GEAR, I heard stories about testing and peer reviews. The two scenarios I will share from GEAR are scenarios I have often heard in traditional development organizations. This kind of information usually emerges when I ask developers what could help them do their job more effectively.

One software developer responded:

> *I know peer reviews are important, but sometimes I just have to make a minor fix to my software. I often work on small projects where I am the only software developer. The company rules require that I get another software developer to peer review my change. Sometimes it's hard to find someone who has the time, and many times that person doesn't know anything about the code I am changing. It just seems like there ought to be some flexibility in the peer review requirements. There are times when I feel the situation doesn't warrant the need for a peer review.*

And a different software engineer made a similar comment with respect to testing, saying:

> *Sometimes I just have to make a small change, but our testing process makes me go all the way back and go through multiple levels of regression testing.*

There should be a way that someone on the project can just say in certain cases this isn't needed. We need more flexibility in our processes.

Let us start with the CMMI model in addressing these comments. First, the Verification Process area of the model does expect you to conduct peer reviews, and to verify selected work products. However, the CMMI does not tell you what you need to peer review and what you need to verify.

SP 1.3 of the Verification Process Area expects you to develop your own verification procedures and criteria.[11]

I want to highlight the word **criteria**. This is the agility-enhancing mechanism.

That word *criteria* is sprinkled throughout the CMMI model. What is the intent when we see this term in the Verification Process Area? The intent is to say to the model user, you need to *think* about what products need to be *verified* and how to best verify them. Ask yourself:

Do all products need to be verified?

If you are reusing a product that has previously been verified, you can reuse that previous verification, and save cost by *not re-verifying it*.[12] The value of reuse can extend beyond just the product development itself.

You must be careful to ensure you *verify* and *validate* your product in the current environment. This is part of what you should be *thinking through* when planning for Verification and Validation. The CMMI model suggests that by establishing *criteria*, you can make *better decisions* when it comes to Verification (and Validation).

The CMMI model does not tell you *when* you need to apply your *Verification criteria*. This is left up to each organization to decide. You can have *criteria* to help you *decide* when testing should be performed, and *criteria* to help you *decide* when a peer review should be held.

You can allow the criteria to be applied at the *start of the project*, at the *start of each increment of the project life cycle*, or it could be *delegated* to a technical lead to apply *just-in-time* at the point when a decision needs to be made in the *middle* of the project.

The degree of flexibility or *agility* on your project is up to each organization to decide based on its business needs, personnel, and culture.

---

11. One could also look at SP 1.1 Select Work Products for Verification as covering criteria of what to verify.

12. This assumes the product will be reused in a similar way and in a similar environment.

Now, let's explore the *ramifications* of these *decisions* by asking a few more questions:

- Is the product mission critical where failure could result in loss of life?
- What are the potential ramifications of a latent defect?
- Do you have verification requirements on the project that the customer has levied?
- Do you have requirements to comply with standards such as DO-178B?[13]
- What maturity is your organization at?
- Can your people apply criteria effectively as intended by the CMMI?

The right answer in your business depends on multiple factors. The CMMI can help by *reminding* you to ask the right questions.

A decision to require a peer review of every line of code change, or go back through multiple levels of testing whenever even a small change is made, should not be based on what you think the CMMI requires. The CMMI only requires that you consider the appropriate factors and decide what is right in your business situation.

Through the use of *criteria*, you can empower those deep in your organization to make *just-in-time decisions*, which can give your organization *great agility*. However, if you take this path, keep the potential *ramifications* in mind as conveyed by the following true story.

7.37 A True Story about the Abuse of Criteria

The use of *criteria* to aid *decision making* is recommended in many cases throughout the CMMI model. If you decide to employ this mechanism to help your organization increase its *agility*, keep the following story in mind.

The Verification Process area expects organizations to *select work products for verification* and to *perform peer reviews*. It leaves the *decision* up to each organization to decide what work products to select and what to peer review. Furthermore, it doesn't dictate *when* you need to make that *decision*.

For years, I have recommended that organizations create *criteria* to help a project leader make more *dynamic "real-time" decisions* with respect to peer

---

13. DO 178B is a development standard required on many projects involving the FAA.

review and/or product verification. I have suggested this because I have often heard frustration regarding *"hard rules"* that don't seem to make sense in certain situations.

What I have suggested is that projects document *criteria* and provide written authority through its project plan to a project leader to make peer review and verification decisions based on that criteria.

While I often recommend this, let me give you a caution. One organization followed my guidance and created the following criteria for when a peer review could be waived:

- Experienced, proven developer
- Low risk change
- Minimal impact to other systems
- Developer working closely with interfacing, dependent personnel

The assigned project leader became busy, and delegated this criteria to his team. When we examined the project later we found that no peer reviews were taking place because all involved were deciding they were experienced, proven developers, their work was low risk, they were working closely with dependent personnel, and there was minimal impact to other systems. There are two lessons here.

First: Project Leaders should **NEVER** delegate such criteria.

Second:

LESSON 7

Criteria can be abused. They can help an organization that desires to increase its agility, but there is responsibility and training that must go along with agility.

CAUTION

Keep this story in mind as you decide whether your organization is ready for the use of *criteria*. Your people need to be ready, too.

The subject of people readiness for *agility* is the primary topic of the DART case study in the next chapter of the book.

7.38 Summary: How CMMI Helps Agile

The following table provides a summary of how CMMI areas discussed in this chapter help Agile.

CMMI Area	How It Helps Agile
Verification (Test, Peer Reviews), SP 1.3, Agile Execution Criteria to aid decisions	On Agile projects, we often make rapid decisions. Rapid decisions can still be made when using CMMI-compliant processes. Documented and trained criteria to aid decision making can improve the quality of those decisions.
Generic Practice 2.9 Objectively Evaluate Adherence, Agile Compliance through well defined "minimums"	Agile projects encourage trust. GP 2.9 of the CMMI supports the development of trust through compliance checks that help us build confidence so we know that trust is warranted.
Generic Practice 2.8 Monitor and Control the Process, Gates	Agile projects encourage trust. GP 2.8 of the CMMI supports the development of trust through monitoring, which helps us build confidence that we know the trust is warranted.
Project Planning, Specific Practice 1.3, Agile Life Cycle Guidelines	Agile projects encourage business people and developers to collaborate. An effective implementation of a defined Project Life Cycle helps the business side and developers communicate more effectively.

7.39 Summary: How Agile Helps CMMI

The following table provides a summary of how Agile approaches discussed in this chapter help the CMMI.

Agile Approach	How It Helps CMMI
Agile approaches promote simplicity. Agile Tailoring Guidelines (Tailor Up) support simplicity.	Traditional tailoring down approaches penalize small projects. Agile tailoring up approaches help us implement the intent of tailoring in the CMMI more effectively.
Agile approaches execute activities in a more integrated way. Thread approach to process development and deployment supports development of more integrated processes.	Thread approach supports training, and continuous process improvement through rapid feedback cycle.

Chapter 8

People Challenges Implementing a "Hybrid" Agile Approach in a CMMI Process Mature Organization

Scenario: You work in a CMMI process mature organization, and believe an Agile approach could help your company. You've talked to your manager and received approval to try a "Hybrid Agile"[1] approach on a new project. Unfortunately, most of your people are unfamiliar with Agile methods. You would like to know the common pitfalls that are likely to be encountered. You would also like to know proven techniques to help your project succeed.

In this case study, we examine the common challenges faced when implementing a "hybrid" Agile approach in a traditional CMMI mature organization. Our focus

---

1. The phrase "Hybrid Agile" refers to a blend of traditional and Agile approaches.

here is to demonstrate how the CMMI can actually help an organization locate its right level of agility. This case study should be of interest to both CMMI- and Agile-knowledgeable people who want to bring more agility to their organization, but are constrained by existing organizational processes and the lack of Agile-knowledgeable people in the organization.

8.1 What You Will Learn in This Chapter

- Why a hybrid Agile approach is commonly used in CMMI process mature organizations moving toward increased agility
- Common risks related to hybrid Agile approaches
- Warning signs to help detect common pitfalls
- Three proven techniques to help traditional organizations successfully implement a "hybrid" Agile approach
- Five examples demonstrating how the CMMI can help implement a "hybrid" Agile approach more effectively
- How management is affected in traditional development organizations by an Agile approach
- How senior management can make a critical difference to the success of an Agile initiative

8.2 Introduction

High-tech industries commonly employ hybrid Agile approaches today. The term "hybrid Agile" means a blend of traditional and Agile techniques[2] [30]. While a hybrid Agile approach might make sense in a traditional CMMI process mature organization, to be effective the consequences of related decisions must be understood.

This chapter presents important challenges faced when a CMMI process mature organization employed a hybrid Scrum/traditional approach[3] [3]. Common pitfalls and related warning signs are highlighted along with recommended techniques proven successful on similar challenges.

---

2. Barry Boehm and Rich Turner discuss hybrid approaches in *Balancing Agility and Discipline*. See Reference.

3. Scrum is a popular Agile method. For more information, see reference.

As previously stated, the CMMI is primarily concerned with "what you must do," rather than "how you do it." But this does not mean you don't need the "how you do it."

In this chapter, we look at three *"how-to"* techniques supporting the intent of specific CMMI practices while also supporting agility. Five specific examples are provided demonstrating how the CMMI could help a hybrid Agile implementation succeed.

8.3 DART Case Study Background

The DART project was a legacy modernization project of a critical business system within a large CMMI process mature high-tech company. A hybrid Scrum/traditional development approach was chosen on the project for multiple reasons. First, a challenging schedule required some degree of process innovation to have any chance of success. Second, a pure Agile approach was not viewed as feasible due to the lack of previous experience with Agile methods and the requirement to follow existing company traditional processes.

DART employed an incremental life-cycle approach where every thirty days, a product delivery was made to a lab environment where customer personnel were trained in the use of the product and encouraged to provide feedback directly to the development team. Frequent *time-boxed*[4] product deliveries were employed to aid customer buy-in and training. DART could not deliver incrementally to a deployed site due to tight coupling of subsystems and criticality of complete system functionality to the business operation.

Senior management had presented the DART team with a challenging six-month schedule target. Using a mix of traditional and Agile techniques, the team and its customer developed a plan that could potentially achieve the aggressive target schedule. I initially worked on the DART team as a senior systems engineer, and as a deputy to the program manager consulting on the *Agile* aspects of the project.

For the first four months of the planned six-month project, DART hit every milestone. With each lab session, the customer's confidence in the new system grew. Team enthusiasm continually increased as we approached the

---

4. "Time-boxing" is a common Agile technique that means we always deliver on schedule. We reduce delivered functionality, if necessary.

planned full deployment target date. Unfortunately, the project ended up taking an additional six months to complete the work and fully deploy the modernized system. Although the customer was pleased with the fully deployed final product, differing views existed among management with respect to how well the project had been managed.

8.4 DART Post-Mortem Project Assessment

Most DART team members believed that the frequent time-boxed deliveries and direct interaction between developers and customer personnel were critical to the eventual full acceptance of the final system by the customer. Many team members indicated a belief four months into the project that they might actually hit the aggressive six-month target. This leads to a question in assessing the effectiveness of the process employed:

> *How could the team members who were so close to the project have missed in assessing the true project status by so much?*

After the project, I gave this question considerable thought and concluded the answer involved multiple factors related to two on-going project activities:

- How the team identified its priority work for each thirty-day increment
- How the team assessed the overall status and reported that status to senior management

The remainder of this chapter focuses on the related *factors*, how those factors influenced project *decisions*, and what could have been done differently to achieve a more successful project outcome.

8.5 More Case Study Background

This was the first *Agile* project for Al who was one of the key programmers on DART. Like other team members, Al had read about Agile methods and was enthusiastic about the opportunity to try them. Mike, one of the DART customers, had an office down the hall from Al. Al knew from what he had read about Agile methods that collaboration with the customer was important. However, Al wasn't prepared for the collaborative challenge he faced on DART.

After the first lab session, Mike began stopping by Al's office. At first, this seemed fine to Al. Al would show Mike the latest product functionality, but Al wasn't sure how to respond when Mike would ask for a change Al believed was beyond the requirements.

Knowing that customer collaboration was a significant Agile practice, and because Al wanted the project to be successful, he began staying late at night and coming in on weekends to work on the new requests from Mike.

This situation is not uncommon when an Agile approach is first introduced in a traditional development organization where developers have not previously experienced a close working relationship with a customer. It should be noted that an experienced Agile coach should have prevented this type of scope creep from occurring. Why this didn't occur is explained as we move forward in this case study.

It is not uncommon when developers have not previously worked closely with a customer to misunderstand "collaboration" as "giving the customer whatever he or she asks for."

CAUTION

Watch for a common sign of misunderstanding collaboration, such as working long hours to please a closely interacting customer.

Effective collaboration requires both sides to have an honest dialogue and to be willing and able to give in a reasonably balanced way. When an *Agile* approach is appropriately implemented, work is planned and executed at a *sustainable* pace. Let us discuss the way an Agile approach is supposed to work with respect to task management, and how we got off track on DART.

8.6 The Way an Agile Approach Should Work with Respect to Task Management

With Scrum (a popular Agile method), there are two important task management items referred to as the Product Backlog and the Sprint Backlog.[5]

---

5. A Sprint in Scrum is the term used for an increment of development that is typically time-boxed to be thirty days long.

The Product Backlog is:

> *A prioritized list of project requirements with estimated times to turn them into completed product functionality[6] [3].*

The Sprint Backlog is:

> *A list of tasks that defines a team's work for a sprint. Each task identifies those responsible for doing the work and the estimated amount of work remaining on the task on any given day during the sprint.*

Both the Product Backlog and the Sprint Backlog should be visible to the entire team at all times. Anyone can add a potential task to the Product Backlog, but it doesn't get to the Sprint Backlog until it is agreed to and planned at a planning session that occurs before each thirty-day sprint. Once we agree to the Sprint Backlog, the work for the next thirty days is fixed. Team members can add new items during the Sprint, but no one from outside the team can add to the Sprint Backlog during the Sprint itself (e.g., customers cannot add to the Sprint backlog during the Sprint itself).

Scrum purists follow these rules in a disciplined way, for good reason. They are proven to work to help a team achieve an agreed-to schedule. Wavering from the rules often leads to trouble like what we saw with Al and Mike. This is an example where using a "hybrid" Agile/traditional approach can lead to trouble if the intent of each practice is not understood, especially those Agile practices you don't follow rigorously. Refer to Table 8-1 at the end of this chapter for key Scrum practices/terminology.

8.7 Mistakes Made on DART

The first mistake made on DART was not keeping all the current work visible to the full team and discussing it each day as a team. Failing to keep all the current work visible is an easy thing to do when you are working closely with a customer who is constantly making requests for new functionality.

This is not an uncommon problem when organizations try to blend traditional task management with an Agile approach. In many traditional organizations, the tasking manager doesn't get too close to the work at the day-to-day level. The problem with this is that with Agile approaches you

---

6. See reference for more information about Scrum-specific rules and terminology.

need closer supervision, especially toward the beginning of a new Agile effort where the customer is interacting on a daily basis.

One of the specific practices intended to help manage the current list of work is the daily go-round where all team members discuss briefly what they have accomplished since the last meeting, what they plan to work on during the next day, and any obstacles they might be facing. The entire team is responsible for the team's work, and members are expected to challenge other team members who might be working issues that have not been agreed to.

This practice motivates the team to stay on schedule. The DART team should have been challenging Al, but they didn't feel there was anything wrong because they thought Al was just "collaborating" with the customer. The DART team members thought Al was doing the right thing because the customer was happy. The team members, all being new to Scrum, had not fully understood their responsibilities as Scrum team members.

LESSON 1

Don't expect your people to know how to collaborate if they haven't worked closely with a customer before. Plan to spend time training them in the practical issues related to "how to collaborate."[7]

8.8 Why Didn't We Prepare Al for His Collaboration Challenges?

To understand why we didn't prepare Al for his collaboration challenges, we need to talk more about DART and the responsibilities of Scrum team members. When using Scrum, work tasks are placed on a visible list. Scrum was originally developed for software projects. I recommended to DART that we tailor this to address all project work.

Even if you include systems products, documentation, and software, some work tasks never make it to an Agile team list. The typical tasks found on a Product or Sprint backlog are tasks such as code, design, test, and documentation.

---

7. A technique to aid collaboration is provided later in this chapter.

> **INSIGHT**   "Less visible" supporting and leadership tasks might be at increased risk on Agile projects, and their need might be greater and/or required on shorter cycles.

Examples of what I mean by "less visible" supporting tasks include analysis leading to a design decision, or analysis leading to making a priority work decision. Examples of "less visible" leadership tasks include monitoring, guiding, and assessing the Product Backlog at the start of each new increment. Now let me give you more information related to how this affected our preparing Al.

8.9 More on the DART Case Study

On the DART project, we had made an initial high-level assessment concerning two subsystems. We originally assessed them as low risk because we thought they would be easy to do. I knew we hadn't done the *detailed analysis* yet to be confident in that assessment. Because of the initial analysis, they had been placed on the Product Backlog as lower priority.

We would eventually have to do more detailed analysis on these systems. Unfortunately Al—who would have been the best person to do this analysis—was also one of our best Java programmers and was doing a great job keeping us on the six-month aggressive schedule by working closely with the customer.

> **INSIGHT**   The effort of actually analyzing the Product Backlog and determining which tasks are most important for the next increment takes time and can be critical to the overall project success.

Because he was getting so much done, I decided to leave Al with his head down working. I didn't involve him in the assessment of the work still to be done on the Backlog because that would have jeopardized our vision to hit the aggressive six-month schedule goal. Al's DART teammates also thought Al was doing a great job. Everyone thought the project was going great, including the customer. But the fact was that Mike wasn't the only customer representative—he just happened to be the one who was communicating with us most frequently during the early phase of the project.

> **CAUTION**
>
> Be aware of your full customer community, even if some are less vocal and less involved early in the project.

As it turned out, the two subsystems that had been deferred ended up being more complex than we thought, driving the schedule six months beyond our target.

> **LESSON 2**
>
> Pay attention to all the work you commit to—including work that is viewed as low priority, especially if it has not yet been fully analyzed.

I now want to present the three "how-to" techniques supporting the intent of specific CMMI practices while also supporting agility. I will also explain more about how these techniques could have helped us on DART. In the second technique, you will hear more specific information related to why we failed to adequately prepare Al for his Agile collaboration challenge and how this technique could have helped.

8.10 Technique 1: 10 Percent Rule

Sutherland 10 Percent Rule

Jeff Sutherland, one of the co-founders of Scrum, has stated when training ScrumMasters that Scrum teams should allocate about 10 percent of project people's time for the analysis and development of the next Sprint Backlog. In hindsight, if I had followed this rule, I now believe we might have had a more successful project outcome on DART. Plan to involve your development team in each incremental planning session, since they have some of the best information regarding prioritization based on their current increment work.[8]

Why didn't I do what I should have done and reprioritize work to free up some of Al's time to analyze these subsystems earlier? There were multiple *factors* influencing my *decision*. I believe now if I had followed the 10 percent rule, the result could have been completing the overall project in less time.

---

8. Refer to the story about "Diddling in DOORs" in the LACM case study in Chapter 3. This experience learned at LACM contains a similar message to Jeff Sutherland's 10 percent rule.

Part of the reason I didn't do this was the pressure I felt to keep one highly visible customer (Mike) happy, and the knowledge that if I pulled Al it probably would have meant we couldn't hit the six-month schedule. This was one decision that, if I had made it differently, could have influenced the project outcome more positively. In the next technique, you will learn about other factors that affected decisions that could have been made differently, leading to more effective project outcomes.

LESSON 3

Always plan for and involve development team members in the next increment of planning and analysis. Always drive to reduce risk of any work you have committed to on the Product Backlog.

8.11 Technique 2: Scope and Collaboration Management

Scope Document and Managing Collaboration

I have raised the issue of training your team how to collaborate. How do you do this? On hybrid Agile projects, I have found that developing and using what I refer to as a Scope document can help with collaboration.

A Scope document serves a purpose similar to the Scrum Product Backlog with one main distinction: It doesn't grow during the project. With "pure" Scrum, anyone can add a new task to the Product Backlog. The problem with this is that if you have a fixed budget and a commitment to deliver full functionality by a given date, you can't allow the baseline requirements to grow without getting budget and/or schedule compensation.

With Agile approaches we don't do all the requirements work up front. We continue to collaborate to ensure we are getting the best value for the customer throughout the project. However, we need to have a way to bound the work, if we are to manage it to a fixed schedule. This is the intent of the Scope document.[9] The Scope document provides a reference for collaboration. For a Scope document to be effective, it must also be used by everyone who is collaborating. This includes both customer and development personnel.

---

9. Initial requirements envisioning and architecture envisioning are followed by roughly 85 percent of agile teams (http://www.ambysoft.com/surveys/projectInitiation2009.html).

Initially, I was in a systems engineering role on DART and one of my tasks was to develop the Scope document. I did this by developing System-Level Use Cases, then having those reviewed and agreed to by the major stakeholders on the project.

On both Agile and traditional projects, one of the most difficult tasks is eliciting the real needs and expectations of customers and getting them agreed to by major stakeholders.[10] By building a Scope document and actively engaging the key stakeholders early in a review and approval cycle, a basis for project success is established.

So the question remains:

> *Since I developed this key document, and since the stakeholders agreed to it, why did we run into trouble with Al doing extra work based on his collaboration with Mike?*

The answer is that while I developed the Scope document and major stakeholders agreed to it, I didn't train Al, or Mike, how to use it.

> *I didn't get to* all *the stakeholders (both up and down the chain).*[11]

How could I fail to meet this responsibility?

8.12 More on the DART Case Study

Besides being responsible for the Scope document on DART, I helped the Project Manager plan the project, and was responsible for developing the test procedures. The Project Manager I was working closely with, Carl, unexpectedly resigned one month into the project. To maintain the aggressive schedule I accepted the additional responsibility of Project Manager, as well as fulfilling my Systems Engineering responsibilities. In taking on the Project Manager role along with the Systems Engineering tasks, every day I had to make *priority decisions* as to where to spend my time.

---

10. This relates directly to Specific Practice 1.1 of the Requirements Development (RD) Process Area of the CMMI model: "Elicit stakeholder needs, expectations, constraints, and interfaces for all phases of the product lifecycle."

11. Generic Practice 2.7 of the CMMI Model, "Identify and involve the relevant stakeholders of the [*fill in relevant process area*] process as planned," provides a continual *reminder* of the need to involve *all* stakeholders.

8.13 How Did I Make the Decision Each Day on What Was Most Important?

To help answer this question, there is an equally important question I should ask first:

> *How did I decide in the first place that I had enough time to take on the Project Manager's role and still meet my commitments as a Senior Systems Engineer on the project?*

A few years ago at the Systems and Software Technology Conference (SSTC), I listened to Judy Bamberger describe five metrics each of us should be collecting and using.[12] These metrics can help anyone decide if he or she can meet a commitment:

1. Task pieces: Do I know all the pieces I must touch?
2. Effort: How long does it take me to do each piece?
3. Availability: What is my availability?
4. Quality: What are my average defects per piece?
5. Effectiveness: Do I meet my commitments?

By asking yourself these simple questions, you can reach a reasonable evaluation of whether you can take on the work. However, this is only true if you first know all the *pieces* to the task. In my case, what were all the *pieces* of the Project Manager's task?

Carl, who was the Project Manager, had been spending a great deal of time working with high-level customer representatives on the high-level requirements. He was working closely with Mike's boss, seeking agreement on the vision of the end product. He was also working with Al, mentoring him daily,[13] and doing some of those "less visible" tasks including *analysis* of lower-priority tasks still on the Product Backlog.

When I assessed my available time to take on the added commitment of the Project Manager's role, I now know I *underestimated* the effort involved in the "less visible" tasks Carl was doing.

---

12. SSTC, 2005 Judy Bamberger, "Five Metrics Each One of Us Should Be Collecting and Using."

13. The reason Carl was doing this mentoring was because he had the skills, including Java programming, that Al needed.

8.14 More about "Less Visible" Tasks That Require More Time on Agile Projects

With any role comes a list of responsibilities, and some of those have more *visibility* and are viewed as more important than others. We discussed the importance of roles and responsibilities earlier in Chapters 5 and 6.[14] Examples of critical "less visible" tasks that Carl was doing include *monitoring* the tasks of others on the project, providing *guidance*, and *reprioritizing* tasks as necessary.

Now here is where the problem comes in:

"Guidance," "monitoring," and "reprioritizing" are critical responsibilities, but the results of these critical activities are "less visible" than missing a schedule deadline with a *tangible product* like the Requirements Specification or a delivered increment of working code.

"Guidance" and "monitoring" are two examples of critical tasks that often require more time, particularly when first moving in the Agile direction. In this situation, we are often asking people to take on new responsibilities and help teammates. This also means people might require more guidance in assessing their own commitments before they commit to helping others with additional work.

For example, on Agile projects we might be asking people to interact more frequently and more closely with customers, as was the case with Al. These could be external or internal customers. From the internal side it could be a Software Engineer working more closely with a Systems Engineer.[15]

More guidance might be required for handling certain situations that arise such as when people can make a *decision* on their own and under what circumstances they should *raise it up* and wait for help from more senior personnel.

"Guidance" and "monitoring" unfortunately are critical tasks but they are "less visible" tasks than those associated with a product or hard milestone schedule. Therefore, these tasks don't always get the priority and attention they deserve.

---

14. Recall from previous discussions that we are reminded of the importance of roles and responsibilities by GP 2.3 and GP 2.4 of the CMMI model.

15. Refer to the "Diddling in DOORs" story in Chapter 3 for a related example.

CAUTION

Don't get caught in the common pitfall of underestimating the less visible work, especially on a new Agile effort. Anticipate increased mentoring needs to help people who are being asked to take on new collaboration responsibilities.

8.15 More about the Importance of Using a Scope Document

The Scope document should have been used by Al during discussions with Mike in assessing any new requests. Al also should have been checking to make sure any requests were on the current Sprint Backlog before agreeing to work on them. When we built the Sprint Backlog at the start of each thirty-day sprint, we used the Scope document to allocate Use Cases from this document to the current sprint. I failed to take the time to train Al in the importance of both the Scope document and the use of the current Sprint Backlog.

I developed the Scope document, and established higher-level customer representatives' approval, but failed to flow it down to developers like Al, or communicate to Mike's boss, on the customer side, that he needed to flow it down to Mike. These are all critical responsibilities that need to receive greater attention as organizations move toward their appropriate level of agility.

CAUTION

Don't get caught in the common trap of building a Scope document, but failing to "flow it down" to those in the trenches who are doing the real collaborating.

No one was checking to make sure we were involving *all* the stakeholders on the customer side and down deep into the organization. What makes this so costly is that it *lacks visibility*, which allows it to impact your program a *little at a time* until all of a sudden you realize the impact is much greater than you ever imagined.

Let us suppose I had done my job training Al how to collaborate using the Scope document, and how to work in a more disciplined way ensuring ongoing work agreed with the current Sprint Backlog. Some who were on this project have argued if we had done this, we might never have gotten DART deployed at all.

The reason they have argued this is that if we had strictly following the Scrum rules, Mike might have gotten upset and might not have ended up being such a strong customer advocate when it came time for full system deployment. While this is

...Glance Forward...

In the next chapter on the Golf Improvement Project, we will see another example of getting into trouble so gradually that it becomes difficult to notice until it is too late to do anything about it. We will also learn techniques that can help you avoid this common trap.

possibly true, there are other options we could have employed to help keep the customer happy and help us manage our work more effectively at the same time. This brings us to Technique 3: Push-Pull.

8.16 Technique 3: Push-Pull

Use Push-Pull to Aid Task Management Decisions

The Scope document is not intended to curtail agility and collaboration, but rather encourage it while creating criteria to help with task management decisions. Let me give an example of what I mean by task management decisions.

Some have claimed that you can't use Agile approaches and a traditional Earned Value Management System (EVMS) together. This is based on the misbelief that when using an EVMS, you can't move work once you have initially planned it. In reality, with all EVMSs, you can control the level of task detail you put in the system, which is key to effectively using an EVMS and an Agile approach together.

The point is not to plan too much detail too far out and to describe the work you will do for each increment in a way that allows implementation flexibility. By creating a system that allows a level of "push-pull" flexibility of tasks when it comes to more detailed decisions, you allow yourself room for customer collaboration and effective decision making within the constraints of the established schedule and budget. Training people who set up the EVMS in how to develop work packages that do not overly constrain the collaborative process is crucial.

Building a system to support our collaborative approach gives us the flexibility to pull work in, if the customer decides something is more important, as long as we can find other work that we can push off of equal value—and as long as it is within the overall agreed to project scope.

> **INSIGHT**   You can use a formal Earned Value Management System (EVMS) effectively with an Agile approach, but to do so requires proper planning, guidance, rules, and training.

> **CAUTION**
>
> Because it is easy to abuse flexibility, clear rules and training must be established before using an EVMS with the Push-Pull technique. Push-Pull must be closely monitored, especially when first implemented.

Unfortunately, too often when Agile approaches are first introduced in organizations (often in a "stealth" way), the consequences on the financial side of the house are not well understood, and therefore the required planning and ground rules are not set up appropriately.

Example rules that need to be clear include: If you push off work, never take earned value for that work unless you pull in work of equal earned value that is within the scope of the baseline effort. Also never take earned value unless the work is done and value is actually earned. These are actually nothing special to "Agile" practices. They are fundamental earned value principles. However, sometimes when we move in an Agile direction it becomes more tempting to "break the fundamental rules."

Pause, Reflect, and Glance Forward

Have you observed within your organization any of the common repeating specific weaknesses discussed?

- Misunderstanding collaboration as working long hours to please a closely interacting customer?

- Failing to involve the full team in assessing work left to do?

- Pushing work out without properly accounting for it on the schedule?

In Part V, you will see criteria to help locate your own repeating specific weaknesses.

A mistake we made on DART was that work Al was doing wasn't pulled forward from the agreed-to Scope document. He was pulling it forward directly from discussions with the customer. This led to effort that was not approved, and partially contributed to the elongated schedule.

> **LESSON 4**
>
> The Push-Pull technique can help your Agile effort succeed, while allowing you to manage cost and schedule even within a formal EVMS. However, you have to plan for it, set up appropriate rules, and train your people to follow the rules.

8.17 How Can the CMMI Help Us Implement an Effective Hybrid Agile Approach?

Saying the CMMI can help a Hybrid Agile approach succeed might surprise some people. What I mean is that by using the CMMI and proven Agile practices together you can develop and deploy effectively the right level of Agile process assets to help your people and organization succeed.

Agile practices are actually disciplined practices. Many organizations fail during an Agile implementation because they haven't trained their people how to execute these practices consistently. The CMMI concept of institutionalization and related generic practices within the model can help Agile projects succeed by providing project personnel with the training and process aids to help effectively execute their agreed-to Agile approach.

Following are five examples that demonstrate how specific CMMI practices could have helped us effectively implement our hybrid Agile approach, and potentially deploy the modernized DART system in less time.

8.18 Examples of CMMI Helping Agile Teams Self-Manage

CMMI Helping Agile Estimate Tasks and Assess Commitments

Agile approaches promote accountability of individuals for task estimates and schedule commitments. They also encourage teamwork. However, to be an effective team member is not always easy. Teamwork requires individual team members to be able to assess how long it will take them to complete their task so they can accurately determine when they will be able to take on more work to help other team members.

On DART, I assessed my Systems Engineering commitments to determine if I could take on the additional Project Manager responsibilities. Looking back, I believe I made the right choice in offering to help. However, I could have made better choices in assessing priorities and reporting impacts. I allowed myself to get caught up in the emotion of the project rather than use objective data to make effective decisions.

How could the CMMI have helped me? Generic Practice 2.3 of the CMMI states:

> *Provide adequate resources for performing the [fill in process area]…*

Generic Practice 2.4 states:

> *Assign responsibility and authority for performing the process…*

So how does one determine "adequate resources"?

Many organizations that use the CMMI address these practices by developing well-defined and documented roles and responsibilities. Individuals are then assigned roles as part of the project planning process.

If I had reviewed a documented list of responsibilities for the Project Manager role—especially a list that would have given me all the tasks Carl was doing on the project—it would have helped me more objectively assess daily priorities and tasks that might have been impacted.

To assess in an objective way how long a task will take, you need to know all the pieces of the task. You need to know the attributes of the task. The CMMI Project Planning Specific Practice 1.2 states:

> *Establish and maintain estimates of the attributes of the work products and tasks.*

I now think of a list of responsibilities as attributes of a task.

Often we don't think this way. However, if something is a responsibility, it usually takes effort to carry it out, and therefore it is an attribute to consider during an estimation process. A CMMI guideline tip states:

> *Consider providing guidelines on how to estimate the difficulty or complexity of a task to improve estimation accuracy…*

Judy Bamberger's five metrics would fit well as an example of such a guideline along with documented roles and responsibilities. Agile practices encourage bottom-up team estimates. The CMMI can help by reminding us to provide documented aids that can help us more accurately estimate tasks by considering all the "attributes" of the task.

This is an example how the CMMI can help our people execute Agile practices more effectively, helping us become better estimators of our work. In the next example, we look at how the CMMI can help us prioritize our work.

CMMI Helping Agile Prioritize

Agile practices encourage the team to focus on high-risk work early, maximizing value to the customer. Risk is based on uncertainty, which is reduced as planned mitigation steps are executed and knowledge is gained. Organizations that use the CMMI Risk Management Process Area develop lists of typical sources of risk to help their people think through and identify the most likely risk areas within their work domain.

Using the CMMI helps organizations institutionalize the process of reviewing risk mitigation plans regularly. Mitigation means to lessen the risk. When organizations first move in the Agile direction, decisions on what work to do early, and what to defer, can be difficult. The wrong decision can inadvertently increase rather than decrease risk. On DART, we deferred work because we thought it was low risk. That work should have been analyzed earlier to reduce uncertainty. This ultimately led to a schedule slip.

How could the CMMI have helped us make a better decision on DART? Using a defined Risk Management Process with guidelines is one way. Other CMMI helpful areas for prioritizing work can be found in the Project Planning Process Area. CMMI Project Planning Process Area, SP 2.1 states:

Establish and maintain the project's budget and schedule.

Traditionally, organizations execute the bulk of the planning activity up front. Nothing in the CMMI requires this. In fact, a related tip in CMMI guidelines book says:

The use of Agile software methods is an important variation. Agile software methods use user or customer feedback in one phase to drive what takes place in the next.

The CMMI also encourages documenting schedule guidelines and involving relevant stakeholders in all activities. Jeff Sutherland's 10 percent rule is an example of a practical guideline for involving relevant people in the next increment planning activity to determine the priority work that should be taking place.

If I had involved Al earlier in the incremental planning to analyze those two deferred subsystems, there is a good chance we would have recognized the added risk in these systems and raised their priority earlier. This would have given us more time to work this issue, by possibly acquiring additional resources, which in turn could have led us to more accurate project reporting earlier with a better overall project outcome.

CMMI Helping Agile Manage Scope

While the team members understood the value of managing a Product Backlog and a Sprint Backlog, we had trouble keeping the real work we were doing aligned with these lists. This was at least partially caused by not training all the team players, including Al and Mike, in the importance of the Backlogs and how their collaboration activities should have been conducted.

We developed the Scope document to help us manage the overall project requirements, but we failed to train the team members how to use it effectively to bound their real work.

The CMMI contains a number of areas that could have helped us with this challenge. First, the Requirements Development Process Area, SP 1.1 states:

> *Elicit stakeholder needs, expectations, constraints...*

We did implement part of this practice through the Scope document, but we fell short with respect to Generic Practice 2.5, which states:

> *Train the people performing or supporting the requirements development process as needed.*

This should have included Al and Mike because their collaboration activities were a part of the requirements development process we were following. We could have addressed this training need by taking the time to walk through the Scope document with Mike and Al.

> **INSIGHT**   Nothing in the CMMI says that training can't be informal and just-in-time. This is often the most effective kind of training, especially when first introducing an Agile approach in a traditional organization.

A related CMMI practice GP 2.7 states:

> *Identify and involve the relevant stakeholders of the requirements development process as planned.*

While we did involve high-level stakeholders, getting them to sign off on the Scope document, we failed to flow the requirements down to involve the people in the trenches.

This is a common weakness I have observed in many organizations and is one of the primary fears management often expresses about Agile approaches—that is, the fear of lost control. By using the CMMI at GEAR, we were able to address this weakness by developing a stakeholder matrix. The matrix was managed at the organizational level to help the company provide the added focus it needed to ensure they were involving the right people at the right time. Project work was bounded by the agreed-to scope. A simple stakeholder matrix could have also helped me as a reminder on DART to involve Al and Mike at the right time.

CMMI Helping Agile Assess Progress

The CMMI does not require a formal Earned Value Management Systems (EVMS), but many large CMMI process mature organizations use them. Some believe the following myth:

> **MYTH**   You can't use a formal Earned Value Management System when using an Agile approach.

The mistake too often made that leads people to believe this myth is setting up work packages and guidelines assuming a traditional waterfall development approach. You can use a formal EVMS with an Agile approach as long as you set up your work packages to agree with the actual work you are planning to do.

> **LESSON 5**
>
> Since those involved on the finance side of organizations often lack experience with Agile approaches, developing guidelines for use of an EVMS when using an Agile approach can help. I recommend such guidelines be developed with Engineering and Finance organizations working collaboratively.

The CMMI Project Monitor and Control process area, SP 1.1 states:

Monitor the actual values of the project planning parameters…

SP 2.1 states:

Collect and analyze the issues and determine the corrective actions…

The CMMI doesn't dictate how to perform these practices. You can provide the guidelines that fit how you monitor your plan and take appropriate corrective action.

LESSON 6

Example finance guidelines for an Agile approach could include level of detail guidance for developing work packages, guidelines in how to plan deferred work, guidelines in planning for evolving requirements, and guidelines in how to use the Push-Pull technique. Guidelines could also include cautions against locking in details for an increment you have not yet planned, and cautions with respect to common misapplications of earned value when using a Push-Pull task technique. Engineering and Finance must collaborate for these guidelines to take hold.

The CMMI does not give you the "how-to" answers for your progress reporting or earned value management system. It does, however, remind us that it is a good practice to define the rules and provide guidelines and training so whatever system you select is used consistently with the life cycle you have chosen for your project. That life cycle can be traditional or Agile. The CMMI leaves that decision up to each company based on what is right for your business.

CMMI Helping Agile Through "Agile Training Scenarios"

Throughout the CMMI framework, the phrase, "establish and maintain" is employed. This phrase's meaning includes the idea of "document and use." However, to use an artifact appropriately means people must be trained in how to use it. Generic Practice 2.5 states:

Train the people performing … as needed.

The CMMI doesn't tell you what form this training needs to take. At LACM (Chapter 2), as the organization continued to align its processes by building streamlined workflows based on what the people really do, they were also streamlining their training by creating what I refer to as just-in-time "Agile Training Scenarios."

Traditional training has often been provided through multiday fire-hose courses that tend to leave the student overwhelmed by the end of the course. Often, not everything in the course turns out to be information the student really needs to know to be effective in doing his or her job. As a result, by the time they need to perform a certain activity, often they have forgotten where they learned it, how to do it, and where to return to refresh themselves on it. What I hear in gap analysis interviews is that people need a quick reference to help them do certain activities right when they need to do them. It was phrased by one client:

Just tell me what I need to know to do my job.

> **LESSON 7**
>
> By breaking up training into "scenarios," each oriented toward a specific role or activity, and making this training available online, students can access and refresh themselves on specific details just when they need it.

Initially I observed this form of training in Agile organizations focused primarily on tool usage. I now find it is growing in interest and use across a broader range of organizations. It is being extended beyond just tool use to include snippets of related principles and rationale along with "how-to" tool examples.

> **CAUTION**
>
> If you start to move your training in the "Agile Scenario" direction, be aware that focusing training just on what people need to know to do their job should not be misconstrued to mean that they don't also need to be concerned about when to involve others. Being aware of interfaces and dependencies involving other stakeholders is part of everyone's job.

While Agile practices are practical and proven in the trenches, the practices themselves fail to address the needs of an organization to ensure it has a staff of personnel trained in the right skills to execute those practices. The CMMI does not give you the training you need, but reminds us of the importance of training. It is a reference to help guide you to the right training answers for your organization.

8.19 How Is Management Affected by an Agile Approach?

Many of the Agile practices we have been discussing in this chapter lead to increased visibility of issues and risks earlier in a project. When uncertainty is allowed to exist late into a project, we increase the chances of significant schedule delays because we have less time to respond with effective mitigation and fewer options. The DART schedule doubled from six months to twelve months partly because we allowed work that was beyond the agreed-to scope to occur early, and because we allowed uncertainty to persist late into the project.

Techniques such as bottom-up estimation by team members, working high-risk areas early, and conducting more analysis of planned future work all tend to reduce uncertainty, but also tend to raise more issues and risks sooner in the project. The good side of identifying issues and risks early is that we have more time to make corrections and get the program on track. By making frequent corrections to the plan, we minimize the risk of the plan getting too far off track. This leads to an important question:

> *How is a manager going to respond when he or she sees more issues and risks raised early?*

For Agile to take hold, it requires a culture of trust, but not blind trust. As one senior manager at BOND put it:

> *I expect my people to bring me problems early, but not to drop them on my doorstep. I expect them to bring solutions, too.*

I have taken away a few important messages from my experiences watching Agile organizations grow increasingly CMMI mature, and watching CMMI mature organizations increase their agility. First, effective Senior Managers in organizations that succeed with agility let their people know that they expect to hear about issues and risks early. They also let them know they expect to hear about the actions that are being taken to address the issues and risk being raised.

There is an important message here for project leaders preparing for discussions with Senior Management.

LESSON 8

Raise up the issues and risks early, but bring your action plans to address them.

You don't need to have every answer, but you do need to show you have thought through the issues and risks you are facing and have mitigation plans in place as well as contingency plans, if appropriate, in case your mitigation fails. The message to project leaders is bring the real status—but also bring your planned solutions.

For Senior Managers there is also an important related message:

> **LESSON 9**
>
> Don't shoot the messenger. No one likes to be beaten up for telling the truth and doing his or her job.

Why Did We Miss Our Real Schedule Assessment by So Much on DART?

I believe the reason was that we all wanted to believe we could do this job in six months. The team was starting to believe it, and I didn't want to be the bad guy and slow momentum and burst the bubble. Therefore—consciously or unconsciously—I did not want to take the time to look at those two subsystems on the Product Backlog. It was easier to just keep believing our original assessment.

If I had changed Al's priorities to spend a little time on this analysis earlier, I knew our immediate milestone would have been jeopardized. Therefore, I didn't assign the proper priority tasks to do the analysis we needed to do when we needed to do it.

> **LESSON 10**
>
> When using Agile techniques, one must constantly reassess the backlog of work and reprioritize that work to make sure you are working the critical issues and reducing risk.

Tom Demarco and Tim Lister wrote a risk management book in 2003 entitled, *Waltzing with Bears* [31]. There is a quote on the back cover of the book I now realize I fell victim to on DART.

> **Demarco/Lister LESSON 11**
>
> "By ignoring the threat of negative outcomes—in the name of positive thinking or a can-do attitude—software managers drive their organizations into the ground."

How Senior Management Can Make a Difference When Moving to Agile

Let me conclude this chapter by sharing a recent story. I was working with a client collecting data for a CMMI appraisal. As I was talking to a systems engineer who was responsible for Requirements Management, I asked him if he had any sample artifacts we could use as evidence that changes to requirements were being appropriately managed.

This relates to Specific Practice 1.3 of the Requirements Management Process Area in the CMMI model. His eyes lit up immediately.

"You bet," he says, *"I've got a great example."*

He then pulls out an extensive Excel spreadsheet showing a list of requirement identifiers and on-going issues being worked against each. It was evident that a great deal of requirements work was under way on the project. This did not surprise me. It is common for projects to work this way. However, when I had previously read their project plan it stated that they were using a strict waterfall development process and that all requirements would be baselined at the system requirements review. There was no plan for evolving requirements work. There was no budget for ongoing requirements collaboration after the system requirements review was completed. So I asked him, as I examined the spreadsheet:

Have you had the system requirements review yet?

He responded:

Oh, yeah, that was completed a few months ago, but we've got way too many issues to baseline the requirements. We'll still be working the requirements until we get to the critical design review.

Then I asked:

Does Senior Management know this?

He replied:

Oh no, they think the requirements are baselined, but I would never tell them what we are doing because they'll just scream at us.

Senior management can make a difference by letting their people know they expect to hear about issues, and by creating an environment where the people feel safe to communicate the truth.

For more information on managing process improvement on the people side, refer to [32, 33, 34].

8.20 The Importance of Personal Safety to Establishing a Culture of Trust

In *Crystal Clear* [4], Alistair Cockburn states:

> *Personal Safety is being able to speak when something is bothering you without fear of reprisal. It may involve telling the manager that the schedule is unrealistic, a colleague that her design needs improvement, or even letting a colleague know that she needs to take a shower more often. Personal Safety is important because with it, the team can discover its weaknesses. Without it, people won't speak up, and the weaknesses will continue to damage the team.*

While the CMMI doesn't directly address personal safety, there are two areas within the model where personal safety could fall within its scope. These areas include Integrated Project Management (IPM) Process Area, SP 1.3, which states:

> *Establish and Maintain the project's work environment based on the organization's work environment standards.*

and Generic Practice 2.5, which states:

> *Train the People.*

Train the People has been included as a generic practice within the model because training is relevant across all process areas and all practices. Too often, however, the training I have observed within organizations has been limited to technical training such as programming skills. The

Pause, Reflect, and Glance Forward

Have you observed any of these common repeating specific weaknesses within your organization?

- Failure to raise key issues in a timely way

- Failure to take timely action

- Communication shutdown between project personnel and Senior Management

In the next chapter, you will see criteria to help identify effective checkpoints to counter your repeating specific weaknesses.

You will also see examples of checkpoints that can help detect and correct common weaknesses before they can damage your project.

scope of the CMMI model is intended to address all training needs relevant to associated practices, including *communication* skills.

In the example just described the systems engineer consciously or unconsciously decided it was safer not to communicate with senior management about the true state of the requirements. It appears to me that this project is likely to slip its schedule. It also appears to me that it is unfortunate that discussions are not happening now between senior management and engineering on *options* to *mitigate the slip* and still provide *best value* to the customer.

Let me say a little more about this recent requirements management story. After it happened, I thought this was an area we could dig into and provide some real process improvement help.

My thought was that we needed to engage a small team that included senior management and engineering and work to align the real requirements process that was going on in the organization with what management was seeing in the periodic briefings. However, when I attempted to do this I was told that:

I "shouldn't push it" and that if I did, "it wouldn't be taken well."

LESSON 12

If people don't feel safe in their work environment, they won't raise valuable issues or provide innovative options.

Clearly, the individual who told me not to "push it" was afraid of something and was not comfortable moving forward to address this real issue in the company.

LESSON 13

It is unfortunate that some of the most valuable potential real improvements in organizations never get addressed due to fear.

One of the reviewers of this book who is a senior manager in a large high-tech company commented on this story, saying he felt that things were "upside down" in most large high-tech organizations. When I asked him what he meant, he said:

We spend all our time trying to make senior management feel comfortable, while the workers are getting more and more uncomfortable. Senior management should be the ones who are uncomfortable, because that is what they are being paid to be—and they should be doing everything they can to make the workers comfortable.

Table 8-1 *Key Scrum Practices/Terminology [3]*

Practice/Terminology	Description
Product Backlog	A prioritized list of project requirements with estimated times to turn them into completed product functionality. Estimates are in days and are more precise the higher an item is in the Product Backlog priority. The list evolves, changing as business conditions or technology changes.
Product Owner	The person responsible for managing the Product Backlog so as to maximize the value of the project. The product owner represents all stakeholders in the project.
ScrumMaster	The person responsible for the Scrum process, its correct implementation, and the maximization of its benefits
Sprint	A time-box typically of about thirty sequential calendar days during which a team works to turn the portion of the Product Backlog it has selected into an increment of potentially shippable product functionality.
Sprint Backlog	A list of tasks that defines a team's work for a Sprint. The list emerges during the Sprint. Each task identifies those responsible for doing the work and the estimated amount of work remaining on the task on any given day during the Sprint.
Sprint Planning Meeting	A one-day meeting time-boxed to eight hours that initiates every Sprint.

Conitnues

Table 8-1 *Key Scrum Practices/Terminology (Continued)*

Practice/Terminology	Description
Sprint Retrospective Meeting	A meeting time-boxed to three hours and facilitated by the ScrumMaster at which the team discusses the just concluded Sprint and determines what could be changed that might make the next Sprint more enjoyable or productive.
Sprint Review Meeting	A meeting time-boxed to four hours at the end of every Sprint at which the team demonstrates to the Product Owner and any other interested parties what it was able to accomplish during the Sprint. Only completed product functionality can be demonstrated.

8.21 Summary: How CMMI Can Help "Hybrid" Agile

The following table provides a summary of how CMMI areas discussed in this chapter help "Hybrid" Agile.

CMMI Area	How It Helps "Hybrid" Agile
Example 1: Project Planning, SP 1.2 Maintain Estimates of Attributes of Work Products	Helps Agile team members with task estimates and meeting commitments
Example 2: Project Planning (PP) Guidelines (e.g., Sutherland 10 percent rule)	Helps Agile team prioritize work
Example 3: Requirements Development (RD) (Scope document)	Helps Agile team members manage scope
Example 4: PMC SP 2.1 Collect and analyze issues (Agile EVMS Guidelines)	Helps Agile team assess progress
Example 5: GP 2.5, Train the People (Agile Scenario training)	Helps team just in time with key skills needed, such as how to collaborate

8.22 Summary: How "Hybrid" Agile Can Help CMMI

The following table provides a summary of how "Hybrid" Agile approaches discussed in this chapter help the CMMI.

"Hybrid" Agile Approach	How It Helps CMMI
Technique 1: Sutherland 10 percent rule	Helps us implement effective Project Planning (PP) on an incremental development project by keeping aware of all commitments, and continually reassessing priorities with latest information
Technique 2: Agile "Scope document" supporting evolving requirements, and training personnel in what real collaboration means	Helps us implement effectively the intent of the Requirements Management and Requirements Development CMMI PAs Helps us implement effective training including "how to" collaborate
Technique 3: Agile "Push-pull" of tasks	Helps us with effective PMC task management—supporting the assignment of the most valuable tasks with best knowledge known today
Focus on personal safely. Providing an environment where people feel safe in speaking up	Helps us achieve the intent of GP 2.10—effective communication with senior management Helps us create an environment where accurate status is reported in a timely way, leading to more effective decisions

PART V

How Real Performance Improvement Is Achieved

This part of the book addresses how real performance improvement is achieved by focusing on how to find repeating specific weaknesses, and what you can do about them.

Chapter 9 is intended to help you think a little "outside the box" by demonstrating the use of an Agile approach together with key CMMI practices to help solve a non-work-related challenge. Through this personal challenge, I draw some nontraditional conclusions—but conclusions backed up by case study data. This case study takes us beyond the fundamentals examining how real "consistent high performance" is best achieved.

In the concluding Chapter 10, we step back, summarize what we have learned from these case studies, and provide an insight into real and consistent performance. This part of the book should be of interest to anyone who is looking for practical and proven techniques to help rise above the competition both professionally and personally.

Chapter 9

Your Repeating Specific Weaknesses: Finding Them, Why They Are Bad, Eliminating Them, and Keeping Them from Coming Back

Scenario: You used to play golf seriously. That was years ago. Unexpectedly, your best friend from your high school golf team has asked you to go with him for a full week of golf to celebrate his sixtieth birthday. You can't say no, but you don't have much time to get your game in shape, and you're still fiercely competitive. What should you do? What options do you have?

9.1 What You Will Learn in This Chapter

- Why focusing on repeating specific weaknesses is critical to rapid process improvement payback
- Four steps to help locate your own repeating specific weaknesses and how to keep them from coming back
- How to integrate short focused practice sessions into a daily routine and why this is critical to real performance improvement
- Perhaps a few techniques to help improve your golf game

9.2 Motivation and Objective

In this chapter, I share a case study where I used an Agile approach and the CMMI together to help solve a personal challenge. My objective here is to help the reader think a little outside the box by seeing how Agile techniques and CMMI practices can be applied in a different domain. Hopefully, you can use this information to help solve your own challenges—professional or personal[1] [35].

Background and Challenge Faced

When I was a teenager, I spent a great deal of time and energy on my golf game because my goal at that point in my life was for professional golf to become my career path. I originally learned the game from my father and a golf professional named Paul Kern. As it turned out, I chose another direction shortly after starting college and didn't play golf at all for over thirty years. When I was about fifty years old, I started playing again when my son asked me to teach him the game. About ten years later in the spring of 2008, a good friend of mine, Bob, who I had played golf with on my high school team, asked if I would go with him and two other friends (Dave and Frank) on a week-long golfing trip. It was planned for the fall of that year in Williamsburg, Virginia (Marriott's Manor Club at Ford's Colony), to celebrate his sixtieth birthday.

I reluctantly agreed, because to enjoy playing that much golf I felt I had to perform at a level of proficiency I was uncertain I could attain given the demands

---

1. An analogy between process improvement and golf is also provided in "CMMI Distilled."

of my time. The challenge I faced was how to get my game to the level I would be comfortable with given the limited time I could devote to it.

9.3 Using the Same Approach I Use to Help Clients

To address this challenge I decided to use the same approach I use when helping clients who come to me with a similar process improvement challenge. My clients desire *real improvement*, but face similar *resource constraints*.

The first step on my golf improvement project was to conduct a gap analysis. I needed to first know the ("as-is") state of my golf game, which would lead me to understand the *gaps* I faced to attain my desired ("to-be") state. Let us start by comparing the approach I used when doing this golf game gap analysis with how I do a gap analysis for clients.

Multiple approaches can be used when doing a gap analysis in an organization. I use the CMMI as reference, which provides engineering and project management best practices. The model can be used for both products and services. My focus when doing a gap analysis is listening to the people in the organization. As they tell me how they do their job, I listen, taking plenty of notes.

I take this approach because I have found that listening to the people who use the processes provides a more accurate assessment of what is really going on in the organization than reading documents that describe how someone thinks the process should be. This approach gives me the best "as-is" process picture from which to build the most effective plan providing *best value* to the customer.

9.4 Determining the "As-Is" State of My Golf Game

So, how did I go about determining the "as-is" state of my golf game? I view my golf skills as a service I provide when playing golf. In this case, I am the one who executes my golf processes. To get the true "as-is" picture of my current golf game, I went out and played a number of rounds of golf, and *took notes* on how I played and how my golf game felt to me after each round. Let me give you some of the words directly from my notes during the first week of this golf improvement project:

Things have been up and down all week. One day my swing feels good. The next day it feels off and the results reflect this. I just don't know what is different from one day to the next.

Examples from my notes taken during the second week of the golf project include:

The second week at the golf course started out badly. I'm playing worse than any time during the previous week. What the heck is going on? My swing feels like it's totally gone. The ball is flying to the left on one shot, and the next shot flies far to the right. I feel like I don't even know how to take the club back. I have no strength. My shots are going very short. Is this because I am 59 years old? Am I just becoming an old man who's losing his distance?

As I was writing these notes during the second week, I remembered something that used to happen to me when I was young. Often, I would only play well for so long, and then something would happen to my swing. I would have no idea what to do. The answer was always to get back to my teacher, Paul Kern. Like magic, he always knew what to do. It would not take more than two shots. We used to stand on the far side of Route 79 in Windsor, New York, where he owned a nine-hole course, and I'd hit balls across the road to the far side of the first hole. I can hear Paul now:

Move that left thumb back to the right. Square up that club-head. Get your body turned around so you're facing the target. Now just let it go. Hit it!

And like magic, the ball would fly straight again right off my club-head every time. Five minutes—that was all it would take. The odd thing was it was always those same three things, but I would never remember on my own. I always had to go back to my teacher.

9.5 The Stages of Mastering a New Skill

Alistair Cockburn, in explaining how Agile software development works [5], has referred to the three stages in Aikido of mastering new skills called Shu, Ha, and Ri.

Shu is the beginner's level where we desire a single procedure that works. Ha is where we detect limitations of that procedure and begin to adapt it to our own circumstances. Ri is the advanced stage where we no longer think about a procedure.

When I was young, I didn't pay close attention to my golf swing. I just went out and played. When things went wrong I knew I could go back to my teacher. At that point, I just wanted someone to tell me what to do. I was clearly in the Shu stage of learning.

Repeating Specific Weaknesses

It was now the third week of the golf improvement project and I was standing on the fairway at Traditions at the Glen in Johnson City, New York (my home golf course), and things were continuing to not go well on this golf improvement project. I recall thinking to myself, "Let's just try a little experiment."

"I'll pretend my old golf teacher Paul Kern is standing right here," I thought to myself. It was late in the evening that night and I was standing in the middle of the thirteenth fairway. There was no one else on the course. I dropped six balls directly opposite the 150-yard marker.

I had been telling my son, Patrick, just a few weeks earlier how frustrated I was with my short distances. I just couldn't figure out why. I hate to admit it, but from 150 yards, I now needed to hit my five iron. I used to hit a five iron 175 to 180 yards. I'm accepting this loss of distance. I know I can't get back everything I once had. I don't need to play like I used to play. I just want to get a little better. I have at this point in my life accepted certain realities of being fifty-nine years old.

I turn the first ball over a couple of times with the face of my five iron to get it to sit up better on the grass. Then I hear my teacher's voice in my head. Pull that left thumb around, square up that club-head, and get your shoulders and feet turned around facing the target. I'm feeling very awkward out in that fairway all alone. The clubface looks to me like it's closed[2] and the ball will go dead left. My left hand feels like it's so strong I'm going to hit a big hook,[3] and my shoulders feel like I'm lined up thirty yards to the right of the green.

Then I hear the voice again, only this time it seems to come from outside my head, "Just hit it!" I give it a rip and the ball flies off my clubface and looks like it's still going up as it passes over the top of the pin dead on line. I fly the green by twenty yards. I'm now standing in the fairway holding onto my

---

2. A "closed" clubface means that the clubface is aligned to the left of the intended line of flight of the golf ball.

3. A "hook" in golf refers to a golf shot where the ball curves from the right to the left for right-handed golfers.

five iron with a single hand and my jaw is almost touching the grass. "I haven't hit a five iron like that in years," I think to myself in total shock. Let's try that again, only I had better make a little change.

I put the five iron in the bag and pull out a six iron and go through the same routine—same result, only this time I only fly the green by ten yards. "I don't believe this," I think to myself as the six iron goes back in the bag and the seven iron comes out. A few minutes later, there are four balls all sitting within four feet of the pin. I'm standing out in the fairway all alone with no one in sight anywhere on the course and start laughing uncontrollably.

> **LESSON 1**
>
> We each have tendencies toward repeating specific weaknesses. Identifying your unique repeating specific weaknesses is the first key step to rapid process improvement payback.

I have found this true for both people and organizations. It might seem hard to believe that after thirty years those same three things still affect my golf swing. I can't explain why, but it's true both in my golf swing and in multiple client organizations. I also believe my repeating specific weaknesses are *unique* to my swing. They are not something I have observed as weaknesses in most golfers learning the game. It is important to understand you can use the process I share, but you can't succeed by using my weaknesses. They are *unique* to me, and of little value to you.

I observe similar patterns in organizations—repeating patterns unique to each organization. For example, at NANO,[4] the pattern of senior management failing to adequately guide the organization at times of crisis, and at GEAR,[5] the failure of engineering to ensure their work remains aligned with the agreed to project management plan. The highest-value priority improvements for GEAR differ from NANO.

I will explain later how you can find your repeating specific weaknesses and how just focusing on these three areas helped to improve my golf game more than I ever imagined possible given the time constraints I faced. First, I want to share what led me to address these weaknesses, and key points I learned related to how those weaknesses would continually find their way back into my game.

---

4. Refer to Chapter 6 for the NANO case study.

5. Refer to Chapter 7 for the GEAR case study.

9.6 A Few Simple, but Critical Steps

What was it after so many years that helped bring these weaknesses to my attention and helped me take the specific actions required for real improvement?

The first thing I did, which was different from what I had done when I played golf as a teenager, and from what I had been doing for the last ten years since my son got me back playing, was to *write down* each night what was happening on the golf course and how I felt about my game. I had *limited time* and I needed to focus my time on the areas that could provide the *greatest value*. The second thing I did was step back and analyze carefully the *objective data* I had gathered. The third thing I did was to take a number of very *specific actions* addressing my now known *specific weaknesses* in a timely fashion. Summarizing those simple, but critical steps:

- Gather objective and specific data
- Analyze the data carefully
- Put plan into action focused on address repeating specific weaknesses in a timely fashion

Note the similarity to the LACM case study discussed in Chapter 3. This might not sound different from what you think you are doing, but the problem in many organizations is that they often never get to the most valuable *specific weaknesses* with *real fixes*. What is most astonishing about this is that this happens even though most people or organizations know exactly what their weaknesses are. Let me illustrate this further.

I will also explain more about my specific swing weaknesses and the actions I took to address them. Let me first say a little more about how I arrived at these actions, and just what I did that turned out to be critical to the success of my golf improvement project.

LESSON 2

By taking notes, stepping back and analyzing the data objectively, I was able to identify and determine the proper specific and timely actions required to remedy my weaknesses.

A Key Observation about Real Performance Improvement

*I believe I always knew I had repeating specific weaknesses, but had never taken the time to determine if there was something I could do about them, **and then do it**.*

What I find interesting is the similarity to what happens when I do a gap analysis. I have found that leaders in organizations are rarely surprised by my findings exposing their most significant weaknesses. In fact, I almost always hear complete agreement with my findings, and hear senior managers tell me they have known what I say is true for a long time.

But why is it that the problems still exist in many organizations when Senior Management has known about them for extended periods of time? In some cases, the reason is that the right fixes appear so straightforward that we end up brushing the issue aside. Sometimes the answer just seems *too simple*. I provide examples of this later in this chapter.

In other cases, the organization might not know how to fix them. Because they don't know how to fix them, they give up without trying and then they just keep coming back. I didn't know how to fix the problem I was facing on the golf project either—that is, until I followed those simple, but critical steps. Let me explain what I did differently to address my golf swing repeating specific weaknesses.

9.7 My Golf Swing Repeating Specific Weaknesses

I had a subconscious tendency over time to allow my left grip to weaken to the point where my thumb was almost resting on the top of the club shaft. The left thumb should be turned so that the V that is formed by your thumb and index finger points over your back shoulder. My V would be pointing at my nose. My second tendency was without thinking to start placing the clubhead behind the ball with an open clubface.[6] Refer to Figure 9-1.

Because this would happen gradually over time, I wouldn't notice it. When I would go to my teacher, he would grab my seven iron and square it up. It always looked to me like the clubface was extremely closed. This would feel very awkward and I would swear it was crazy to hit a ball with a clubface so

---

6. An "open" or "closed" clubface refers to the angle the face of the club makes with respect to the intended line of flight of the ball. "Closed" means that the face of the club is lined up to the left of the target. An "open" clubface means it is lined up to the right of the target.

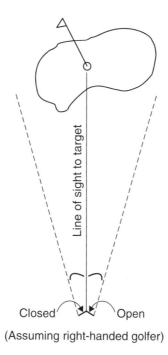

Line of sight to target

Closed   Open

(Assuming right-handed golfer)

Figure 9-1 *Open and Closed Golf Clubface*

closed. The last tendency I had was to gradually open my stance so that my left shoulder would be facing far to the left of the target. The net effect of all this was to cause one of two things to happen when I would swing—pulled shots to the left or sliced shots to the right. Along with these symptoms, I always lost power because the power of my shoulders was moving left in the wrong direction. I was misaligned with the target.

9.8 Repeating Specific Weakness Lessons

This realignment always felt odd. It was all in the setup. My swing was rarely fundamentally bad. Once he got me aligned and said, "Just hit it!" the ball would fly straight and long directly toward the target. However, it would always take a few days for this alignment to begin to feel natural.

> ### LESSON 3
>
> When you've been doing something wrong for an extended period, the right way feels wrong.

This lesson isn't really new to many people. Furthermore, it isn't the most valuable lesson I have found, but it does explain why organizations have trouble changing.

I continued practicing and collecting objective data. One night after reflecting on this data, I was able to change course by taking the *right actions* at the *right time* leading to real improvements. Following are more words from my notes:

I realize I come out here, hit the ball well, start to build some confidence, and then my swing tempo picks up. It happens very gradually. I don't notice it each night. Each night there are imperceptible increases in my swing speed. By the end of the week, I realize I am swinging much faster and my consistency has substantially degraded. The ball is flying left, then right, and I am playing worse than at the beginning of the week.

How to Find Your Repeating Specific Weaknesses...

Use the following criteria to help locate your own repeating specific weaknesses:

- Often first appear as small, almost imperceptible issues, making them easy to ignore

- Tend to occur during times of stress

- Create clear obstacles to achieving objectives

> ### LESSON 4
>
> The way you get to that place where you are doing it wrong often happens so gradually that it becomes difficult to notice until it is too late to correct.

One of the reasons I believe this occurs is because we start to take success for granted and stop paying close attention. The next thing you know we are just "going through the motions" without the proper thought, and

"Going through the motions" does not work.

Let us examine some analogies to business.

9.9 Golf Weaknesses and Analogies to Business

GEAR and NANO revert to behaviors not in their best interests during times of crisis. Senior management at NANO becomes consumed with the current problems and stops *guiding* and *communicating* with the rest of the organization. At GEAR, engineering stops *communicating* with project management. Both organizations know these patterns exist, but they don't seem to be able to stop. This is similar to where I found myself on the golf improvement project during the second week when I wrote:

> *My swing feels like it's totally gone. The ball is flying to the left on one shot, and the next shot flies far to the right.*

When I get to this point on the golf course, I might as well go home for the day. I have not found a good way to recover from this situation. I need to put the *right actions* in the *right places* at the *right time* to keep me on the road to recovery. I had to find my "good swing" and learn how to keep that good swing from getting so far off that I couldn't get it back quickly.

LESSON 5

The key is to put the right actions in the right places, and execute them at the right time to ensure we never get to the place from which we don't know how to recover in a timely way.

Measurable Objectives: Right Actions, Right Places, and Right Time

Part of the answer to putting the *right actions* in the *right places* and executing them at the *right time* is locating traditional trouble spots where I can sense a potential problem and correct it before it occurs. This was my goal on the golf project—to get my game where it needed to be, and then to teach myself how to keep my game from degrading to that point of lost control using key *checkpoints*. This would allow me to play with the level of confidence desired during the marathon golf week in Williamsburg.

So what kind of a plan did I put in place to help reach this goal?

I needed to put changes in place that would allow me to detect what my teacher could detect in five minutes. Now I needed to do it myself. I needed to teach myself to do it in the middle of a round of golf so my game never degraded beyond my established *objectives*. I will explain how I set my objectives, and how I *aligned* my *measures* with my objectives in a moment.

When I was young, I didn't pay close attention to my golf game. Although I could play well I didn't play well consistently. It was routine for me to get to a point where I was playing poorly before I would figure out I needed help from my teacher.

Now I didn't have my golf teacher to run to so I needed to be my own teacher. I also didn't want to risk a bad round or two. I wanted to make sure I was ready to perform consistently well for an entire week. In a way, I was placing more stringent requirements on my game from a *consistency* point of view than when I was young.

This is where I employed a fundamental *Agile* approach, and *CMMI level 4 and 5 practices* together. This is where I moved from the Shu to the Ha stage of learning by developing *my own rules* to address *my unique swing weaknesses*.

9.10 Agile Approach

A common Agile approach I employed on the golf improvement project was *continuous self-assessment* (similar to Agile daily standup meetings), together with *on-going small adjustments* (continuous refinement of the plan). The reason these assessments needed to be continuous was to ensure I was avoiding my known trouble spot of letting the *imperceptible* changes creep up, allowing my game to get to that out of control point. For this to work I needed to be sure I was continuously assessing the *right things*. This leads us to the important topic of *specific checkpoints*, and how you pick the right ones.

9.11 Selecting Specific Checkpoints

Now I had to be my own teacher. Agile teams continuously self-assess and make small process adjustments as needed.

In this case, I created a routine to help me monitor my known recurring weaknesses so I could rapidly sense the need for adjustment and take timely action.

I created a *pre-shot routine* where I deliberately looked at my grip to see if my thumb was sliding. Over the next few weeks I caught myself a number of times trying to move that thumb back up on top of the shaft. I don't know what makes me do it. But I know now how to correct it before it does much damage to my round. I have added a similar pre-shot checkpoint for the other two known weaknesses that are common with my swing. This *pre-shot set-up with conscious checks* appeared to have gotten this issue under control.

9.12 Measurement Objectives and Aligned Measures

My game didn't need to be perfect, but I wanted to keep it within a tolerance I could manage. To accomplish this I employed a *measurable objective*.[7] When I was a teenager, I used to play close to par golf (shoot in low seventies on most par seventy-two golf courses). At fifty-nine, given the amount I play, I would be satisfied to play well enough to have a reasonably good chance to break eighty each day. That was my *measurable objective* for the project. A more *specific measure* I derived from that objective[8] was "*thumb position*." This was something I could monitor by visually checking prior to each shot.

9.13 Another Checkpoint on the Golf Improvement Project

Another observation I found in my notes about my swing was my tendency to bring the club-head too far inside on the backswing. Chris Demarco, a touring professional has a habit during setup of taking the club back halfway and then looking at it. I have found using a similar practice swing and checkpoint helps to ensure that I break my wrists up soon enough, keeping the club on plane while starting the backswing. As a result, I have also added this *checkpoint* during my *pre-shot routine*. Let us consider the business side.

9.14 A Critical Distinction: Traditional CMMI and Agile Approach

You can think of my *specific checkpoints* as data gathering from *subprocesses* of my golf swing that I have selected and placed under statistical management.[9]

---

7. The Measurement and Analysis Process Area, Specific Practice 1.1 states, "Establish and maintain measurement objectives that are derived from identified information needs and objectives."

8. The Measurement and Analysis Process Area, Specific Practice 1.2 states, "Specify measures to address the measurement objectives."

9. Refer to the previous discussion on Quantitative Project Management in Chapter 3.

However, I am doing more than just "monitoring" the subprocess. By catching my thumb variations early in my alignment process, I am *managing this subprocess, and keeping it within my defined limits.* Inherent to the success of the method being employed is that I am not just collecting data about the position of my thumb on the golf club, but rather I am providing *rapid feedback and action* to realign the thumb to help the very next shot.

My goal on the golf project was to *play golf more consistently*, not just collect data about my weaknesses. This subtle but critical distinction is often the biggest point of contention between many traditional implementations of the CMMI, and an implementation that employs an *Agile* approach. Agile approaches demand rapid feedback and problem resolution. This is a crucial piece of information that must be taken into consideration if you want to achieve your objectives faster with real improvement.

> **LESSON 6**
>
> An effective improvement project must have timely integration of real solutions—not just data collection and analysis.

From a CMMI perspective, this could be stated as:

> *An effective implementation of Quantitative Project Management practices (QPM) leading to real improvement must be integrated with Causal Analysis and Resolution (CAR).*

This is why I have often recommended that organizations should not wait to implement level 4/5 practices until they have formally achieved a CMMI staged level 3, as many do. This is also why many organizations fail to achieve significant real process improvement payback from their investment.

Finding the Right Place, Time, and Checkpoints for Your Organization

Where should the checkpoints be in your organization? Just like my golf swing, it depends on your organization's specific weaknesses. This is why a gap analysis is critical and needs to reflect how you are really operating, not just what your documented processes say.

> **LESSON 7**
>
> I had to find the right checkpoints that would keep my specific weaknesses in check, but not intrude on the overall rhythm of my swing.

Again, you can't use my weaknesses—too many organizations try to do this. Many just try to address everything in the CMMI model equally, or pick data to monitor because they have heard it is what other organizations are using.

Recall the lesson from LACM in Chapter 3. I actually found myself slipping into this common weakness multiple times with my golf project. That is, I tried to work on too many different things that really were not key to my unique weaknesses. I found that real improvement resulted when I limited myself to primarily the core issues.

> ### *How to Find Effective Checkpoints*
>
> Use the following criteria to help identify effective checkpoints to counter your repeating specific weaknesses:
>
> - Nonintrusive
> - Support rapid feedback
> - Support continual small corrections

At GEAR,[10] the signs of trouble often do not occur until integration, but the root cause is traceable to the seemingly *imperceptible* "small" *decisions* that occurred along the way. Examples at GEAR include *decisions* related to completion criteria for a design, or completion criteria for a peer review. Many people knew the "minimum acceptable standards," but because they had not explicitly documented them or put the processes in place to enforce them, it became too easy to allow one situation after another to slip by without meeting the known organizational standards.

Each *decision* on its own often did not appear to be significant. A specific example I heard about during the gap analysis at GEAR was a *decision* to move forward with coding a software design despite open issues that had not been resolved relative to *ambiguous requirements*. I also heard about a decision to proceed into coding despite a design review not having been held. In some of these cases, the decisions could be valid given specific circumstances, but without a clear written standard, and an objective compliance process, it became too easy to allow such cases on a regular basis with no one *stepping back* to observe, measure, and report the *cumulative effect* on the overall project.

Like my golf swing, these gradual almost *imperceptible* variances from the planned process tend to have a cumulative effect that we often don't notice until the project reaches a point where we *no longer have control* to bring it back into alignment.

---

10. The GEAR case study is discussed in Chapter 7.

Example Checkpoints

Use the following examples to help develop your own checkpoints:

- Minimum required attendees at key meetings

- Reminder to keep design work aligned with requirements

- Reminder to ask yourself each morning, "What should I be working on today given my role and responsibilities?"

- Reminder to ask the questions ahead of time that Senior Management will soon be asking

- Reminder to involve the full team in assessing work

- Reminder to communicate status accurately up the chain

- Consider placing key checkpoints in visible places (e.g., hang them on the wall in your office) to help you not forget during times of crisis

To be successful, we need the specific checkpoints continuously starting early (i.e., requirements reviews, design peer reviews).

Examples of "specific checkpoints" addressing GEAR's specific weaknesses include:

Checking on the minimum required attendees at specific required meetings (i.e., product reviews, team meetings, project kick-off meeting) that had been agreed to and documented. This check reminds the organization to include the "right people" and not to hold the meeting if the right people don't show up. This addresses the specific weakness identified with respect to the effectiveness of meetings at GEAR being dependent on "who shows up." Another example is providing a documented checklist for design reviews, which includes ensuring traceability back to requirements exists for components identified during the design activity. This check reminds the organization that design work must remain aligned with the agreed-to requirements scope. This addresses the tendency in the engineering organization to give the customer capabilities that might be beyond the agreed-to scope, which in the past had caused GEAR to get into cost and schedule overrun difficulties.

However, as I learned with the golf improvement project, checkpoints must do more than detect. They must also include timely correction if they are to make a real difference.

That is, don't just observe the left thumb moving in the wrong direction. Actually move it back! Don't just observe that critical attendees are missing at a review. Cancel the review! Don't just observe work going on

outside the agreed-to scope. Take action to correct it! Don't just measure a process deficiency. Resolve it!

Too often, process improvement efforts are weakest on this most important follow-through step. This is another reason why I claim selected CMMI level 4/5 practices should be implemented earlier in an improvement project life cycle.

> **MYTH**   If an organization gets to CMMI level 3, it can consistently perform by continuing to do the same thing over and over.

While it might appear counter-intuitive, consistent performance results from continuous small changes. Becoming aware of my three repeating weaknesses did not in itself stop them from repeating. I found myself continuing to fall back into the same pattern. I believe this was caused by an unconscious belief that just focusing on those three repeating weaknesses was too simple[11] a solution. This resulted in my failure to pay close attention to them. As a result, they continued to gradually work their way back into my game.

I finally realized, after trying other checkpoints that weren't critical to my specific weaknesses, that when I had too many things to think about the checkpoints did not work. The noncritical checkpoints became too intrusive, negatively affecting the overall rhythm of my swing. I realized that by consciously paying close attention to a *smaller number of key checkpoints*, the overall *consistency* of my game improved.

9.15 Were the Checkpoints for the Three Repeating Weaknesses Sufficient?

Let me now share more from my golf notes to help you understand another aspect of checkpoints. The following notes are from the eighth week of the golf project:

> *My swing is off today and I notice something. My weight is shifting to my back foot and it isn't transferring back at the point of impact. I believe I know what started this. I read an article in Golf Magazine [36] that I really liked. It was by Stewart Cink and was entitled "All-Feel, No-Think Shots."*

---

11. Note the similarity to the observation I have made with how Senior Managers in many organizations have responded when they hear my gap analysis report.

In this article, Stewart says:

> *Golf is a thinking man's game, but when it's time for action you need to hit "delete" and allow instinct to take over.*

Then he describes a few drills in the article he uses and believes in. I'd been losing distance, and I thought I had it solved through my alignment fixes. Then over the next few weeks, gradually my distance decreased again. I kept checking my setup and it was good. I couldn't figure out what it could be until I read this article. In the article, Stewart gave us three techniques for hitting long and straight. He uses the following words in describing his three techniques:

1. Create as much freedom as possible between your grip and waist at address.
2. Start your backswing with the club-head moving first and let your arms and hands push back. The important thing is that your swing feels "big and slow."
3. At the top, your shoulders and trunk should feel fully turned.

I went out and tried Stewart's recommendations one night on the golf course and was amazed with the results. I was quickly back to my twenty yards added distance with all my clubs.

What I determined from this exercise was that over the previous few weeks, my swing had gotten shorter. To keep from allowing the swing moving inside on the backswing, I was focusing on cocking my wrists at the right time to keep the club aligned, but I wasn't thinking of keeping the swing "big." So, over time, my swing became restricted. I wasn't watching to ensure I was taking a full backswing and shoulder turn, so I was losing distance because my swing was smaller.

LESSON 8

A single set of checkpoints is never perfect. Whenever you solve a weakness, expect another to surface.

9.16 Analysis

What I learned from this experience was that when we focus on solving specific weaknesses, often other weaknesses surface. A common example in large high-tech organizations occurs when individual departments work internal improvements, causing weaknesses to surface involving dependencies with other departments. This is one of the primary reasons for the lesson highlighted in Chapter 3 related to selecting subprocesses that cross multiple organizational boundaries. It also relates to the recommendation I made at GEAR discussed in the last chapter for using the "thread" approach to process development and deployment. Following is a discussion on how I addressed this issue on the golf project.

9.17 How Did I Address the Problem of My Golf Swing Getting Shorter?

To address the problem of my swing getting shorter, I added another piece to my pre-shot routine, which I refer to as *Visualization and Integrated Practice*. This actually turned out to be an effective aid to address a number of potential future weaknesses as well.

The Power of Visualization and Integrated Practice

Before doing my alignment checks, I step back behind the ball at least four to five yards so I can visualize the shot I want to hit. After I have visualized the shot, I take a practice swing. I don't take this swing without careful thought. The partial Chris Demarco half-swing is first made to refresh the *backswing path* in my head. A second more complete practice swing is made consciously thinking about the Stewart Cink "big and slow" *feel*. This prevents my swing from getting short, and reminds me to maintain my rhythm to counter the potential gradual imperceptible speed increases.

9.18 Rhythm in Golf and High-Tech Organizations

For my body to work well hitting a golf ball, each of the parts must do its piece to maintain an overall rhythm of the swing. Nick Price and Lanny Wadkins have very fast swing tempos, but their rhythm is consistent so it works for them. Ernie Els and Retief Goosen have slow, flowing swing tempos. Because their rhythm is consistent, it works. To play golf well and consistently, each player must determine his or her own *unique* rhythm and then maintain that rhythm throughout a round of golf.

Organizations have rhythm, too. To maintain your organization's rhythm, all departments or team members must meet their commitments, or it can throw off the overall organization rhythm. This is because other groups might be dependent on your output to complete their commitment. At LACM, we saw the trouble that was caused when the procurement department missed their commitment and how it affected the overall rhythm of the project.

A Misunderstanding Between Agile and CMMI Communities

When I think of rhythm in my golf swing, the words *consistency* and *repeatability* come to mind in a *positive* way. Some Agile proponents have viewed the notion of a repeatable process in a negative way. Ken Schwaber, co-founder of Scrum, has argued against the notion of *defined* process by stating that software development is an *empirical* process in the sense that we are constantly learning and feeding back improvements in the process. [3]

While this idea of continuous learning and feedback for improvements has been used as an argument against the notion of defined process in the CMMI, in reality this is what "defined" actually means in the CMMI. That is, tailored from the organizational assets and *feedback* to both those executing the immediate process to help them determine whatever adjustments are called for, and feedback to the organizational assets to help others improve.[12]

Where the real conflict comes is in the *frequency* of feedback and improvement. With Agile, the cycles are short, and many believe this is counter to the CMMI—another myth. It is only counter to how many have chosen to implement the model in the past.

> **MYTH**   The short continual iterations encouraged by Agile approaches are counter to the CMMI.

The fact is that the CMMI doesn't dictate any length of time, or exact frequency for tailoring and improvement cycle feedback. It says you need to do it. You decide the appropriate length of the cycle. Each organization has its own rhythm. Each organization can define its own approved life cycles, and these should be based on its business needs.

Ask yourself key questions to help decide what is right for your organization. For example, how fast must you get product out the door in your organization?

---

12. Reference Generic Practice 2.8, Monitor and Control the Process, and Generic Practice 3.2, Collect Improvement Information.

As we start to understand that tailoring of processes is something that can be done on shorter cycles, we begin to see continuous process improvement in a new light—a light that starts to look more "Agile."

We also begin to see "process improvement" in a more *integrated* way with "product" development, monitoring, and control. This is one reason why at GEAR I recommended a more integrated approach to process development and deployment.

9.19 What Business People Can Learn from Golf Professionals

Many golf professionals start by stepping back away from the ball and visualizing the shot they are about to hit. Then they take their own *uniquely* constructed practice swing (e.g., Chris Demarco), which has been developed to address specific known repeating weaknesses within their own golf swings.

If you watch golf professionals on television, you will notice after completing a swing they often hold their pose continuing to watch the ball until it stops. They are registering a picture in their mind of the result (gathering the latest objective data, and conducting an immediate analysis). If it is a good shot, this will help to reinforce the next swing, as a good memory has been created. If there was something in the execution of the shot that didn't go as planned, you will often see the professional take another practice swing right there after the stroke has been made.

They want to make the correction and register the slight refinement immediately to reduce the risk of the initiation of any downward cycle in their game. This is rapid feedback and correction, which are key techniques with Agile approaches. The short cycles of planning, monitoring, controlling, and feedback with Agile approaches are effective "how-to" techniques to achieve the CMMI practices within the Project Planning (PP), and Project Monitor and Control (PMC) Process Areas.

LESSON 9

The most effective checkpoints occur in very short cycles and include all three elements of data collection, analysis, and actions to improve performance.

> **INSIGHT**   The most effective checkpoints are integrated with rapid improvement and as close to "real-time" as possible, but not so close as to intrude on performance.

This could be viewed from a CMMI perspective as "mini-continuous process tailorings." These techniques often help golf professionals save a potentially bad round, and turn it into a great round. The same techniques can have similar effects in business. An argument often heard against this approach is that continuous change will lead to chaos. This is why you need the *minimum* "must-do's"[13] defined first to make the boundaries clear in your organization.

Drawing More Lessons from Golf Professionals to Help in Business

The visualization golf technique is analogous to the project leader keeping the end goals of the project constantly clear for all team members. The practice swing is continuous training, which is essential to counter the natural pressures that often arise taking us away from our end project goal.

During workshop training sessions I hold with clients, I often use "what-if" scenarios to help attendees visualize themselves and prepare for real project situations. I have also suggested using these techniques each day at work possibly early in the morning before the day gets started to consider the likely "what-if" scenarios for that day. This becomes your "practice swing" before you execute your "real swing" that day at work. You are preparing yourself, just like a golf professional prepares for each hole and each golf shot.

9.20 How the Checkpoints Helped to Achieve the Golf Project Goal and More

My goal on the golf improvement project was consistent performance to a well-defined level. The checkpoints I selected helped maintain my golf swing tempo and my rhythm throughout the marathon golf week in Williamsburg. They were placed at key points where I could sense a problem starting and correct it before it reached a point where I could no longer control it. These points were based on my past swing weaknesses, which never

---

13. Refer to Chapter 4 for more information on the minimum "must-do's."

surfaced during the week due to the continuous monitoring and constant refinements the checkpoints provided.

The checkpoints were chosen in a way as to be as *nonintrusive* as possible during the actual execution of the swing. Most of the checkpoints were in *preparation steps*, allowing the swing itself the freedom I needed to confidently perform.

During the actual marathon golf week with my friend Bob, and his friends Dave and Frank, I shot one round early in the week in the low eighties, and after that all rounds were in the seventies, with my game and scores *consistently* improving as the week progressed. I believe picking the right checkpoints and implementing them in a disciplined way was key to the project's success.[14]

LESSON 10

Real consistency of results is the product of continuous small changes constantly addressing specific weaknesses that never completely go away.

Steps to Finding the Right Checkpoints for Your Organization

To summarize the steps I used to find key checkpoints:

Step 1: **Talk to the people who use the process and take notes. Even if what you are hearing sounds like nothing special, write it down, because experience has shown that over time, patterns emerge that are critical to locating proper actions. Don't trust your memory or let yourself believe what appears obvious is unimportant.**

Step 2: **Take the time to objectively analyze the data, extracting key repeating weaknesses unique to your situation.**

Step 3: **Identify and implement practical specific checkpoints.**

Step 4: **Most importantly, for real improvement, timely action must be integrated with ongoing real-time performance.**

---

14. On the final day of our marathon golf week I shot a seventy-six* at the BlackHeath course at Ford Colony. But Frank told me I needed to put an asterisk next to that score because in the middle of the round I had to skip two holes (they gave me two pars on my score card) because I had to teleconference into a technical working group meeting at NANO.

9.21 Revisiting CMMI Level 4/5 Practices and Their Relationship to Agility

MYTH   The higher CMMI level practices are theoretical and too far a field from real projects to have real value that can help a project in a timely way.

This myth is the result not of the CMMI practices themselves, but the way many organizations have chosen to implement them. I have made the point often in this book that the CMMI is a reference model that helps us understand what to do. But it doesn't mandate "how" or "when." Agile and lean techniques provide effective "how-to" techniques that can work with the CMMI.

In Chapter 3, I provided an example of *gathering, analyzing, and acting* on data in a timely fashion, leading to an effective solution through the procurement case study at LACM. In this chapter, we see a similar case study on the golf improvement project where *gathering, analyzing, and acting* in a timely way proves key to real process improvement.

The CMMI level 4/5 practices can help move your skill level from Shu to Ha, and you have to move from Shu to Ha if you want to get better.

MYTH   Consistency is achieved by doing the same thing over and over.

Consistency is actually achieved through *continuous small changes* addressing specific weaknesses that never end…

9.22 Summary: How Agile Can Help CMMI

The following table provides a summary of how Agile approaches discussed in this chapter help the CMMI.

Agile Approach	How It Helps CMMI
Taking notes constantly (daily team communication)	Helps us gather the right specific data needed for effective improvement and more effective decisions (MA, QPM)
Timely action plans addressing specific weaknesses (removing obstacles on short cycles)	Helps us achieve effective corrective action (CAR)*
Implementing well-placed checkpoints (rapid feedback and correction)	Helps us ensure our corrective actions (CAR) are effective and as nonintrusive as possible on team performance

* It is interesting to note that CMMI Version 1.3 might feature CAR-like activity descriptions at lower maturity levels (e.g., CAR-like subpractices added to IPM SP 1.5 and QPM SP 2.3). At the time of writing this book, Version 1.3 had not been released, so this could change.

Chapter 10

Summary and Conclusion

10.1 What You Will Learn in This Chapter

- The major Agile "how-to" options and CMMI "reminder" practices summarized
- What we have learned about measurement
- Three lessons and one insight related to consistency and high performance

10.2 What Can We Learn from the Case Studies in This Book?

The overarching lesson I hope readers take from this book is the knowledge that you have *options* when using the CMMI—more than you might have known before you opened this book. Table 10-1 is a high-level summary of the major *Agile* "how-to" options to traditional approaches discussed in the book. These can help an organization find its right level of agility to be competitive in today's rapidly changing world while maintaining appropriate *discipline* and *control*. You will also see a reference to CMMI Practices that can be used as "reminders" to help ensure we are not forgetting proven practices in times of high project stress.

Table 10-1 *Summary: How CMMI and Agile Help Each Other*

Associated Agile Supporting Artifacts	CMMI Area	Chap Ref
Pruning Process Assets Leaning Peer Review Process	OPF SP 1.1, Establish Org Process Needs, Helps Effective Decisions with Limited Resources	2
Small Teams, Specific Measures, Rapid Action, Focus on "Handful" of Keys (Simplicity)	CAR, SP 1.1, Select Data for Analysis, SP 2.1, Implement Action	3
Select Subprocess "Threads" That Cross Organizational Boundaries	QPM, SP 1.3, Select Subprocesses to Statistically Manage	3
Agile Organizational Repository Structure Agile "Must Do" Process Packaging	OPD, SP 1.3, Helps apply tailoring —balancing "unique needs" and "meaningful consistency"	4
Formalizing Informality— "Doorway" Risk Management	RSKM, SP 3.1, Helps achieve real intent—timely mitigation	4
Agile TWG	OPD, SP 1.1, Helps develop processes that reflect what people really do	4
Agile Integrated Project Management Plan (PMP)	PP, SP 2.7, Helps capture planning decisions, rationale for people selection	5
Agile Senior Management Brief Guidelines	GP 2.10, Helps Senior Management see more accurate objective data	5
Agile Action Items Guidelines	PMC, SP 2.3, Helps keep actions from falling through cracks	5

Table 10-1 *Summary: How CMMI and Agile Help Each Other (Continued)*

Associated Agile Supporting Artifacts	CMMI Area	Chap Ref
Agile Stakeholder Involvement Matrix/Guide	GP 2.7, Helps proactively involve remote teammates	5
Agile Measurement Repository	MA, SP 2.4, Communicate Results— Helps us "carry the measures forward"	5
Agile PPQA Mentor/Helper Approach	GP 2.9, Helps leverage collaboration culture	5
Use of Roles and Responsibilities to Share Authority and Responsibility	DAR, SP 1.2 Criteria, Aids in more effective decisions	6
Training People to Use Measures in Everyday Decisions	MA, SP 2.4, Communicate Results, Helps use informal measures in every day decisions	6
Plan Reflects Real Plan, Updated When More Accurate Information Available	Pp, Sp 1.2, Help Establish More Accurate Estimates By Considering project-specific factors	6
Agile Roles and Responsibilities Starting with Talents of Current People	GP 2.4, Help assign responsibilities more effectively by accessing unique talents of people	6
Agile "Pre-Tailoring Project Types" Option	GP 3.1, Helps tailor more effectively in support of unique project needs	6
Agile Compliance Through Well-Defined "Minimums"	GP 2.9, Helps us know when to say no through clear go/no-go criteria	7
Agile Life-Cycle Guidelines	PP, SP 1.3 Helps align management and engineering	7
Agile Tailoring Guidelines (Tailor Up)	GP 3.1, Helps establish defined process more efficiently for all projects	7
Agile Execution Criteria (Peer Review, Test)	VER, SP 1.1 and SP 1.3, Helps establish criteria in support of right level of Agile decision making	7

Continues

Table 10-1 *Summary: How CMMI and Agile Help Each Other (Continued)*

Associated Agile Supporting Artifacts	CMMI Area	Chap Ref
Sutherland 10 Percent Rule	PP, SP 1.2, Helps more accurate estimates	8
Agile Scope Guide	REQM, SP 1.3, Helps manage scope creep	8
Agile Push-Pull Guide Agile Master Schedule Guide	PMC, SP 1.1, Helps implement earned value, evolving requirements and collaboration	8
Agile "Scenario" Training	GP 2.5, More effective just-in-time training	8
Personal Safety Guide	GP 2.10, Helps communication with Senior Management become more accurate and effective	8

10.3 What Have We Learned from NANO and GEAR?

Alistair Cockburn has said:

> "As much as I love to trust people, a weakness of people is being careless. Sometimes it is important to simply trust people, but sometimes it is important to install a mechanism to find out whether people can be trusted on a particular topic."[1] [5]

Currently as I conclude writing this book, I am still involved actively helping NANO and GEAR. To rapidly make a positive difference in both of these organizations and help them achieve their business objectives fast, we are deploying process assets incrementally based on new project start opportunities. Our approach is to release less process functionality if necessary—and focus on the highest-value processes/practices based on specific identified weaknesses. This allows us to help projects more quickly where help is needed most.

---

1. Refer to page 181 of *Agile Software Development, 2nd Edition.*

My latest lesson from both the NANO and GEAR experiences indicates that PPQA should be implemented early and incrementally, especially in "Agile-like" organizations that have misunderstandings of agility and are in need of increased *discipline.* However, in doing so, PPQA checklists must remain consistently *aligned* with the *incrementally* deployed practices.

10.4 What Have We Learned about Measurement?

Measurement is critical to both Agile approaches and the CMMI. The CMMI reminds us of the importance of measurement through the Measurement and Analysis (MA) and Quantitative Project Management (QPM) Process Areas. From MA, we learn the importance of establishing measurement objectives first, and then aligning our measures with those objectives. From QPM, we learn the importance of selecting subprocesses for statistical management.

From the Agile side and our experiences (LACM procurement case study, golf improvement project), we have learned the importance of deriving context-relevant specific measures and the importance of acting on that data in a timely manner to achieve real improvements that help people every day.

Often in large high-tech organizations, effective use of measures tends to focus on the long-term trends and improvements. This is certainly an important aspect of measurement. However, the CMMI model was not intended to be limited in its use to only long-term improvements. It can and should be used to help projects and people every day. This is a value Agile can bring to help the CMMI.

From our Agile Principles, and our experiences, we have learned that measures can be implemented at varying degrees of formality, and that less formal measures used every day in making decisions are often best implemented by knowing what questions to ask, who to ask, and when to ask them. Refer to Figure 10-1.

Throughout this book, I have shared many practical and proven measurement techniques implemented by asking the right question at the right time. The CMMI helps us know what the right questions are. Our Agile experiences help us better understand when those questions should be asked, and when related actions should be taken.

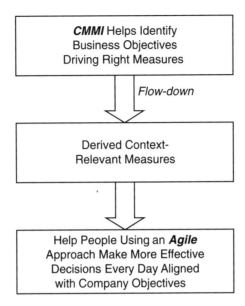

Figure 10-1 *CMMI and Agile Together for Effective Measures*

10.5 What Have We Learned by Thinking Out of the Box (Golf Project)?

There are three overarching lessons from the golf improvement project.

First is the importance of identifying those "handful" of specific areas to focus on (*unique repeating specific weaknesses*) that could provide the greatest payback for the limited investment available.

Second is to find whatever technique works to ensure you don't fall into just "going through the motions," which is the root cause of lost control. I will explain in a moment a counter-intuitive technique I have found works best for me.

Third is to never underestimate the importance of *integrated and continuous on-going practice* such as the pre-shot practice swing and visualization technique. In the business world, this equates to taking time to plan each day, including going through your own potential "what if" scenarios and preparing to make the most effective *decisions* with the *most current objective data* available. This has been found to be a practical and valuable form of continuous training.

As you start each day with these "what if" scenarios, ask yourself what is most important for you to be doing today given your *responsibilities and commitments.*

As you make this assessment, never underestimate the value of the "less visible" tasks of *monitoring, analyzing, prioritizing, and guiding.*[2] Because I now believe these techniques are critical to real and consistent performance, I have developed a way to keep myself from falling back into the "going through the motions" trap.

10.6 The Value of Small Changes to Aid Real and Consistent Performance

I have found that by making *small changes continually* to my golf game checkpoints, it allows my checkpoints to continually keep working. This is counter-intuitive. The natural thought is:

> *If these checkpoints were working so well, why would I consider adjusting them?*

What I have found is that continually making very small conscious adjustments keeps the gradual imperceptible creeping changes that are not in my best interest—and have in the past caused my golf game to slip out of control—from actually occurring.

As an example, I now know exactly where my left thumb should lay on the golf club, but each time I place it there I move it just slightly one way or the other from where I think ideally it should be. This causes me to stay conscious, "always checking in with myself" to ensure I have not strayed too far either way with the left thumb.

The reason I do this is that the only way I know to keep myself from falling into the "going through the motions" trap is to keep changing things just a bit, which in turn forces me to pay attention.

By allowing things to move "a little," I keep things from moving "a lot."

LESSON 1

Continual small changes can counter the normal tendency over time to fall into the "going through the motions" trap, which is the root cause of lost control.

---

2. Refer to the DART case study in Chapter 8 for more information on "less visible" tasks.

10.7 Supporting Small Changes in Business: The Two Sides of Tailoring and Criteria

I mentioned earlier in this book that one reason my client NANO[3] might not be doomed is that the CMMI level 5 organization trying to take their business away takes three times as long and costs twice as much as my client does.

One question I received from the initial reviews of this manuscript was why high CMMI mature organizations tend to have higher costs and longer schedules than would seem to be warranted, and if this needs to be so. My immediate response was:

> *No, it doesn't need to be so and this was part of why I wrote this book.*

In the beginning of this book, I talked about the tendency to read things into the CMMI model that are not really there, thus creating *non-value-added* work. But this doesn't account for all the cost and schedule inefficiencies I have observed. Let me give you an example.

I have heard the following comment made by a CMMI lead appraiser, which on the surface sounds positive and accurate:

> *This organization is clearly CMMI level 3 because we saw the evidence of projects using the organization's common assets through the use of a common project planning template and the use of a standard approach to estimate work products and task attributes.*

This same lead appraiser raised a concern about the direct evidence provided by one project with respect to the *Project Planning Specific Practice 1.2:*

> *Establish estimates of work products and task attributes.*

The comment made was that the evidence provided was:

> *"Too project unique," and the lead appraiser wanted to see more evidence that the project estimated using the "company standard approach."*

Now admittedly, this is a balancing act.

To achieve a CMMI level 3, you need to adequately address *Generic Practice 3.1*, which tells us we need to:

---

3. Refer to Chapter 6 for the NANO case study.

"Establish and maintain a description of the defined process," where *"defined"* means:

Tailored from the organization's set of standard processes according to the organization's tailoring guidelines.

The balancing act is explained in a "tip" in the CMMI guidelines book [1] under the *Organizational Process Definition (OPD) Process Area, Specific Practice (SP) 1.3, Establish Tailoring Criteria and Guidelines.*

The tip states that the challenge of tailoring is:

To provide guidance that has sufficient flexibility to meet the unique needs of each project but at the same time ensure meaningful consistency.

Unfortunately, the tendency I have seen in a number of high maturity organizations has been to downplay the "unique needs of each project" and up-play "consistency" to the point where I have witnessed the addition of unnecessary effort in the name of "consistency."

If we go back to that example project where the lead appraiser didn't like the project-unique estimation evidence, it turns out that by considering project-unique information (i.e., work that already had been done on that project, and knowledge key people on the project already had) that project was able to develop a lower bid to do the work than the company standard approach would have led to.

> **LESSON 2**
>
> Consistency often turns out to be the easiest thing to do, but it can also be the most expensive thing to do in specific situations.

How can you gain real efficiencies when using the CMMI model? The answer is through the *tailoring process* and the use of *criteria*, which are left up to each organization to define.[4]

In this particular case, a "small tailoring" of the company standard estimation process—or the use of a set of *criteria*—allows you to make an effective *decision* considering appropriate factors, such as taking into consideration the project-specific knowledge that could help gain cost and schedule efficiencies.

---

4. The answer can also be to adjust what you select to standardize to include additional factors important more generally to a class of projects. A benefit of this approach is that other projects then directly benefit from what was previously learned, and the standard process evolves to better reflect the appropriate set of "minimums" without unnecessarily sacrificing deeper understanding.

This type of tailoring or use of criteria can only happen if the culture, processes, and training in the organization supports it. Refer to Figure 10-2.

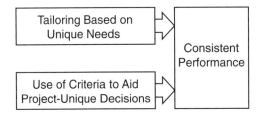

Figure 10-2 *Key Aids to More Consistent Performance*

However, on the other side, please keep in mind the following caution:

CAUTION

Any organization that moves in an "Agile" direction by supporting continual "small adjustments" must be aware of the potential consequences if its workforce doesn't have the necessary skills and maturity to use criteria and tailoring appropriately.

LESSON 3

Tailoring your processes and the use of criteria provide your best opportunities to gain cost and schedule efficiencies and are supported through the CMMI model. Furthermore, they are both consistent with Agile approaches.

10.8 Conclusion

The guidance in the CMMI book under tailoring refers to the "balancing act" of consistency and project unique needs. Another tip under Organizational Process Definition (OPD) in the CMMI states:

Finding this balance usually takes time as the organization gains experience from using these assets.

Consider the following thought as you look to determine the right balance of consistency and uniqueness for your organization.

The greatest golfers in the world first achieved a level of consistency by learning the fundamentals of the game. However, those fundamentals were not enough to allow them to rise above the competition.

Jack Nicklaus, playing in an era when one of the fundamentals of golf was, "keep your right elbow close to your body on the backswing," was known for his flying right elbow at the top of his backswing. Arnold Palmer was known for his unorthodox knock-kneed putting stance.

I see this same focus on *uniqueness* separating great high-tech organizations from their competition today. LACM[5] is currently at the top of their game and are doing everything possible to stay there by focusing on—in the words of their VP—the "unique value" their organization brings to their customer.

Similarly, recall the conversation at NANO when one of the leaders said:

> *We need to define Project Lead consistently across the organization.*

The Director immediately replied:

> *No, we don't. What we need to do is change the word.*

He then said:

> *I don't want you to change what your people do as "Project Leads," but we do need to use another word to describe it.*

NANO did have an organizational standard set of responsibilities for a Project Lead. However, they had tailored the Project Lead role for the different project types taking into consideration project-unique factors and the strengths and weaknesses of the current project personnel. As an example, this led to a tailored set of responsibilities for a Project Lead on an install project (which had no new software development) that differed from a Project Lead's responsibilities on projects that were software development intensive. It is important to note that with this tailoring there still existed a "core" set of responsibilities common to all Project Leads across the organization.

If the Director ignored the organizational standard roles directing each individual without reference to previous training and tasking, it would have led to chaos and ultimately degraded organizational performance. At times, the Director had been guilty of this, and he knew he needed to change his behavior.

---

5. Refer to Chapters 2 and 3 for the LACM case study.

At the same time, if they did not tailor the organizational roles recognizing the strengths and weaknesses of the current personnel and the specific needs of each project type, it is likely they would not have been able to achieve the performance that had kept them ahead of their competition. Their challenge was to locate the right balance that achieved the business objectives today while supporting sustained growth in the future.

We tend to think of uniqueness and consistency as being at odds when we think of it as a "balancing act." For example, if I am doing something in a unique way, I am most likely not being consistent with the organization. But there is another way to view uniqueness.

On the golf improvement project, I spent a great deal of energy and time understanding the uniqueness of my personal habits that caused repeating specific weaknesses in my swing. By understanding better these repeating weaknesses,

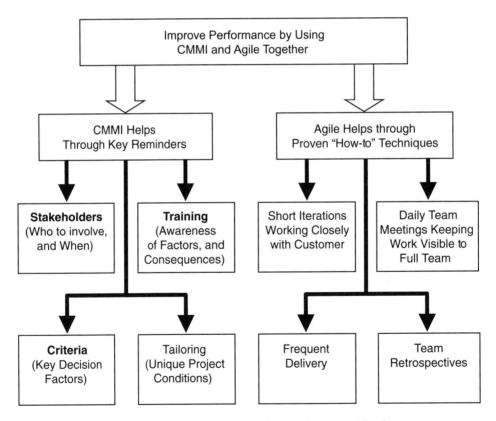

Figure 10-3 *CMMI and Agile Together for Improved Performance*

I was able to put *unique tailored rules* in place that actually helped me *improve my consistency*.

The point is they can work together. You can use your uniqueness to aid the achievement of more consistent results. And here is the key point—often, your greatest unique value rests in the talents of your people. Refer to Figure 10-3. For more information on integrating Agile and traditional development approaches, refer to [37, 38, 39, 40, 41].

> **INSIGHT** While consistency is an important starting point, it is often the unique talents of your people that distinguish organizations that achieved greatness.

That Director at NANO recognized that "consistency" had a place, but also recognized the unique talent each of his Project Leads brought to the job was allowing him to stay ahead of the competition, and he did not want to lose that edge. That is why he started with his people when refining his roles and responsibilities.

The Agile Manifesto states:

> *Build projects around motivated individuals. Give them the environment and support they need, and trust them to get the job done.*

The CMMI framework can support our Agile principles by providing a reference framework that helps us ask the right questions at the right time, leading to the right actions to help us create an environment where we can confidently trust our people to get the job done.

Epilogue

What Does Passion Have to Do with Performance?

Let me give you another perspective on consistency and performance. As I started to become more consistent at reproducing the mechanics of a good golf swing on the golf improvement project, I found myself asking *longer-range questions*.

These included questions related to what I was really doing out on the golf course. Was it just an exercise to make sure my friend Bob didn't beat me during our marathon golf week to celebrate his sixtieth birthday? If so, what would happen after? Was I going to just walk away from the game again when all this was over?

By asking these questions, I realized that consistency would not be enough to keep me interested in this game. The way my mind works, once I figure something out I often get bored and move on to something else. I realized I was at risk of giving up the game again as I did forty years ago. I have seen this same pattern in many organizations. At LACM, consistent project performance wasn't enough to keep people from leaving the organization. What more did they want? What more do I want?

I got my golf game back to a reasonably consistent level. But I know myself and I know I will lose interest in a second if the only reason to come out to the golf course and play tomorrow is to try to do again what I did today. There has to be more to it. And this brings us to the subject of *passion*.

When I went to my job interview for the first company I worked for out of college, I went in my tennis shorts. And for years when I was an employee working in the defense industry, I didn't feel committed or even motivated toward my career. I was just "having fun."

During that period of my life, every time the job started to lose its "fun-value" I actively sought out a change to get the "fun-value" back up. In my twenty-five years in industry prior to starting my own consulting business, I was never bored because my jobs always had some level of new challenge associated with them. During that time, I learned what it meant to play roles, including that of software engineer, systems engineer, technical lead, department manager, chief engineer, project engineer, internal consultant, and training/workshop facilitator.

One reason I finally made the decision to go out on my own was that the *options* to continue to keep my job as exciting and have fun were starting to diminish. After working in industry for twenty-five years, I was starting to feel like I had fewer rather than more options to keep having fun—to keep it new, exciting, and fresh.

As a result, I made a *decision* that opened up more options and therefore more fun again. Throughout my consulting years I have always taken the jobs I want to do, not the jobs that pay the most. My rationale for this is simple: I have figured out if it isn't fun, it's a risk, because I will lose interest and that means I won't do it well. If I find it fun, it will create energy and I'll do it well. Although I wasn't taking this approach early in my career because I thought it would help my career, I believe it turned out to be the best thing I could have done for my career.

Of what benefit can this knowledge be to managers in large high-tech organizations? Am I suggesting we all just go have fun, and forget the hard work?

Of course not. However, I am suggesting that some changes could be made in high-tech industries in how we help people figure out what they should do with their careers.

We can't make every job fun all the time. However, often there are signs when people just don't fit in the job they are currently doing. In such cases, we often hear managers say there is nothing they can do, but this is not always the case.

I have observed situations where managers were constrained in their options, but creatively found ways to make small changes in an employee's responsibilities leading to performance improvement. Even small changes show employees someone cares and can spark new interest in a person who might just be tired of doing the same thing.

It has been my experience that if you look at any organization that is successful and is maintaining that success, you find people who are passionate about what they do. In small and innovative organizations, I frequently observe this passion. What I believe keeps this passion alive is a child-like fascination that comes from a never-ending desire to learn.

Unfortunately, this is not what I am seeing today in many large companies, although I see no reason why it couldn't be this way—or at least why we cannot begin by making some of those small changes that can start us on this path.

What is happening? Kids who have parents working in high-tech industries hear their parents coming home from work saying:

I'm tired.

I can't wait for my retirement so I can get out of there.

I don't like my job.

True passion must come from within. It cannot be driven into someone from the outside. While we can't drive passion into someone, we can help people find their passion often just by little things we do to help them. Small changes can help today even in environments where trust and collaboration are lacking. Small changes can help to keep people interested in a job they are growing tired of. And while keeping people interested in their work might not give them passion for it, it can provide a first step toward passion. Refer to Figure E-1.

I am passionate about what I do—but I don't feel like I found my passion. It isn't that simple. It isn't like the light went on one day and I realized what I was passionate about. I feel like I am passionate about what I do, not because of what I do, but the way I do it. The way I keep it interesting is by continually changing it and looking at it a little differently so I can learn more about it. I feel more like I am creating my passion every day, and if I stop, it will stop, too.

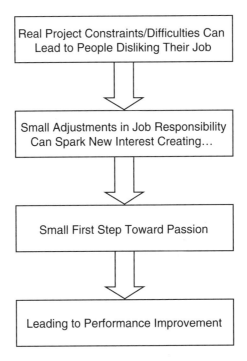

Figure E-1 *A First Step Toward Passion and Performance Improvement*

One reviewer of the initial manuscript of this book said he was disappointed to hear me say I didn't feel like I "found" my passion. People want to know how to find passion. Parents want to know how to find passion so they can help their children find their passion. My wife worries about our son, and what will happen if he never finds his passion. This led me to think about what happened in my own life.

I had originally planned on golf being my career. My first *decision* to change my life led me to work in the U.S. defense industry for twenty-five years after college. But early in my career in the defense industry, I also started to dream about going out on my own, and I didn't just dream about it. I actually wrote my first business plan close to ten years before I started my business. Then I started making *decisions* that would position that plan to one day become real. The plan wasn't long. It was less than ten pages, and it contained just a handful of keys that I knew would be critical to success.

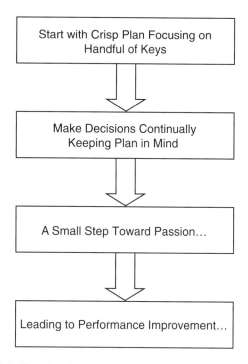

Figure E-2 *Road to Improved Performance Through Passion*

That same reviewer, who is a senior manager in a large high-tech company, told me he frequently tells young engineers they should write a twenty-year career plan. Many young kids, like my son, might not think they could possibly do this, especially if they had no idea what they wanted to do with their life. But I believe there is a way.

Just ask yourself if—somehow by magic—you could become anything you wanted to be, where would you like to see yourself in twenty years? Allow yourself to dream. Then write down your dream, and after you write it down, don't allow yourself to get sidetracked.

Focus on that handful *of keys* that you know rest at the heart of your dream. Go back and read what you wrote about your dream regularly. If you start with a dream, and then start making *decisions* with that dream in your mind you won't be able to keep yourself from finding your passion. Refer to Figure E-2.

Appendix A

Twelve Principles Behind the Agile Manifesto[1]

1. Our highest priority is to satisfy the customer through early and continuous delivery of valuable software.
2. Welcome changing requirements, even late in development. Agile processes harness change for the customer's competitive advantage.
3. Deliver working software frequently, from a couple of weeks to a couple of months, with a preference to the shorter timescale.
4. Business people and developers must work together daily throughout the project.
5. Build projects around motivated individuals. Give them the environment and support they need, and trust them to get the job done.
6. The most efficient and effective method of conveying information to and within a development team is face-to-face conversation.
7. Working software is the primary measure of progress.
8. Agile processes promote sustainable development. The sponsors, developers, and users should be able to maintain a constant pace indefinitely.

---

1. Reference from Agilemanifesto.org.

9. Continuous attention to technical excellence and good design enhances agility.

10. Simplicity—the art of maximizing the amount of work not done—is essential.

11. The best architectures, requirements, and designs emerge from self-organizing teams.

12. At regular intervals, the team reflects on how to become more effective, and then tunes and adjusts its behavior accordingly.

Appendix B

Example Agile Project Management Plan (PMP) Template

Key Points to Aid Use of Template:

- This annotated example PMP template is provided to help your Agile and CMMI integration effort get started on the right track
- Guidance in using this template is provided in Chapter 5 in a discussion of the five simplified steps to planning.
- Rationale supporting template sections in the book is referenced from sidebars on the left side of each template page.
- The relationship of template sections to CMMI model practices is provided through sidebars on the right side of each template page.

Project Management Plan (PMP) Template

[Insert Date Here]

[Insert Version Number Here]

Authored by: _____

Approved by: _____

Key Points to Aid Use of Template:

- A record of change pages can provide evidence for multiple CMMI expected practices.
- For example, a change revision section as seen here can provide evidence that a plan is maintained. This ties to CMMI Project Planning (PP) Process Area, SP 2.7 Establish and maintain the plan.
- As another example, the reason for change field can provide evidence for Project Planning (PP) GP 2.7 Involve Relevant Stakeholders (in this case, the reviewers of the plan).

Record of Changes

Change Rev	Change Date	Affected Pages	Reason for Change
Initial Draft			For Review
Rev A	April 04, 2009		Incorporate comment from functional lead

1 Scope and System Overview

System Overview

DISCUSSION:
Ch 5 Step 1: "The What"

[Provide here a high-level overview of the System, its purpose, physical components, users, and statement about its long-range vision and vision for early releases. Include a referenced diagram, and identify where a work breakdown structure can be found.]

PP SP 1.1:
Scope, Work Breakdown Structure

2 Organization and Staffing

Organization

DISCUSSION:
Ch 5 Step 2: "The Who"

[Provide here a description of the project organization. Include major roles and responsibilities, such as Program Manager, Project Engineer, Chief Architect, and Task Performers. Include a description of key project teams.]

PP SP 2.4:
Plan Project Resources

Staffing

[Provide here the planned staffing plan, or reference staffing plan in external document, or location.]

Role	Assigned Personnel	Required Skills

GP 2.3:
Provide Resources

GP 2.4:
Assign Responsibility

Training

[Provide here a statement about the training plans for the staff.]

GP 2.5:
Train People

3. Life Cycle and Schedule

Life Cycle Model

DISCUSSION:
Ch 5 Step 3: "The When"

[Provide here a description of the life cycle model chosen for the project.]

PP SP 1.3:
Project Life Cycle

Project Schedule

[Describe the plan to develop, review, approve, and maintain the project schedule. Include the location where the Project Schedule will be maintained and frequency of update.]

PP SP 2.1:
Schedule

4. Project Monitor and Control

Tasking

[Describe the process by which tasks are communicated to task performers. Include written and verbal techniques, and where task descriptions are maintained.]

PMC SP 1.6:
Conduct Progress Reviews

PMC SP 1.7:
Conduct Milestone Reviews

Periodic Progress Reviews

DISCUSSION:
Ch 5 Step 4: "The How"

[Describe planned periodic progress reviews. Include information such as day, time and frequency of meetings, issues discussed, minutes taken, and action item processing.]

PMC SP 2.1:
Analyze Issues

PMC SP 2.2 and 2.3:
Corrective Action

Milestone Reviews

[Describe when the milestone reviews are planned, and the purpose of each milestone review. Milestone reviews are typically held to communicate accomplishments and issues to major stakeholders with a focus on maintaining buy-in.]

Note:
Practices achieved by following the plan

Peer Reviews

DISCUSSION:
Ch 4 Peer Reviews

[Describe, or reference, peer reviews planned and products that must be peer reviewed. Identify, or reference, personnel required to attend peer reviews. An example table format is provided here.]

VER SP 2.1, 2.2, 2.3:
Peer Reviews

Note:
Practices achieved by following the plan

Review Product	Required Personnel
System Requirements Document	Author, Chief Engineer, Functional Lead, Customer Rep
System Architecture Document	Author, Chief Engineer, Functional Lead

Risk Management

DISCUSSION:
Ch 4 Risk Management

[Describe, or reference, the process by which risks are identified, documented, managed, and how risk mitigation approaches are initiated, when deemed appropriate.]

[Example: Core Team members are encouraged to raise risks and issues at daily standup meetings. The team lead uses the following criteria … to aid determination when risks should be raised for higher visibility.]

PP SP 2.2
Identify Risks

RSKM
Multiple Specific Practices

Note:
Practices achieved by following the plan

Work Environment and Tools

[Identify tools used on the project. An example table format is provided here.]

Tool	Purpose of Tool

Configuration Management

[Identify, or reference, products to be controlled by the Configuration Management System.]

GP 2.6:
Manage Configurations

Quality Assurance

DISCUSSION:
Ch 7 Compliance

[Identify, or reference, how management achieves objective insight on process and product quality.]

GP 2.9:
Objectively Evaluate Adherence

Maintenance of this Plan

[Describe the process by which this plan is maintained. Include who is responsible for its maintenance.]

[Example: This Project Management Plan (PMP) is maintained by the Project Lead. The original version is reviewed and agreed to by the Project Core Team, and is approved by the Project Manager. The document is updated as necessary at the start of each project major increment. Minor updates are maintained by the project lead between releases in a folder located at …]

5. Metrics

DISCUSSION:

Ch 5 Measures

[Describe the metrics planned to be collected on the project. Include how the metrics are collected, frequency of collection, how analyzed, stored, and communicated. An example is provided here.]

MA:

Multiple Specific Practices

Metric	Description
Requirements	Current Actual, and changes since last reporting period
Schedule	Updated weekly. Schedule is maintained at…
Cost	Current Burn Rate
Staffing	Current Planned and Actual Staffing

Appendix C

Example Agile Organizational Process Asset Guidelines

1 Structure and Definition of Organizational Process Assets

Organizational Process Assets include three entities:

- Process
- Process Guidelines
- Enablers

DISCUSSION:
Chs 4 and 6 OPD & OPF on establishing "minimum" content of process assets

A process description identifies the activities that must be accomplished related to the process. Guidelines provide helpful hints and options when tailoring a process to the needs of a given project. Enablers include any aids that can be employed to help carry out the activities of a process. Enablers can include templates, forms, and best-case examples.

OPD:
SP 1.1 Establish Standard Processes

2 Guidelines for "Process"

DISCUSSION:
Ch 4 Organizational
Process Asset Library

A documented description of each process must exist and must contain the following information:

- Cover sheet that includes date and version/revision information
- Author, Expert, and Required Approvals
- Identification of roles responsible for carrying out the process
- A Purpose of the process statement
- Stakeholders involved, or required to be notified when carrying out the process
- Required activities when carrying out the process
- Products or services produced by the process
- Required reviews and approvals of products or services produced
- Requirements for control of product or services

OPD:
SP 1.5 Establish
Organizational Process
Asset Library

3 Guidelines for "Process Guidelines"

DISCUSSION:
Ch 7 Tailoring

Guidelines for a process are optional, but encouraged. Guidelines might not be needed for processes that have supporting enablers such as a Project Planning process that has a project plan template. If a guidelines document is developed, it is recommended to include the following information:

- Version/Revision information
- A Purpose of the guideline section/statement
- Helpful hints, things to think about when using the process, things not to forget
- Guidance in choices when tailoring the process for a given project
- Information concerning related tools and enablers

OPD:
SP 1.3 Establish
Tailoring Criteria and
Guidelines

4 Guidelines for Enablers

Enablers for a process are optional but encouraged. Enablers can replace a guideline. Example enablers include templates and forms, or any aid, including a best-case example, in carrying out the process.

Appendix D

Example Agile Process Asset Approval and Release Process

1 Purpose

DISCUSSION:
Ch 6 Need to start with OPF and OPD

The purpose of the Organizational Process Asset Approval and Release Process is to document the process to review, approve, and release into the Organizational Process Asset Library (PAL) new or updated process assets.

2 Activities

There are four (4) primary activities in this process.

DISCUSSION:
Chs 6 and 7 on OPD and OPF

1. The first activity after assigned process asset work is completed is to provide the draft assets to the Organizational Repository Administrator (ORA)

who will coordinate the review and approval process prior to releasing the new or updated assets into the repository.

2. The ORA ensures appropriate review of assets in accordance with Management Steering Group (MSG) direction.

3. Subsequent to review and approval, the ORA ensures all process assets are appropriately marked with updated date and revisions information and approval signoffs.

4. The ORA ensures the repository is updated appropriately and alerts relevant stakeholders in accordance with the Organizational Process Definition (OPD) process.

Note that the inputs to the first activity can be initiated by anyone in the organization or through maintenance, but are subject to the approvals described in the project management plan under roles and responsibilities.

OPD:

SP 1.5 Establish Organizational Process Asset Library

Note: "Establish" means "establish and maintain." This means document and use, which also means update to keep current.

The approval and release process supports the intent of "establish and maintain."

Appendix E

Example Agile Organizational Process Focus Process

Key Points to Aid Use of Template:

- Policy statement included in this process. As an option, this statement could reference another location where the policy exists (at NANO, this was edited to reference the existing policies within the Enterprise Plans).
- Note the reference to the Organizational Process Needs description. This addresses SP 1.1 of OPF.
- Note that the format of this process is consistent with the Process Asset Guidelines (found in Appendix C of this book).
- Note this process requires the feedback of project experiences to the organizational level.

Process Title: Organizational Process Focus (OPF) Policy and Process

Author:

Expert:

Required Approvals: _____

Policy Statement: It is the policy of the *[Name of Relevant Org]* Organization to maintain a Process Management Steering Group (MSG) with the responsibility to oversee the organizational processes and related repository. It is the responsibility of the MSG to ensure the organization's processes are maintained in accordance with the Organizational Process Focus (OPF) Process described below.

Purpose of Process: The purpose of this process is to ensure process improvements are planned, implemented, and deployed in support of the needs of the *[Name of Relevant Org]* organization based on periodic organizational assessments and approved improvement recommendations.

Process Stakeholders: This process is owned and carried out by the MSG on behalf of, and through the support of, all team members.

Organizational Process Needs:

- The *[Name of Relevant Org]* Organizational Process needs are established through the *[reference existing process needs documentation and location]*.

Process Improvement Recommendations

Process improvement recommendations are encouraged to be submitted to the MSG by any *[Name of Relevant Org]* team member whenever candidate improvements are identified. Contact the *[insert role name for organizational repository administrator]* for more details on the appropriate method to identify a problem or recommended improvement.

Required Activities (carried out by MSG members or supporting team members):

DISCUSSION:
Ch 4: The "must-do's" are not tailorable

1. Periodically review Organizational process needs, objectives, and related metrics with a focus on the current business needs, and initiate/oversee appropriate process improvement actions and plans.

OPF:
Most Specific Practices for OPF are covered through "must-do's" in this process document

2. Oversee the Organizational Process Repository, ensuring appropriate review and approval of process artifact changes prior to release.

3. Ensure the organizational processes are periodically appraised (e.g., independent gap analysis) and appropriate process action plans are initiated and implemented based on identified weaknesses.

4. Review organizational process improvement recommendations and initiate/oversee appropriate process action plans.

5. Ensure approved processes and supporting process assets (e.g., templates, guides) are deployed to projects and that the associated goals and metrics are understood.

6. Ensure project specific experiences using processes are fed back and considered for future process improvements. Feedback to project might be in the form of lessons, products, and/or measures.

Products:

The primary products of the OPF process are process improvement action plans, approved updates of process artifacts, and feedback of process-related experiences (lessons, products, measures).

Required Reviews, Approvals, and Product Controls:

Required reviews and approvals and product controls are provided through the Organizational Process Asset Approval and Release Process, which can be found in *[reference location where process documentation maintained]*.

Appendix F

Example Agile Organizational Process Definition Process

Key Points to Aid Use of Template:

- This process ensures resources are provided and assigned to maintain the organizational process asset repository.
- The "must-do's" of this process invoke the defined process asset approval and release process.
- This process defines the process to tailor the organizational process assets.
- This process invokes the organizational process asset guidelines to ensure process development follows a consistent format and rules.

Process Title: Organizational Process Definition Policy and Process

Author:

Expert:

Required Approvals:_____

Policy Statement: It is the policy of the *[Name of Relevant Org]* Organization to maintain an Organizational Repository containing work environment standards and process assets in support of on-going projects. This organizational repository includes project products, lessons, and measures and is stored in *[fill in location]*.

OPD GP 2.1

Establish Policy

This repository is supported through the activities identified in the Organizational Process definition process described below.

Purpose of Process: The purpose of the Organizational Process Definition is to ensure standard processes, approved life cycle models, tailoring criteria and guidelines, and work environment standards are established and maintained. This process identifies the activities conducted in support of the maintenance of key process assets and the organizational repository.

Measurement: The process assets within the organizational repository have been packaged in support of measurement. Process guidelines are separated from process descriptions. The process descriptions include only required activities. Refer to *[insert location to find process asset guidelines]*. Process compliance to process descriptions will be monitored, measured, and reported.

Process Stakeholders: Process asset responsibility is distributed throughout the *[Name of Relevant Org]* organization. However, nothing is allowed into the Organizational repository prior to appropriate review and approval by relevant stakeholders. Required process assets are based on an approved plan, and its current status is tracked and monitored by the *[insert name of role for Organizational Repository Administrator (ORA) or assigned process improvement project manager]*. It is the responsibility of the *[insert role name (e.g., ORA)]* to ensure the activities identified in this process are carried out.

Required Activities:

1. Standard Organizational Processes are maintained in the Organizational Repository, which is accessed through *[fill in specific access method]*.

2. All new releases of process assets, or changes to existing process assets, are conducted in accordance with the *[reference Organizational Process Asset Approval & Release Process]*.

3. A description of the approved life cycle model can be found in *[fill in location where approved life cycle models maintained]*.

4. Tailoring the processes at *[Name of Relevant Org]* is handled as part of the project planning that happens in the beginning of each project per the organizational project management processes.

5. The process assets that are maintained in the Organizational Repository include both process

descriptions and process guidelines. The process description identifies the activities that must be accomplished (these are not tailorable). The guidelines provide the options that are used to help in tailoring the process during the planning phase of the project. The results of tailoring are captured in the project plan.

6. When a project is completed, the resulting products, measures and lessons are stored in *[fill in location]* where they can be accessed and used to aid future project planning and execution.

7. Work environment standards are found *[fill in]*.

Products:

The primary products of the OPD process are the approved process assets stored in the Organizational Repository, and the products, measures, and lessons provided from on-going projects in support of future project planning.

Required Reviews, Approvals, and Product Controls:

Required reviews and approvals and product controls are provided through the Organizational Process Asset Approval and Release Process, which can be found in *[fill in location—could be in Process Improvement Project Management Plan]*.

Appendix G

Terminology Used in This Book

Agile approach: The extension of Agile concepts to include the critical domains of Systems Engineering, Project Management, and software.

Agile-like: Organizations that are trying to use an Agile approach, but are missing key ingredients of true agility.

Agile organization: An organization that uses an Agile approach on the majority of its projects.

align: In agreement with, or consistent with.

CMMI compliance: Achieving the intent of the CMMI practices.

disconnect: An inconsistency.

high maturity: Includes maturity levels 3, 4, and 5. As a point of clarification, today when the SEI refers to "high maturity," it is now reserved for levels 4 and 5.

hybrid Agile: The use of a blend of traditional and Agile techniques.

level 3:   CMMI Maturity level 3.

myth: A belief about the CMMI model, or an Agile approach, that most people know is not true, but often organizations behave as if it were.

process asset: Any artifact that supports people in carrying out their jobs, such as a template or guide.

stealth Agile: An informal Agile initiative that isn't part of a documented and approved plan.

value: Usefulness with respect to achieving business objectives.

wannabe Agile: Organizations that are trying to use an Agile approach, but are missing key ingredients of true agility.

References

[1] Chrissis, Mary Beth, Konrad, Mike, Shrum, Sandy. *CMMI: Guidelines for Process Integration and Product Improvement*, Second Edition. Boston, Addison-Wesley, 2007

[2] Glazer, Hillel, Dalton, Jeff, Anderson, David, Konrad, Mike, Shrum, Sandy. "CMMI or Agile: Why Not Embrace Both!" Technical Note CMU/SEI-2008-TN-003, November 2008

[3] Schwaber, Ken. *Agile Project Management with Scrum*. Microsoft Press, 2004

[4] Cockburn, Alistair. *Crystal Clear: A Human-Powered Methodology for Small Teams*. Boston, Addison-Wesley, 2005

[5] Cockburn, Alistair. *Agile Software Development: The Cooperative Game*, Second Edition. Boston, Addison-Wesley, 2007

[6] Beck, Kent. *Extreme Programming Explained: Embrace Change*. Boston, Addison-Wesley, 2000

[7] Ambler, Scott. *Agile Modeling*. John Wiley & Sons, Inc., 2002

[8] Beck, Kent, Fowler, Martin. *Planning Extreme Programming*. Boston, Addison-Wesley, 2001

[9] Beck, Kent. *Test-Driven Development*. Boston, Addison-Wesley, 2003

[10] McMahon, Paul. "Lessons Learned Using Agile Methods on Large Defense Contracts," *CrossTalk, The Journal of Defense Software Engineering,* May 2006

[11] Jakobsen, Carsten Ruseng, Johnson, Kent, Sutherland, Jeff. "Scrum and CMMI Level 5: The Magic Potion for Code Warriors." Agile 2007 Conference, Washington, D.C., IEEE

[12] McMahon, Paul. "Are the Right People Measuring the Right Things? A Lean Path to Achieving Business Objectives." *CrossTalk, The Journal of Defense Software Engineering,* May 2008

[13] Humphrey, Watts S. *A Discipline for Software Engineering.* Reading, Addison-Wesley, 1995

[14] Florac, William A., Carleton, Anita D. *Measuring the Software Process: Statistical Process Control for Software Process Improvement.* Reading, Addison-Wesley, 1999

[15] Wheeler, Don. *Understanding Variation.* Second Edition. 2000

[16] Goldratt, Eliyahu. *The Goal.* The North River Press Publishing Corporation, Third Revision, 2004

[17] Kennedy, Michael. *Product Development for the Lean Enterprise: Why Toyota's System Is Four Times More Productive and How You Can Implement It.* The Oaklea Press, April 2003

[18] George, Mike, Rowlands, Dave, Kastle, Bill. *What Is Lean Six Sigma?* McGraw-Hill, 2004

[19] Siviy, Jeannine M., Penn, M. Lynn, Stoddard, Robert W. *CMMI and Six Sigma: Partners in Process Improvement.* Boston, Addison-Wesley, 2008

[20] Cockburn, Alistair. "What Engineering Has in Common with Manufacturing and Why It Matters." *CrossTalk, The Journal of Defense Software Engineering,* April 2007

[21] Hilden, Delinger. "Implementing CMMI in a Diverse Organization." SEI web site

[22] McMahon, Paul. "Are Management Basics Affected When Using Agile Methods?" *CrossTalk, The Journal of Defense Software Engineering,* November 2006

[23] Cohn, Mike. *User Stories Applied: For Agile Software Development.* Boston, Addison-Wesley, 2004

[24] http://www.ambysoft.com/essays/agileLifecycle.html

[25] Cohn, Mike. *Agile Estimating and Planning*. Boston, Prentice-Hall, 2006

[26] McMahon, Paul. *Virtual Project Management: Software Solutions for Today and the Future*. CRC Press LLC, 2001.

[27] Highsmith, Jim. *Agile Project Management: Creating Innovative Products*. Boston, Addison-Wesley, 2004

[28] Highsmith, Jim. *Adaptive Software Development: A Collaborative Approach to Managing Complex Systems*. Dorset House Publishing, 2000

[29] McMahon, Paul. "Defense Acquisition Performance: Could Some Agility Help?" *CrossTalk, The Journal of Defense Software Engineering*, February 2009

[30] Boehm, Barry, Turner, Richard. *Balancing Agility and Discipline*. Boston, Addison-Wesley, 2004

[31] Demarco, Tom, Lister, Tim. *Waltzing with Bears*. Dorset House Publishing, 2003

[32] Curtis, Bill, Hefley, William E., Miller, Sally A. *The People Capability Maturity Model: Guidelines for Improving the Workforce*. Boston, Addison-Wesley, 2002

[33] Humphrey, Watts S. *Managing Technical People: Innovation, Teamwork, and the Software Process*. Reading, Addison-Wesley, 1997

[34] McMahon, Paul. "Uncommon Techniques for Growing Effective Technical Managers." *CrossTalk, The Journal of Defense Software Engineering*, Online Only Feature, November 2006

[35] Ahern, Dennis M., Clouse, Aaron, Turner, Richard. *CMMI Distilled: A Practical Introduction to Integrated Process Improvement*, Second Edition. Boston, Addison-Wesley, 2004

[36] Cink, Stewart. "All-Feel, No-Think Shots." *Golf Magazine*, September 2008

[37] McMahon, Paul. "Integrating Systems and Software Engineering: What Can Large Organizations Learn From Small Start-Ups?" *CrossTalk, The Journal of Defense Software Engineering*, October 2002

[38] Paulk, Mark. "Agile Methodologies and Process Discipline." *CrossTalk, The Journal of Defense Software Engineering*, October 2002

[39] Highsmith, Jim. "What Is Agile Software Development?" *CrossTalk, The Journal of Defense Software Engineering,* October 2002

[40] McMahon, Paul. "Bridging Agile and Traditional Development Methods: A Project Management Perspective." *CrossTalk, The Journal of Defense Software Engineering,* May 2004

[41] McMahon, Paul. "Extending Agile Methods: A Distributed Project and Organizational Improvement Perspective." *CrossTalk, The Journal of Defense Software Engineering,* May 2005

About the Author

 **Paul E. McMahon,** Principal, PEM Systems (Binghamton, NY), helps large and small organizations as they move toward increased agility and process maturity. He has taught software engineering at Binghamton University, State University of New York; conducted workshops on engineering process and management; and published more than 35 articles, including several on Agile development in *CrossTalk: The Journal of Defense Software Engineering*. Paul is also the author of a book on collaborative development, *Virtual Project Management: Software Solutions for Today and the Future* (CRC Press, 2000).

A frequent speaker at industry conferences, including the Systems and Software Technology Conference, Paul's observations and insights reflect 24 years of engineering and management experience working for such companies as Link Simulation and Lockheed Martin. He has been consulting independently since 1997.

Paul holds a BA, Magna Cum Laude, in mathematics from the University of Scranton, and an MA in mathematics from Binghamton University. He is a Certified ScrumMaster.

E-mail: pemcmahon@acm.org

Index

CMMI Training and Support:
Helping hands with a global reach.

Do you need help getting started with CMMI adoption in your organization? Do you want to learn more about CMMI, SCAMPI, or high maturity practices? Regardless of your level of experience with CMMI tools and methods, the SEI Partner Network and SEI training can provide the assistance and the support you need to make your CMMI adoption a success.

The SEI Partner Network is a world-wide group of licensed organizations with professionals who are qualified by the SEI to deliver SEI services. SEI Partners can provide you with training courses, CMMI adoption assistance, proven appraisal methods, and teamwork and management processes that help you implement CMMI in your organization.

Advanced and specialized training is also available from the SEI. Courses offered by the SEI include executive seminars, an overview of process improvement, courses covering level 2 concepts and level 3 concepts, an intermediate level course, a high maturity course, and training for CMMI instructors, SCAMPI Lead Appraisers, and SCAMPI Team Leaders.

To find an SEI Partner near you, or to learn more about this global network of professionals, please visit the SEI Partner Network website at http://www.sei.cmu.edu/partners.

To learn more about CMMI training, visit the SEI Training site at http://www.sei.cmu.edu/training/find/ to search for all CMMI-related training courses.

Get Started with Agile

Addison
Wesley

Agile Software Development

Alistair Cockburn

One of Agile's leading pioneers introduces his powerful model of software development as a "cooperative game of invention and communication."

ISBN-13: 978-0-321-48275-4

Succeeding with Agile

Mike Cohn

This is the definitive, realistic, actionable guide to starting fast with Scrum and Agile—and then succeeding over the long haul.

ISBN-13: 978-0-321-57936-2

Agile Adoption Patterns

Amr Elssamadisy

Proven patterns and techniques for succeeding with Agile in your organization.

ISBN-13: 978-0-321-51452-3

Agile Product Management with Scrum

Roman Pichler

Leading Scrum consultant uses real-world examples to demonstrate how product owners can create successful products with Scrum.

ISBN-13: 978-0-321-60578-8

Agile Project Management

Jim Highsmith

Best practices for managing projects in agile environments—now updated with new techniques for larger projects.

ISBN-13: 978-0-321-65839-5

The Software Project Manager's Bridge to Agility

Michele Sliger / Stacia Broderick

Shows experienced project managers how to successfully transition to agile by refocusing on facilitation and collaboration, not "command and control."

ISBN-13: 978-0-321-50275-9

Also of Interest

Balancing Agility and Discipline • Barry Boehm / Richard Turner • ISBN-13: 978-0-321-18612-6

For more information and to read sample material, and to see our complete list of agile titles (print and eBook formats) visit **informit.com/agile**.

Titles are also available at safari.informit.com.

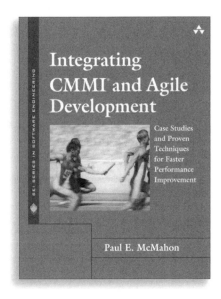